SHOOTING SKILLS

CLAY PIGEON SHOOTING

SHOOTING SKILLS

CLAY PIGEON SHOOTING

JOHN HUMPHREYS

Illustrated by Derick Bown

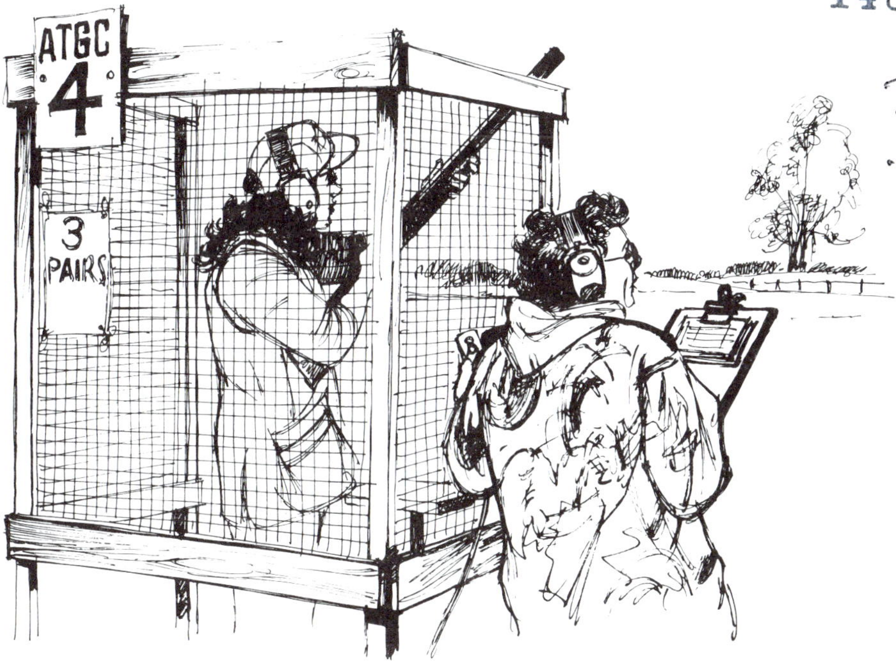

BLANDFORD

SHOOTING SKILLS

A BLANDFORD BOOK
First published in the UK 1995 by Blandford,
an imprint of the Cassell Group
Wellington House
125 Strand
London WC2R 0BB

Distributed in the United States by Sterling Publishing Co Inc
387 Park Avenue South, New York, NY 10016–8810

Distributed in Australia by Capricorn Link (Australia) Pty Ltd
2/13 Carrington Road, Castle Hill, NSW 2154

British Library Cataloguing-in-Publication Data
A catalogue record for this book is available from the British Library

Photographs supplied by Centaur Photography

ISBN 0 7137 2513 3

Typeset by Litho Link Ltd, Welshpool, Powys, Wales
Printed and bound in Great Britain by Hillman Printers (Frome) Ltd

CONTENTS

Conversion table

1 in = 2.5 cm

1 ft = 30.4 cm

1 yd = 0.9 metre

1 mile = 1.6 km

1 acre = 0.4 hectare

1 oz = 28.3 g

1 lb = 0.4 kg

1 ton = 1.016 tonnes

1 gallon = 4.5 litres

$°F = \frac{9 \times °C}{5} + 32$

INTRODUCTION

Clay pigeon shooting as we know it today has roots which run back a century or so. On paper it is a simple enough sport, the basics of it being the knack, art and skill of hitting a moving, inanimate target, of co-ordinating hand and eye sufficiently well to strike from afar. The sport may be simply described as the hitting with a charge of shotgun pellets a disc of baked clay which shatters when struck, indicating in the clearest and most public way a clean hit. The target is propelled by a device operated by a powerful spring and the disc is shaped so that it skims easily and can be made to fly a considerable distance.

In practice, it is far more complicated than it sounds, for refinements of the target, the way it is thrown, its speed and the shotguns that are available to the participants have developed to a high technical level. Fame and fortune accrue for those who become expert in it; competition runs at international level and the sport is known throughout the world.

It was not always so, for it started as a convenient method of practising game shooting. Game shots pride themselves on their marksmanship for there has always been an unspoken element of competition, but the shooting field itself is not a place to practise. The clay pigeon is the ideal compromise, for it is not affected by close seasons and 'birds' can be shown at any angle and in any numbers. Weaknesses of style can be identified and ironed out and certain shots which always caused a problem can be corrected so that the game shooter can take his or her place at the covertside or on the grouse moor and be able to shoot with confidence.

For others, with neither the opportunity nor the desire to shoot live quarry, it became a sport in its own right. Certain types of 'bird' were identified and named so that 'down the line', 'springing teal' and 'skeet' became specialist clay birds with only a passing mimicry of the real thing. In time each discipline, as they became known, developed its own techniques, experts and even its own weaponry. A gun for down the line shooting would not be suitable for shooting at, say, skeet. Coaches, clay grounds clubs, teams and international squads followed quickly and the UK was able to field teams which frequently proved to be world beaters. Competition is enjoyed at every level from international to a few shots at the local country fair. The sport is popular with women, more so perhaps than field shooting, and there are special classes and competitions for women only.

The popularity of the sport is indicated by the estimated half a million folk who take part in it on a regular basis. They may be found in a small number in a corner of a farmer's field with one portable trap they have provided themselves, having a few shots before the pub opens and keeping themselves sharp for the pheasants later in the year. They may be found at shooting schools having lessons, or attending one of the hospitality corporate days which have become a business feature of the last few years. They may spend every evening at their club enjoying a round of mixed birds or polishing their skills for a forthcoming competition. A keen performer might fire 1,000 cartridges in a week, the next person might fire 50 in a year, but each is a clay shooter an each takes what enjoyment there is from the sport.

The various disciplines can appear complex to a newcomer used only to game shooting. They will be described in full later in this book, but the complexities of universal trench, the bolting rabbit, FITASC sporting or even ZZ target shooting each has its challenges, its own rules and, at competition level, is judged by a stern overseer. When any sport becomes competitive, rules appear and in their wake comes the adjudicator, the referee or umpire as he or she is sometimes known.

By the same token a governing body is required, one which administers the sport and, using membership money, funds various competitions and developments in the sport. For clay shooting it is the Clay Pigeon Shooting Association, the CPSA, which was founded about 60 years ago. There is a team of professional officers on hand to deal with queries and a useful booklist of minor publications. Paid up members are covered for third party insurance, and such cover is essential for anyone involved in the sport of shooting. Guns can be dangerous things and accidents do happen. The CPSA has enjoyed fluctuating fortunes lately; having been in the doldrums for a while, it is currently thriving under new management and has been revitalized. Anyone who intends to take up clay shooting on any but the most casual level ought to become a member.

The sport has produced stars as big, though not as well paid, as the footballing icons. The likes of George Digweed, Joe Neville, Peter Boden and others are household names where clays are talked. Like many physical sports it can be cruel and the winners rise, flourish and fade. Sadly but truly the giants of yesterday become names from the mythology of the sport and suddenly new stars appear on the horizon.

Beginners might be confused by the different styles adopted by the experts and sometimes also by coaches. Weight on the front or the back foot for the high overhead? Elbow up or down? Gun raised to the face or cheek dropped on to the stock? All are vexed questions and beginners each find their own individual style. Styles needed in clay shooting are not the same as those used in game shooting, where the challenges tend to be different. Even so, good clay shots are usually excellent game shots whereas the reverse is more rarely the case.

It is said that regular practice in all things makes perfect and this ought to be true of clay pigeon shooting. Even here there is some disagreement for there is a school of thought which claims that really good shots are born rather than made. Both have a point and while practice can lift a performer to the best of his ability there are those with such a natural aptitude that they will be the world beaters and achieve a level which a moderate performer, with all the practice in the world, will never achieve.

This little book is a short, introductory stroll through the world of clay pigeon shooting which is a fine sport, enjoyable at many levels, suitable for young and old alike, where you meet new friends and interesting people, develop personal skills, self-awareness and confidence and, quite simply, have fun. It might be that you will one day shoot for your country or you may end up at the end of the field with a trap you took there in your car boot and a member of your family to work it for you. Whatever the case you are joining a sport which is alive and vibrant and certainly here to stay.

I have mentioned that this is a sport by no means confined to men only and where, for the sake of brevity, I write 'he' or 'him' I address my remarks equally to men and women without intending any distinction.

1

History and Background

As long ago as the time of Henry VIII, the skill of shooting a moving object was a valued military attribute. Archers practised at what they called the popinjay which, while often a static stuffed bird on top of a pole was, in more sophisticated versions, a tethered live bird or bundle of feathers which would move with the wind.

Shooting with a gun at anything which moved was developed in a simple form in the reign of Charles II. A book by Thomas Page entitled *The Art of Shooting Flying* was the users' guide of the time. The first clay pigeon was a wooden disc hung on a giant washing line. A serf was instructed to run along pulling a cord attached to this disc which shot along the line as fast as he could run. The marksman had to aim and fire at this. Today such a feat sounds quite easy, but at the time they would be using flintlock guns.

The flintlock was detonated by a flint striking a steel which ignited priming powder in a pan which, in turn, set off the main charge. The time lapse between deciding to fire and the shot reaching the target was considerable and to add to their problems they suffered from what were known as hang fires, a delay in ignition caused by damp powder, a weak spark or a blockage in the touch hole. Page advised the shooter to keep well ahead of his target and hold the lead even when the gun failed to fire when he pulled the trigger. It might well go off a moment later due to a hang fire, so Page advised to '. . . continue in the same motion for some time after, in case the gun hang fire or not fire as quick as it ought to'.

In the late eighteenth and early nineteenth centuries top hat shooting replaced the disc on the string. For this a live bird was placed on the ground and covered by the top hat of the shooter who stood by with his piece loaded and primed. The sport was to stoop, take up your top hat, place it on your head, raise the gun and shoot at the bird which was now rapidly departing. The weaponry had advanced since the days of flint, but was still primitive by today's standards and this was never an easy shot. It must be remembered that a great deal of sporting shooting at the time was at sitting targets which the shooter could stalk and fire into the thick before they knew he was there.

In the early part of the nineteenth century, the redoubtable wildfowler and partridge shot, Colonel Peter Hawker, had his man throw up inanimate objects at which he could shoot and in his lifetime he saw the arrival of the percussion cap which was a far more reliable ignition method than the old flintlock. The percussion gun was a most successful invention which served the shooting public well for a century.

The top hat system was replaced by a man hiding safely behind a wall who would, on command, throw up live birds. Their flight was unpredictable and this was deemed good sport. The bird thrower was already known by the name we use today, a trapper. An even better method was to have the bird in a collapsible box on the ground some distance in front of the shooter. This box, which opened on the pulling of a cord, was known as the trap – another word which survives and now refers to the machine which throws the modern clay pigeon.

The final sophistication of the single trap was to have a series of five of them in a line, each with its release string running back to the trapper. The trapper could add an element of the unexpected by pulling whichever of the strings he chose, requiring the shooter to make some rapid adjustments before he fired. This sport became popular and wagers were made on results and judges were appointed to interpret the rules. Live trap shooting flourished until 1921 when it was banned in the UK, although it continued overseas and to this day is practised in some places.

The latter half of the nineteenth century saw the sport along with the technology of shooting expanding rapidly. Encouraged by royal example, the gentry were going in for game shooting in a big way; their bags of birds and rabbits running into some thousands a day. Game rearing was done on a large scale and some shooters were in the field every day of the week except Sunday – they would have been out then also had it been permitted to shoot game on the sabbath. They started with the grouse in mid-August and did not cease until the last pheasant was shot on the following 1 February.

Guns and cartridges had improved to match these new requirements and percussion, that old favourite, had given way to the centre-fire gun, the prototype of which

was first seen at the Great Exhibition in 1851. There had been a brief flirtation with the pinfire gun, in which the firing pin was incorporated in the cartridge and could be seen protruding over the breech of the loaded gun. This ammunition was deemed unsafe and the gun was not popular, but the pinfire was an important bridging period between percussion and full centre-fire.

It was not until the turn of the century that the shotgun as we know it today was in full production. Some of the weapons made then are still giving good service today and the basic design has yet to be improved upon. All guns then were made with the two barrels side by side, the later popularity of the over-and-under gun being no more than a refinement on the established theme. Today all serious clay pigeon shooting is done with an over-and-under gun. There are special classes and competitions for game shots who prefer their side-by-sides.

Famous gunmakers flourished in London and Birmingham, names such as Purdey, Holland and Holland, Lang, Churchill, Watson and a host of others had full order books. Not many of them survive today, for the cheaper, imported guns have largely replaced what remain the best examples of the gunmaker's art in the world. Only a few examples of their work survive them. One famous gun made by Boss of London was used at Birmingham to test shotgun cartridges. In its lifetime it fired more than a million and a half cartridges but the barrel wear from all that punishment was less than one thousandth of an inch. There could be little better tribute to the quality of workmanship and the materials used.

At least one of the great firms, Holland and Holland, which is still in business, set up a shooting school in 1835 with the purpose of fitting customers with guns and giving them some practice shots and expert coaching. They were still using released live bird

targets, but the results of coaching and practice soon showed themselves in the shooting field. The result was that more shooting schools sprang up, but there were problems with supplying sufficient live birds to make the running of a popular shooting school viable. The search was on for an inanimate target which could be made to fly well and which would replace the live bird.

This was a time of active experiment. Metal propellers, lumps of wood, flying darts and many other objects were tried, each propelled from a device powered by a strong spring. Popular for a time were glass balls full of feathers. These flew well and a shot could easily be recorded by the palpable shattering of the ball and the flying out of a cloud of feathers which mimicked the real thing. However, they were found to be unsatisfactory because they littered the ground with shards of broken glass.

The breakthrough came in 1844 when an American, Ligowsky, saw children skimming clam shells over the water and noted how the

The Ligowsky clay trap, one of the earliest produced.

shells flews and glided. This discovery was the clay pigeon shooter's equivalent of Newton and his famous falling apple, and Ligowsky made clay targets from discs of hard baked clay. These flew spinning from a trap, were dynamically stable and could be made to fly at various trajectories. He invented a trap to throw them and the early version retailed at £1 15s (175p), while a box of a hundred clays set you back eight shillings and sixpence (about 42p).

Before long the shooting schools were offering a choice of a mixture of clay pigeons and real birds. At Charles Lancaster's London school you could shoot clay birds or pheasants released from a high tower. One of Lancaster's most illustrious early clients was Annie Oakley, the American sharp-shooter immortalized in *Annie Get Your Gun*. She shot game when in England and Lancaster made her some fine sporting guns.

By the turn of the century the school at Holland and Holland had become highly sophisticated. The shooter could try the pattern of his or her gun on a steel plate, clay birds could be presented which mimicked anything from driven grouse to high, curling pheasants and a gun could be made to measure using a device still in use known as a try gun. 'Birds' could be thrown over the shooter from the high tower and what is more, there was expert coaching available. There was a luxurious pavilion on site for the rest and refreshment of the gentleman and lady shooters. Visit the famous Holland and Holland school today and you will see that little has changed in the last 90 years.

Shooting clay targets received an enormous boost when King George V visited the West London Shooting School to shoot sporting clays. He was already a renowned game shot. Edward VIII was said to have had a clay trap installed on a battleship so that he could practise as he toured the world on his royal duties.

It was but a little step from the shooting school and clay target designed to help only the game shot, to the development of clay

shooting as a sport in its own right. In the 1920s down the line (DTL) or double rise became a speciality and clubs were set up to deal with that specific type of shot. In 1925 was held the first of many international clay pigeon shooting matches. It was at Carlisle between England and Scotland and Scotland won.

The over-and-under gun and the semi-automatic were brought over from America and designed by John Moses Browning. Made in a factory in Belgium, Browning remains a popular and well-made gun. The over-and-under caught on rapidly and many shooters found their performances improving when they used the narrower sighting rib. The theory was that instinctively you would point at a distant object with one finger, a sighting tool not unlike the single rib of the over-and-under. To point with a side-by-side was akin to pointing with two fingers, a thing no one ever does. The over-and-under was here to stay as the clay shooter's favourite gun.

At the same time clays improved. Now made of a mixture of lime and pitch, they come in different sizes and even colours. You can shoot at the tiny mini, the midi or the full size standard. You may try your hand at skimmers known as battues, shoot at orange ones against dark backgrounds or even special ones designed to hop along the ground like rabbits.

Clay traps have become highly technical and varied. They can be fully automatic, electrically powered and throw any type of bird at the touch of a button. They can make clays behave in any conceivable way from imitating closely the real quarry species to showing birds which are designed for the specialist clay shooter.

Various disciplines evolved, each with its own special techniques, rules and regulations. The sport is enjoyed by those who are members of an international team or who still use it for what it was originally intended, a convenient method of improving game shooting skills. The sport enjoys huge popularity. After a century of development it is here to stay and with the uncertainties facing all field sports, including live bird shooting, its future looks assured.

2

The Disciplines

There are three main disciplines involved in formal clay shooting: trap, skeet and sporting shooting. Within each one there are various permutations and sub-divisions.

Trap shooting

Trap shooting derives its name from the old pigeon trap in which a live bird was held, released on the signal and shot so that it fell within a defined area. Live birds are no longer used, of course, but modern trap shooting owes much to these roots.

In modern trap shooting, going away targets are shot from a trap set in front of a line of five or more shooters. Each shooter takes turns to fire at the going away bird, they change places so that each target varies slightly from the one before. The name 'down the line' derives from the practice of shooters moving down the line for each set of shots. This is a highly popular form of clay shooting and one at which a shooter of limited experience can perform reasonably well. The angle and speed of the target is limited and to shoot one, or two, even for a beginner is not impossible. Those who consistently shoot them all have the powers of concentration needed for international competition, or for skeet shooting.

Down the line trap shooting has many variations on the basic theme. Olympic trap is probably the hardest, for each shooter has three traps in front of him so that there are 15 of them in all. This greatly widens the variety of angles of shots presented. This sport is recognized at Olympic level and is considered by experts as the cream of trap shooting.

Other variants include ZZ trap which is growing in favour but not yet universally popular, single barrel, handicap by distance, double rise, automatic ball trap and universal trap.

Each discipline has its own specialists and the reader may well find himself settling for one in favour of the rest.

• **Down the line** is often a starting point for most aspiring clay pigeon shots. It teaches mental discipline and gives a good grounding in stance, footwork, swing and concentration. The targets come from one trap situated 16 yds in front of five shooters. Their speed is moderate compared to many other clay birds and the angle of the birds from position to position varies only slightly. Each shooter will fire at five birds from each position, giving him a total of 25 shots in a round.

Since this is considered an easy target, high scores are expected, and remember we are looking now at a seriously competitive sport. A score which would be thought good at a harder discipline would not be acceptable at DTL. A competition with 100 targets calls for intense concentration. One or two careless misses could cost a place due to loss of points. To shoot 'a hundred straight' is a not uncommon achievement as shown by the many clay shots with badges on their vests claiming that feat.

In DTL a first barrel kill scores three points, a second barrel kill scores two. A miss, of course, scores nil. To score top points of 300 you must, therefore, shoot every single bird with your first barrel.

To shoot DTL well it is important, as in all forms of shooting, to get the feet and stance right before you call for a bird. As usual the front foot will be pointing in the direction at which you expect to fire. Aim may be taken and the gun mounted before the bird appears and about 2 ft above where you expect to shoot will be about right. Each target is slightly different and usually the extremes of the arc are the most difficult shots. Positions five and one show the bird angling most sharply and due allowance must be made in anticipation of the shot by correct foot placing and initial aim.

When all is already you call for the bird. You see the target, swing the gun smoothly using your body from the hips up rather than the arms to provide the movement. You blot out the target with the muzzles and kill the bird. Hit or miss, your only thought now is addressing the next target.

Each shooter will develop his own style with experience. The high gun mount does not suit everyone and trial and error will establish which is the best style for you. You will learn which are the trickiest targets for you and learn to overcome the problem presented. The beginner should have no

difficulty in hitting at least some of the birds so that instant success brings encouragement.

In time there will be new challenges such as the refinements of automatic ball trap or even the international disciplines such as Olympic trap or universal trench. The DTL bird is subject of innumerable variations.

This type of shooting calls for intense concentration. The trick is not to worry about what others are doing, not to count your score as you go along and not to allow yourself to be distracted by anything but the job of hitting the next bird. On no account will you indulge in idle chatter or listen to any spectators who are so thoughtless as to be talking while you are concentrating. Should you happen to miss, put the matter out of your mind: there will be another similar bird along in a minute.

It is said that many game shots have trouble with the going away bird, the grouse or partridge which has passed the butt and is fleeing to the far horizon. A few half hours with a DTL trap, which is easy to set up on any safe piece of ground, would cure that fault quickly. Failing that, a session at a shooting school with a good coach would have the same effect.

Many clay shooters concentrate on trap shooting in one or all its forms to the exclusion of all other shooting.

• **Olympic trap** is a refinement of down the line and is one of the two disciplines which are competed for at the Olympic and Commonwealth Games giving the good performer the incentive and opportunity to represent his country.

There are five shooting positions and in front of them, 16 yds away, is a long trench in which is a series of five banks of clay traps,

each bank in front of one of the shooting positions. At each trap point there are three traps, making 15 in all. Each trap might throw a bird anywhere within a 45 degree arc. To establish such an Olympic trap set-up is expensive for the traps are fired acoustically and not many clubs can, or will, commit the outlay for such a sophisticated and specialist system. There is one in Beverley in Yorkshire, one in North Wales at the Sealand ground, a noted one in the Midlands at the Garland Shooting Ground, one in South Wales and another near Loch Ness, so the enthusiast might find himself travelling many miles to practise.

The birds come in a bewildering variety from a combination of so many traps and shooting positions. The shooter will be thrown a target from any one of his three traps. He may shoot twice at each target and, unlike DTL, there is no penalty for a second barrel kill. The targets are thrown at set angles to distances of up to 87 yds. The stance is optional gun up or gun down. The referee is positioned just behind the middle of the line of shooters so as to have an uninterrupted view of the proceedings.

• **Universal trench** is similar to Olympic trap with five firing points but there are only five traps. The shooter may be thrown a target from any one of the five traps. In other respects such as scoring and gun position it is similar to Olympic trap. This discipline is especially popular on the Continent.

Unlike Olympic trap, birds will be angling far more widely. The shooter has to cover a far greater distance and will need to scan the whole area and not be committed to an arc of fire which might not be the right one when the bird shows. Its proponents claim that universal trench is harder to shoot than Olympic trap. As in all down the line shooting, concentration is important, for this is competitive sport and scores mean everything. The position of the feet, the stance, the relaxation but at the same time intense concentration and speed of reaction are some of the qualities which make the difference between the good and the mediocre.

• **Automatic ball trap** is a third variation on the DTL discipline. For this the set-up is similar to that of Olympic trap except that there is only one trap on the ground the usual 16 yds in front of the five shooting positions. The clay is thrown at unpredictable angles and elevations to a distance of up to 87 yds. Scoring and other rules are similar to those of Olympic trap.

Automatic ball trap is popular; it is easy and cheap to install on a clay ground so that opportunities to shoot it abound. The shooter has full use of the gun, lots of straight going away birds and tricky angled shots especially on the end shooting positions 1 and 5. It can be seen as useful training for Olympic trap but in its own right it has international status, so that the good shooter has the chance to represent his or her country.

Automatic ball trap is shot by a squad of six shooters each of whom takes a target from one of the five positions before moving one pace to the right to shoot again from the next peg. Each shooter will fire at 25 targets in a sequence, each shooting and moving quickly to the next position so that the event builds up a rhythm.

The expert advice is to allow the bird some law before mounting smoothly, chasing it and taking it. Concentration and swift reactions are, as in many clay disciplines, essential.

Starshot and pro trap.

• **Double rise.** Among the fringe clay disciplines, this is where two targets are thrown simultaneously rather than one. The gun may shoot once at each target and scores five for a double kill and two points for a single.

• **ZZ target** is another minority sport but it is popular in France where professionals make a great deal of money. The target is not a conventional clay but a three-bladed propeller with a detachable plastic centre. It needs a special trap to make it fly. The shooter faces a bank of five traps any one of which will release a bird. To score, the plastic centre must be knocked out of the propeller by the shot and fall within a defined area.

• **Single barrel** is a version of down the line but only one shot is allowed at any target.

• **Double trap** is a new Olympic discipline introduced in 1988. The shooter must take two birds fired from different trap positions as they might be set up for Olympic trap, but in the case of double trap there are only three traps used. Gun up or down is optional but most prefer to have the gun into the shoulder before calling for the bird.

• **The flush** is where a team of shooters stand in a short line and shoot at clays thrown over them in any numbers and all combinations of speed, height and angle. Fifty clays and three shooters might be involved and the fun is fast and furious as clays come over while shooters are trying desperately to reload. Tactics may be used and a battle plan in which each gun is designated certain birds (left-hand man takes those to the left, etc.) can work well and the experts seem to manage it. All too often, however, the arrangement breaks down half way through and it tends to be each one for himself.

• **Starshot and pro trap.** It would be wrong not to give passing mention to starshot. For this the clay is fired across a giant half wheel bolted on to a trailer. The wheel is divided into defined areas and to kill the clay in the more difficult segments (i.e. those closer to the trap) scores more highly than those killed on the outer perimeter which are easier. This sport was made popular on television in the 1980s when various stars from the world of sport and entertainment competed. This did the sport of clay shooting a lot of good and no doubt attracted many new entrants.

Pro trap is popular and along with starshot may be found at country shows. For this a series of traps throws a run of birds on a computerized program. The shooter will have 25 targets and will shoot from one fixed position.

Skeet shooting

Skeet shooting is a popular discipline which shows much American influence. In the UK it falls into either ISU Olympic skeet or English skeet, the latter being both easier and more popular than ISU. There is a D-shaped layout with seven marked points on it, usually in the form of paving slabs sunk in the ground on which the shooter will stand. In ISU there is an eighth point midway between the traps.

At either end of the D are situated two trap houses 40 yds apart, one higher than the other (known as high house and low house), which throw a succession of birds in pairs on fixed and known trajectories, the first from

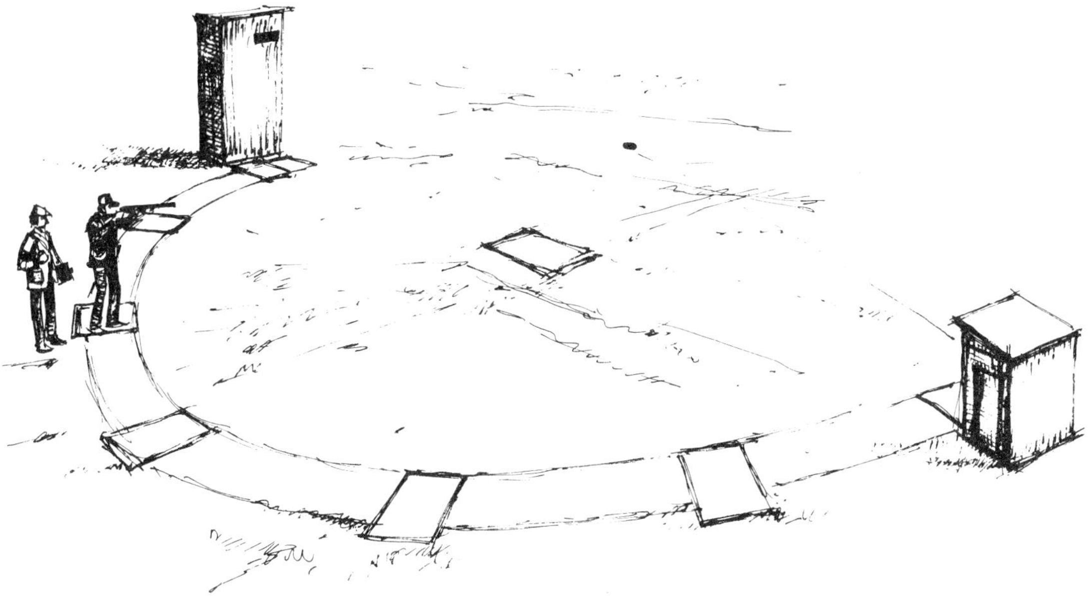

the high house trap followed immediately by one from the low house, taken at each of the seven stations. Also there will be simultaneous doubles taken at stations one and two, the high house target showing and being shot first. Another double at station four may be shot in any order but the shooter has to state which bird he will take first. Doubles are thrown also at stations six and seven where the low house target is shot first. This makes a total of 24 targets and a final one (making 25 in all) may be a repeat of the first target to be missed or, in the case of a clear round, the optional last bird is open from low house 7 or high house 1 from station seven

The shooter will move from place to place in an arc so that at each position the birds appear at different angles. In position one, for example, he would have a bird travelling almost directly away from him like a DTL target while the other extreme is one which comes quartering towards him like a sporting bird.

In this way, in 25 shots the shooter is presented with every type of target, quartering, crossing, going away and driven. Skeet shooting encourages good footwork and mounting, speedy reflexes, sound technique and confidence. More than anything a round of skeet teaches concentration. Those who excel at it and who know they can hit every target in a round require a special kind of concentration to keep their performance consistent.

There are three types of skeet currently shot in the UK. In English skeet the bird is released the moment it is called for by a shout of 'pull' or 'mark'. The gun may be held in any position. One round is 25 targets per shooter which are addressed from seven different shooting positions.

The International Shooting Union (ISU) skeet, also known as Olympic skeet, is very difficult and is not for beginners who should start with English skeet. This is shot with the shooter holding the gun butt at hip level and there can be a delay of no more than three seconds between the call and the appearance of the clay. A round of ISU skeet is 25 targets shot from eight different shooting points by each competitor. The clays should travel some 71 yds at predictable angles and elevations.

American skeet is also shot from eight rather than seven shooting positions. In this case the bird is released the moment the call is given and should fly 60 yds at predictable angles and elevations. There are the usual 25 targets and in American skeet the gun position is optional.

The English skeet clay travels a shorter distance and therefore more slowly than the ISU or American versions. Therefore it is easier to hit and makes an excellent grounding for those finding their way in the sport. The shooting basics are vital for success so that proper footwork, co-ordination, balance and concentration all play their part. Skeet also helps with timing and anyone who can perform well on English skeet should find it a good apprenticeship for other disciplines.

There are various schools of thought as to whether it is better to hold the gun to the shoulder or down when calling for the bird. Advocates of the former claim that gun-up reduces the number of movements necessary before shooting and helps concentration. The gun-down lobby holds that premounting commits the shooter to what might be a wrong line and that adjustments have to be made. It is easier to mount and swing, they say, than to swing after you have bedded the gun into the shoulder. The bird should be called and the whole body go into one smooth movement of picking up the clay, swinging and shooting.

Similarly, opinion is divided between maintained lead or mounting swinging from behind the bird and shooting instantly. Maintained lead requires the shooter to know exactly where the gun barrels are in relation to the shot, to hold and swing them the right distance in front at the speed of the bird and shoot when all the co-ordinates come together.

For the beginner, either style will work and it is a question of using the one which suits. Some shooters instinctively move ahead of the target while others will feel more comfortable coming up to it from behind. Maintained lead is favoured by many American skeet shooters, whereas Joe Neville, said to be the UK's finest skeet shot, writes:

> My technique is simple but effective. I swing the gun from slightly underneath the bird and out in front as the gun comes up to my shoulder. As the stock actually comes into my eye and shoulder together the muzzles are in the place they need to be to kill the target. I always start my swing slightly behind the bird so that the timing of the shot is precise.

Much the same may be said of the position of the feet. While it is important to get them in the right place with the general principle that the front foot (the left for the right hander) should be pointing in roughly the direction where you expect to take the bird, it is much more important that the shooter should be comfortable. Some crouch in what to the classic game shooter is an unattractive posture, though effective. Others go for the straight front leg, rigid front leg, both legs bent or any combination of all three.

The way to start from basics is to shoot from position one at the incomer which some find one of the easier birds. With the aid of a coach and taking as long as necessary – it may be a month – the shooter works round the various stations using low house. The nearer the middle, the more the bird becomes a crosser and the problems about maintained lead or swing from behind can be addressed. Having reached station 7 the shooter retraces the course, learning the techniques for the high house bird.

In the event of a sudden loss of form and confidence a shooter should be moved back to a position where he or she had success, usually on a high house, until able to hit them again. The double from station 4 can be a problem to many. The second bird is the harder one to hit. The competitor is allowed two practice targets and experts recommend that they should be high house singles from position one which, being an early bird, acts as a confidence booster.

Once some experience has been gained and you are hitting a good share of birds, look for a chance to join a squad. As in team games you tend to play up to the level of the company you are in, even if it is the opposition. The chance to fill a gap in a crack squad is not to be missed for you will shoot better in good company and learn by watching experts in action. Each squad will have a leader who starts on station one. He will see some trial birds and be satisfied that they are being shown in accordance with the CPSA rules. In serious competition squadding is done by a draw and you have to go where you are put. Although each is shooting in company, skeet is a private affair, each person competing against himself, using the tools he has been given. Some wear blinkers to eliminate outside distractions while ear muffs will drown any extraneous noise as well as protecting the ears so that the shooter is isolated in a private world.

Skeet shooting has many attractions. A moderate performer can have fun and hit some birds without taking it too seriously. Those ambitious to progress may take up ISU and possibly shoot for their country. This is one of the clay disciplines which may be taken as seriously as each shooter wishes.

Sporting shooting

This is probably the most popular branch of clay shooting. In this the clays are presented to imitate real live quarry such as would be met with in the field. Birds may be thrown from in front of the shooter to come over the head in pairs or singles and this represents driven partridge or grouse. Another will shoot vertically up in the air in front and this becomes springing teal which flies off in that manner when startled. Pheasants are represented by clays thrown off a high tower to come straight over the head of the shooter or to angle across in front. Some will cross in

front from right to left and left to right. Bolted rabbit is a special clay bowling along the ground in front to be snap shot before it vanishes behind an earth bank. Walked-up birds may be shown as the straight going away clay like a down the line target.

Thus any number of variations are possible unlike some of the more formal disciplines where the shooter knows exactly what to expect. In addition it is customary to mix the birds used. Hence it is possible to introduce the midi, mini, battue and rabbit to vary the flight and present the sort of variety and unpredictability which a game shooter would encounter on a driven or walked-up shooting day.

Another attraction of English sporting is that no permanent trap layout or set of shooting standards is needed, thus making it cheap and easy to set up. The most basic competition is at 20 mixed birds, the sort of shoot that you might meet at a country fair where guests and visitors are encouraged to 'have a go' for a modest fee. At the other end of the scale there is the British Open Championship where 100 far more testing targets offer a challenge to the experts. The standards of shooting between the proper 100 bird set-up and the modest local affair are very different.

To shoot sporting well calls for much practice, a study of the basics such as footwork, concentration and good gun mounting and the ability to 'read' a target correctly. The keen shot will visit many grounds for at no two will the targets be exactly the same. A shot who masters his or her own local ground might be in trouble at the ground in the next county. George Digweed is a great sporting champion and his advice is to learn another discipline to reinforce the basic skills needed. In his case it was skeet which he felt helped him greatly.

I started shooting skeet as a diversion from sporting and in two years I shot nineteen 100 straights including one on my first appearance in the England team. I am certain that shooting in this discipline has contributed to my success at sporting and it has definitely helped my concentration.

Another interesting feature of sporting is that birds may be shown in any number of combinations. A high pheasant might be followed by a bolting rabbit 'on report', i.e. released the moment the first shot is fired. Sometimes targets will appear from opposite sides of the arena and this calls for some nifty footwork to be correctly positioned for them both.

A wise ground manager uses the topography of the land to make the birds more interesting. Any small hills or hollows, wooded rides or banks of tall trees have obvious uses. Surprise woodcock may be shown from low bushes, and pheasants over the high trees. Any water makes a shooting ground more attractive and clays approaching over the corner of a lake or stream, presented to simulate duck, are always interesting birds.

For those aspiring to the ultimate of the full 100 targets shot from 10 stands which you would expect at a championship shoot, it is considered wise to have a look at the targets before starting. Just to walk from stand to stand and watch the birds, deciding the flight paths, where each is to be taken and what the problems are likely to be can be an enormous help to those ambitious to do their best. Some birds will need to be taken early; it is no good finding this out when you are in the hot seat and it is too late. 'Walking the course' is as wise for the sporting shooter as it is for the show jumper.

Expert advice is not to call for the bird with gun mounted. You cannot predict the flight well enough to do this with consistency for the second of time saved by an early mount is of little advantage and may even be a handicap. Better to wait and watch the bird as it appears and mount and swing smoothly as it flies past.

Targets are presented after a maximum of three seconds. The shooter should call loudly for the clay so that all present, especially the judge who will be wearing ear protection, will be able to hear. The referee will call 'kill' or 'lost' at each bird and a shooter who disagrees with a 'lost' verdict should speak out there and then and not after the round is over.

The shooter should allow the trapper time to reload and cock the trap before calling for the next bird. A decent delay takes the pressure off the trapper, especially when throwing doubles. At the end of the round the shooter opens the gun, takes his card from the referee, thanking him as he does so, checks that his score has been correctly recorded and moves away.

The targets may be roughly divided into four categories: the incoming bird, the going away bird, the left to right crosser and the right to left crosser.

The incomer may be angled from left or right and may be high or low. Too low birds are not popular due to the possible danger of a low shot and the falling of sharp fragments of broken clay round the ears of shooter and spectator alike. The easiest bird is the straight overhead which is smoothly blotted out with the muzzles and killed. Once this technique is learned then various angles and heights may be introduced until the methodology is mastered.

The bird going away must be addressed quickly. An error at the muzzles, even a tiny one, will be compounded by the time it reaches the target and will result in a handsome miss. As in the incomer the straight bird is the easiest to hit and this is the one on which to learn. Once this has been mastered the angled shot to left and right may be attempted.

The crossing shots from right to left and left to right should be tried with the simple right-angled bird. For the right hander the right to left bird will be easier than the reverse for the front hand is pulling rather than pushing the muzzles through the target. This is a more positive action. The master eye is important with these two birds. A switch to the wrong eye can cause misses in front. In the case of the left to right-bird a takeover by the left eye in a right-handed shooter will result in such misses. When shooting doubles as crossers the rear bird should be taken first despite the temptation to take the leader. Once the rear bird has been hit the swing continues smoothly to overtake and kill the one in front.

English sporting is easy to find for all clay grounds and most village fetes and country shows have a layout. If the beginner decides to carry on with the sport and take it up seriously, there is no substitute for a good coach on a proper clay ground. There will be no shortage of advice from bystanders and self-appointed experts although this is sometimes conflicting and causes more confusion than anything else.

Sporting clay shooting goes well with real quarry shooting. Game shots or wildfowlers can sharpen their reflexes, learn how to handle the birds which always seem to catch them out and keep their eye in with sporting shooting, even if it is done at a modest level with a single trap and a few friends in the evening. Wherever in the country you happen to live you are unlikely to be far from a sporting shoot on most Sunday mornings and you are sure to be made welcome. How far you progress thereafter and whether you become a second George Digweed and shoot your 100 straight is largely a matter of your ability, how far you want to take it, how much money you can afford travelling and practising and the depth of your commitment.

FITASC sporting

This is the ultimate form of sporting shooting, which reproduces the shooting field as closely as possible. It is administered by *Federations Internationale de Tir aux Armes Sportives de Chasse* which is the Paris based body responsible also for the trap discipline of universal trench, a superior version of English sporting, held by many to be the most challenging clay discipline as well as one which can be most exciting. A sporting layout is set up with a series of varied and testing targets. The shooter is put in a squad of six competitors who move round the course taking turns to shoot first at each firing point; the squad is accompanied by a scorer and a referee. Firing technique is precise. The butt must be clear of the shoulder until the target is up and flying and you are not allowed to move before you see the target – any anticipatory twitches as you hear the trap are outlawed.

The original FITASC set-up was a 25 bird layout with three shooting stands and four or five traps. (On the major 100 bird competition there are four stands.) The common pattern is for four singles and two doubles at each stand. An extra single may be shot on one stand to make up the total for the round to 25. In the event of a tie with two or more shooters scoring the same, a shoot off of a new round of 25 will be held until a clear winner is established.

Only one squad is allowed on the layout at any one time so that two stands are unoccupied while the third is being shot. A new variant has been created on the old FITASC pattern. One reason for this was the increasing popularity of FITASC. This resulted in pressure on grounds and the fact that all but one of the stands stood idle at any one time.

For the new version each stand has its own set of traps rather like in English sporting – indeed, it has been likened to squadded English sporting. There is no rule against more than one squad being in the field at the same time so that when stand one has been vacated and the squad moved on to stand two, a second squad moves in. This means that more shooters can be occupied at the same time and there is a more economical use of trappers' time and maximum use of ground space.

English sporting is a good apprenticeship for FITASC and it is recommended that at least two years are spent mastering that discipline before moving on to the more severe challenge. A good performance at one does not guarantee success with the other. FITASC is expensive and complicated to stage and many traps and trappers are needed. Not many grounds are equipped for it and a two-day session could cost the competitor a considerable sum.

Many UK shooters excel at FITASC and we have a number of distinguished champions at British, European and world levels. FITASC is popular world wide: in the 1990 championships at Le Rabot in France, for example, there were 720 entrants in the competition coming from nine countries.

It counts as a branch of sporting shooting and is considered by its proponents the ultimate challenge. Those addicted to it often forsake all other disciplines in its favour. As far as imitating a stand in the real shooting field it is without equal, for in one round a shooter can experience every type of bird that is likely to be encountered in live quarry shooting. It follows that many expert FITASC men and women are also very good game shots.

3

Guns

The gun used for clay shooting will be no larger than a 12-bore. The larger gauges usually associated with wildfowling carry more shot, have longer range and might be deemed to give the user an unfair advantage over the more lightly armed. The barrel length will vary from 25 in to 34 in – the lower legal limit is 24 in.

The most popular gun for clay shooting is the over-and-under (OU), which has one barrel vertically above the other. Although the best British gunmakers made such a gun for field shooting long ago, it has only become popular well within our lifetime. The availability of many reasonably priced and well-made imported guns placed them within reach of everyone.

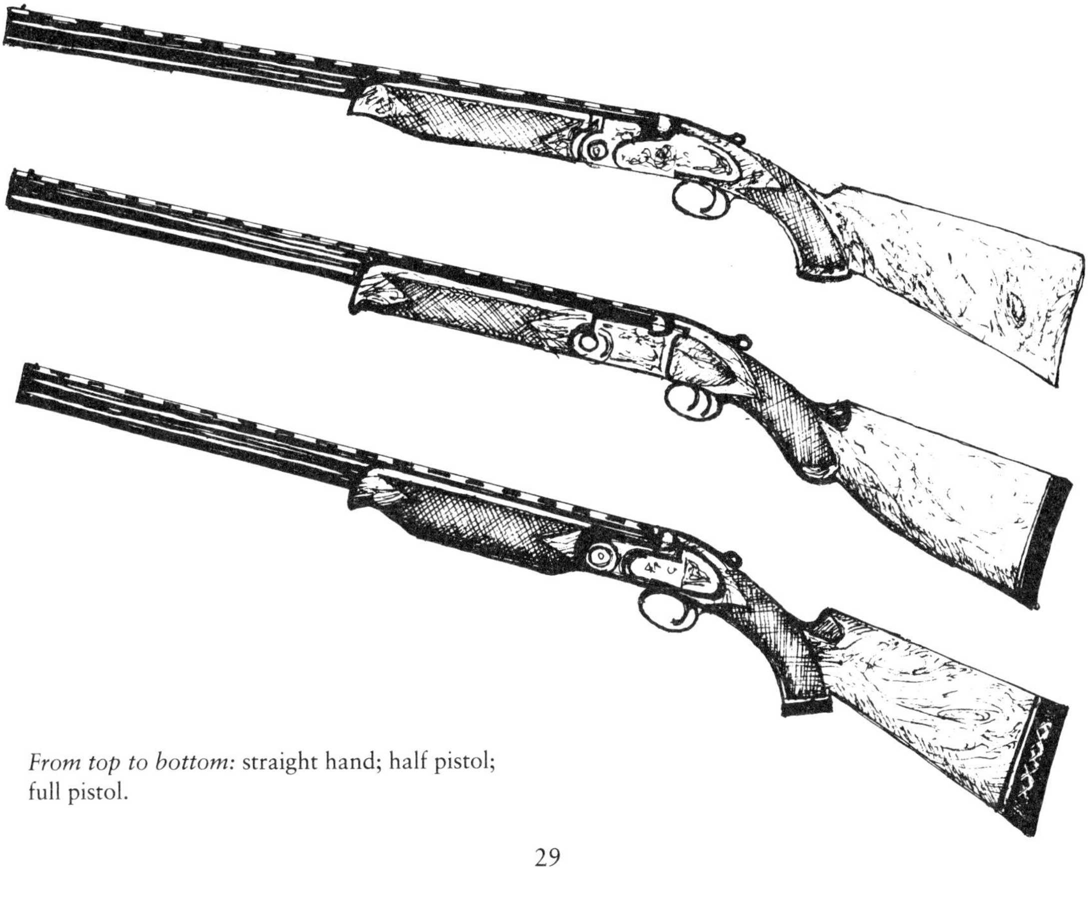

From top to bottom: straight hand; half pistol; full pistol.

This type of gun is available in any variety of combinations. The stock may be Monte Carlo, straight hand, half pistol, full pistol, with or without a rubber recoil pad. The stock may be cast on or off, to fit or be straight. Fore-ends come in any style from beavertail to splinter and special adaptations. Triggers are single selective, double, or single non-selective.

Unlike the game shooter the clay shot tends to use no safety-catch. This is because the gun is never closed and loaded unless it is going to be fired within the next few seconds and from a safe position. Just once in a shooting lifetime a safety-catch left on by mistake might cost a competitor a bird and with it a championship. Clay guns with non-automatic safety-catches can be adapted easily by a competent gunsmith.

The chambers may be made to suit and the chokes (see p. 32) bored to requirements although many modern clay guns have interchangeable screw-in chokes which may be replaced as needed. Boxlock, sidelock, ejector and non-ejector are all available. Top ribs and side ribs come in any combination from none at all to ventilated, narrow rib or wide rib. Sighting beads can be plain steel or fluorescent compound, the better to catch the eye on a dull day. In other words a well

The over-and-under – in this case a top grade Beretta sidelock – is the universal favourite for clay shooting.

stocked gun shop can offer the buyer a gun to suit every need or whim and length of purse. Among the especially popular makes of OU clay gun are those manufactured by Beretta, Browning, Miroku and Perazzi. Some old favourites such as Winchester and Nikko are no longer made although they may be bought second-hand.

Side-by-side hammer guns may be used but are rarely seen except at purely sporting birds where an owner might like to try out an old friend and see if it still shoots straight. The side-by-side hammerless gun may be ejector or non-ejector. The best British versions of this gun are among the finest in the world and tend to be used almost exclusively on the game shoot rather than the clay layout. Some competitions are aimed specially at side-by-side owners and are named as such, but they tend to be one-offs for the benefit of game shots who want to try their hand at artificial birds.

The side-by-side is not popular on the clay ground for it is deemed too light for regular clay shooting and the barrels are not as pointable as the single sighting plane of the over-and-under. The game gun is responsive and light enough for game shooting and was designed for that purpose. No top competitor uses one today for competition shooting. The going away bird, for example, would be hard for a side-by-side shooter. The light barrels would flick up at the first shot and a precision shot at a quartering bird would be difficult indeed.

On the other hand, the OU is quite acceptable and effective for game shooting and after some early years of suspicion by traditionalists they now appear regularly in the field. The lesson is that the beginner who can afford only one gun for all purposes, but wants to concentrate on clays with the odd day at game, needs to buy an over-and-under. The beginner committed to clays has little choice but to take the same path.

Your gun should be the best you can afford. While it may be the case that all guns superficially appear the same there is a deal of difference between a good one and a bad one. The feel, balance and handling qualities can vary enormously depending on how much you pay. It is better to buy a quality second-hand gun than a new one of inferior quality. Guns are made to last.

While the single barrel gun is too restricted for general use in the UK, the hammerless single such as the Ithaca is popular in the USA where down the line shooting limits the shooter to a single barrel. However, the single barrel semi-automatic has its place on the clay ground. Barrels may be interchangeable or screw-in chokes are available. Most semi-autos are designed for right handers but this means that the empty case and bits of debris are thrown across the face of the left-handed shooter after each shot. Remington make a semi-auto with the port on the left hand side for such shooters.

The correct type of ammunition must be used with the auto since not all types are compatible. Care must be taken to choose carefully and experiment before going in for competitions. The main worry with this type of gun is the uncertainty of such a highly mechanical system. It might break down and let you down at a critical moment. Most models are very reliable but the worry that something might go wrong at the very next shot can be off-putting.

One advantage of the semi-auto is that it has very little recoil. Thus it is often used for youngsters or beginners or those of light

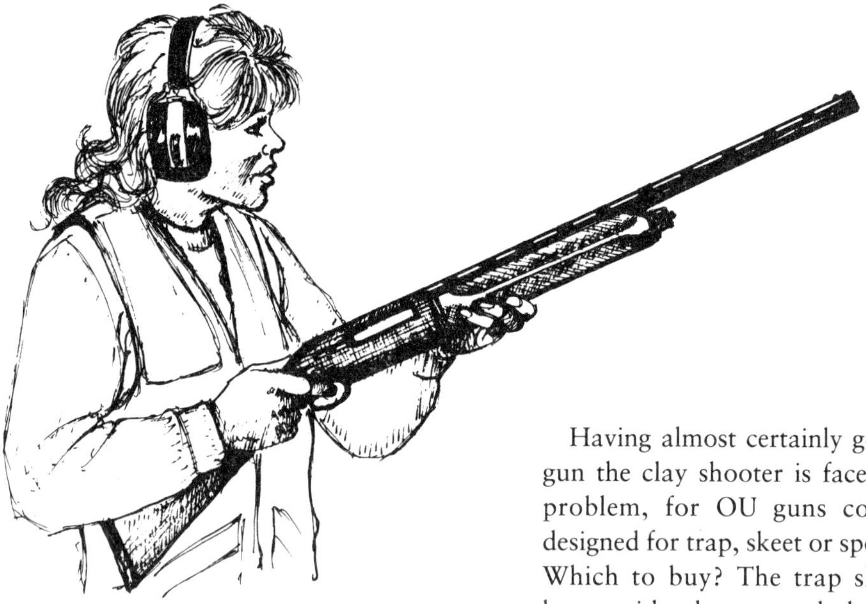

build like some women shooters. A heavy recoil can be tiring, especially as in one day on a clay ground a shooter may take 200 shots. On the debit side, worries have been expressed that, while a break action gun may be clearly seen to be unloaded and safe, this is not so with a semi-auto. The breech block should either be open at all times or it is possible to insert a special bung with a red flash on it showing to the world that the gun cannot be fired. The limit now is two cartridges in the magazine and one in the chamber. The clay shot in competition is limited to a maximum of two shots.

The pump-action shotgun is far less popular in the UK than in the USA. In other respects it has much in common with the semi-auto although the fresh cartridge is pumped in by the shooter's left hand rather than being fed in automatically, powered by the recoil. For double shots this takes the shooter off true aim and can be distracting.

Having almost certainly gone for the OU gun the clay shooter is faced with another problem, for OU guns come differently designed for trap, skeet or sporting shooting. Which to buy? The trap shooting gun is heavy with a longer stock, low comb height, a recoil pad and long barrels of probably 30 in. It may have screw-in chokes but will more likely be bored tight at full and three-quarters. Choke is a constriction in the last inch or so of the barrel; it holds the shot together and makes the pattern of shot effective at longer ranges than if there were no choke. True cylinder is the most open and full choke is the tightest. The clay shot would use full choke for the trap bird and open choke for skeet.

The general-purpose model is the sporting multi-choke. Choke may be changed to suit the target so that skeet may be shot. Before the days of screw-in multi-chokes there was a

A cross-section of the shotgun showing screw-in chokes.

specialist skeet gun, light with short barrels and open borings for the close shots to be taken. The sporting gun will do for both sporting and skeet, unless the owner wishes to become a specialist skeet shot.

The length of barrel and fit of the gun are two very important factors. It is possible for the average man to wear an off-the-peg suit but to be immaculately clothed he needs something bespoke and made to measure. The same is true of guns, for while most average shots can perform creditably with any gun they do very much better with one that fits them. As for the all-important stock, your face should lie about 1½ in from the comb. The stock length will be determined by the thickness of your neck and depth of your cheekbone, the measurement being taken from the middle of the butt to the point at which the finger touches the trigger.

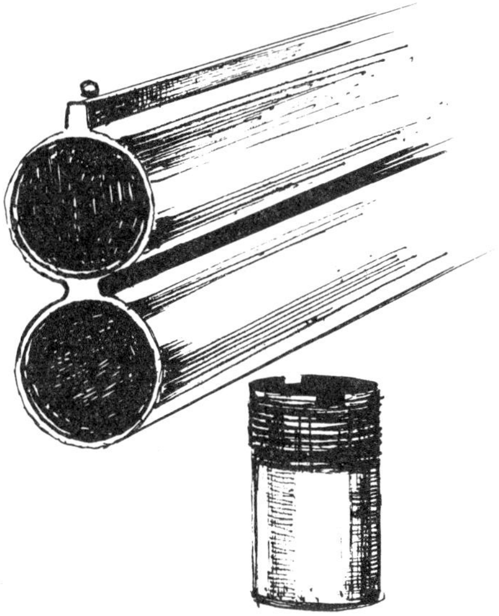

The comb determines the height of the gun and when the stock is to the shoulder the cheek should rest on the comb so that the master eye is looking straight down the barrels at the sight. The OU tends to shoot high. The distance between the line of the barrels and the comb should also be 1½ in. The drop at the end of the stock, known as the heel, will be about 2 in.

Cast is the bend in the wrist of the stock which brings the barrels in line with the dominant eye. In most cases this is the right eye, for which the stock is said to be cast 'off'. For the left-handed shooter it is bent the other way and so is cast 'on'. Problems arise for the right hander with a left master eye. There are two options here, either to change shoulders and shut the better eye or to use a cross-eyed stock which allows the gun to be mounted on the good shoulder while the barrels align with the better eye. In my view this is a desperate (and expensive) resort sometimes used by game shots but rarely, it seems, by clay experts.

When considering the choice of triggers, the single selective is by far the favourite. The selector button is usually incorporated in the safety catch. The weight of trigger pull, i.e. the pressure required to fire the gun, should be about 3½ lb on the first trigger and 4¼ lb on the second. Trap shooters prefer the pull to be a little heavier to prevent premature discharge.

The most popular barrel length is between 27 and 28 in. Shorter barrelled guns are harder to use for they tend to fly everywhere and are hard to swing steadily. Some game shooting guns are made with 25 in barrels but these are rarely seen on clay grounds. The longer barrel allows easier control and makes for a better swing. The experts tend to use the longer barrels, 30 in being popular, but for the beginner the shorter length will give a better all-round performance until you become proficient. The rib, from which there are many to choose, is purely a matter of personal preference.

I have explained the matter of choke: the more you have the closer the shot hangs together and thus the harder it is to hit a close target. The beginner should keep the chokes open with improved cylinder (open) and quarter choke (a little tighter) in the two barrels. For targets within easy range up to 30 yds these give a far better killing pattern. A shot taken with a full choke barrel might miss entirely whereas exactly the same chance taken with improved cylinder would result in a hit. The specialists shooting FITASC prefer chokes much tighter for they tend to take long shots.

The choice of gun and its various pieces of furniture and fittings can be bewildering for the beginner. Much of the choice must lie with what you feel most comfortable using. You would need to be very choosy indeed to opt for a side-by-side, a single barrel or an auto if you intend to shoot clays seriously. There is nothing wrong with any of them, as I have explained, but to start you off it is safest to follow the well-worn path.

As a beginner you will need an over-and-under gun, barrels of 28 in, stock to fit as described, fore-end to suit, top rib ditto, single selective trigger and barrels bored improved and quarter (or multi-) chokes. With this you will be able to perform creditably at most clay targets – when you become an expert then is the time to start playing around with new measurements and more specialist guns.

4

BUYING A GUN

Having read the literature, talked to other shooters, watched at some clay grounds and maybe had a shot with a friend's gun, the beginner feels ready to lay down his hard-earned money and purchase a gun. The most likely choice is an over-and-under with medium length barrels and one which fits. The buyer will have decided whether it is to be for a particular type of clay shooting or a general, all-purpose gun which will be about right for most things just to get started. This decision must be made before going into a shop or the buyer might be decoyed by quite the wrong type of gun just because it is the sort used by the famous A.J. 'Smoker' Smith.

There are three sources of guns: gun shops, mail order or private purchase. Gun shops can be good in that they offer expert advice and have a back-up service in case of trouble. Most shops will do this, so beware of those without such a service. The assistant behind the counter may not be an expert, and he may only be standing in for the regular man on his day off – so be careful.

It is a wise move to take with you a friend who has experience of clay shooting and gun buying, for moral support of this kind can save you from making a horrible mistake. You will know your budget and just how much you have to spend. It should be the most you can afford but do not overreach your resources and end up with a debt you cannot repay. On the other hand, do not be deceived by the cheap and shoddy just because it looks all right on the outside and the price is rock bottom. You get what you pay for. Set a top limit and stick to it; make your first visit one of reconnaissance and do not expect to walk out with your new treasure wrapped in oily paper. Check the field and be prepared to go more than once.

If you buy a new gun there are some advantages. The gun will come with a guarantee so that a no-question-asked replacement service will be available in case of a maker's fault. Also the new gun will certainly be 'in proof'. It is against the law to sell a gun out of proof, one with barrels worn, pitted or damaged so that they would no longer pass the proof test. Proofing is carried out at the Proof Houses in London and Birmingham. Continental guns also have their own proof marks which meet the exacting UK standards. The mark of proof is stamped on to the flats of the barrels and may be easily interpreted.

The gun should be minutely examined before buying. You may have come into the shop with the notion that you want to join the army of Browning or Beretta owners and you want a 28 in barrel multi-choke. The shop ought to have a good selection of such a popular model. Make sure there are no blemishes or damage to the woodwork, especially the thin wood in front of the action on the fore-end where cracks can appear.

The blacking on the barrels should be consistent and dense. Inside the bores should be polished with no signs of dents. Take the fore-end on and off a few times to ensure it does not stick. Open and close the gun. It is likely to be stiff but this will wear off after a few boxes of cartridges. Any stiffness should be smooth, with no signs of a catch of metal on metal. Modern guns are made to high standards but damage may occur in transit or in the shop where it may have been dropped.

There is a strong temptation to buy a second-hand gun; the same money which buys a new one will go further and buy you something superior. However, there is a risk that the gun has seen too much action or may have been damaged or neglected. There are many good second-hand guns on the market and many a bad one too. Like buying horses and second-hand cars it is very much a case of 'let the buyer beware'.

As with a new gun, you will have set your sights on the barrel length, type of grip, model, etc. and you will still have a top price above which you will not go. Some gunshops offer a back-up service and a guarantee for second-hand as well as new guns. It is sensible to make sure that this comes with the package. You will have read the advertisements in the sporting press so you ought to know what you will expect to pay for the gun of your dreams.

One or two guns on the rack will catch your eye. At first glance they look right, they are the sort of thing you are looking for and there are no obvious signs of breakages or bumps. Have a check list and your expert friend with you as you examine the gun. Go over it logically, barrels, action and stock, and apply a few simple tests. Have the bores and the barrel wall thickness measured on the spot (the gunsmith will have a tool for this purpose) and make a note of the measurements. The gun must be in proof and this test will confirm that the bores have not become enlarged through use or abuse. There is no regulation about the thickness of barrel walls but you will not wish them to be too thin, no matter how well the internal measurements look.

Hold the barrels up to a light about a foot away and rotate them through 360° looking down them as you do so. In this way you will see any dents, signs of lead deposits or pit marks, i.e. small pock marks inside the barrels caused by corrosion. Do the same looking at the outside of the barrels where ripples, dents or bulges will be exposed by the light. Examine the ribs for signs of dents – a special hazard in ventilated ribs. Also look for weakness in the solder which fixes the rib to the barrels. Tiny holes sometimes appear and water will leak in and set up a rust trap between rib and barrel which you can neither detect nor cure.

If screw-in chokes are fitted, take them out and examine them for thread damage or any build-up of dirt. The barrel lumps should be clear of any tiny grooves or scratches where grit has worn away the metal, indicating that the gun has not been well cleaned. Check any protruding metalwork such as the cross pin, the bite and other sharp edges for signs of wear or rounding of any corners that are supposed to be square. This is often a good test of a gun which has had heavy use. The face of the barrels should be pit free and the extractors should move freely, with no catching or signs of undue wear.

Turn next to the stock and assess its general appearance. A well-figured stock is a joy to see and a matter for owner pride, but it is no good if it is cracked or chipped. Look closely at all places where the wood is slim, such as the hand or wrist of the gun, where the strap is screwed in. Chequering should be sharp and clean, although in a second-hand

gun you would expect to find some wear. Chequering can conceal a tiny crack, as I know to my cost. My gunsmith found a tiny crack under the chequering when I took my gun in for an annual service. I had not noticed it, although I had examined the gun each time I had cleaned it, and I needed a complete new stock at a price which made my insurance company wince.

The wood ought to be slightly proud of the metal and not discoloured by regular soakings in oil. This is particularly damaging, softening and swelling the wood, making the wood fit poorly to the metal. There should be no gaps between wood and metal. The main stock wood should be free of bad dents or deep scratches. It is impossible to have a pristine stock on a second-hand gun, but bad or unsightly damage which cannot be repaired must be noted. It might not put you off buying the gun but it might be reflected in the price you pay for it.

The action should appear unmarked and clean. There should be no, or few, marks round the striker holes and the pins should appear undamaged. The knuckle of the gun should have no wear marks and be smooth. This is the main hinge of the gun and a part likely to take most wear. Most of the works are hidden inside the action so that even a superficial check will not be possible. Check all screw heads and pins for signs of damage which might indicate that some amateur blacksmith has had a go at taking it apart. This can be an ominous sign. The general bright and tidy appearance of the action is a good guide to a cared-for gun.

Test the trigger pulls with your forefinger and two snap caps in the breech. Squeeze gently so that you can assess the strength you need to discharge the gun, whether there is drag, if the pull is too light or if you need to heave on the trigger before the lock snaps. Trigger pulls too light and too heavy are equally dangerous and adjustments will have to be made in the shop.

The action/barrel fit should also be checked. Put barrels and action together leaving off the fore-end. Lay the gun flat on the counter on a cloth and try to move the

barrels from side to side. Next take the gun up and give the stock some firm thumps with your hand and then shake it from side to side holding it at the wrist. There should be no detectable movement from side to side or up and down.

Try the ejectors by firing one barrel, jogging the stock to set the second barrel and firing that. Open the gun slowly and note the timing of the ejection. If the case catches the face of the action in either barrel the timing is faulty. If neither case ejects at all then some drastic therapy is called for. One may eject but not the other. The perfect ejector shoots both spent cases clear of the gun simultaneously and you need to test no more than twice. It has been known for cases to eject when snap caps are used, but not with real ammunition. This indicates more severe wear and you will need to take up your warranty.

You should now have completed your check list and may be in a position to make a decision. A good gun dealer will allow you to take the gun away for a day or two for field trials and there are many who will encourage this. This allows the ultimate test of satisfaction, not only that the gun is sound but that you can hit things with it. If there are any minor faults the gunsmith will rectify them – but do not neglect to retest before you collect your purchase. Remember that you will need a shotgun certificate to buy a gun as well as cartridges and changes of gun ownership must be reported to your local constabulary.

It is possible to buy guns privately second-hand. All the above tests must be carried out with even more care, for the world of second-hand gun selling is full of trickery. No honest seller will be afraid of having the gun examined by a qualified gunsmith and this would be my strong recommendation.

The days of guns increasing in value by huge amounts overnight have gone. Most guns will hold their value well if you look after them and when you come to change or trade-in you ought to get a large part of what you paid for it as credit against your next purchase. The gun should be serviced once a year, cleaned properly (a matter I deal with in detail in the next chapter) and kept in a secure place, along with the cartridges, in order to comply with the law.

Your gun will become your treasured possession, and with it comes responsibilities. Your safety, the care of it and the way you handle it are all down to you. Accidents must not be allowed to happen and you must act in a sensible manner at all times. The pleasure you gain from it, shooting your chosen targets, will be worth the care of looking after it and paying so much for it. A good gun is one of those things which you enjoy using but which loses no value while you are doing so.

5

Gun Cleaning and Care

If you look after your gun it will look after you. We have seen how to identify signs of neglect or misuse in guns appearing on the second-hand market and it is important that your gun does not end up in a similar state with pitted barrels, loose action and damaged or discoloured woodwork. It is virtually impossible to wear out a gun by normal use. There are guns in existence which have fired an estimated million shots, the resultant wear in the inside of the bores barely measurable and the barrels still well in proof. Leave your gun uncleaned after a few wet days or fail to lubricate the moving parts and more damage will occur in a month than in a lifetime of shots.

A cared-for gun will not only serve the owner well and not break down in action, which can be a disaster if you are in the middle of a competition and maybe doing well, but it will maintain its value for the second-hand market. Clay pigeon folk tend to chop and change their guns more than game shooters so you need to present the dealer with something which is attractive.

The popular, fleece-lined gunslip can be a problem. While soft and kind to your gun as you convey it from place to place, the wool will absorb any moisture which happens to be on the barrels. Leave the gun in the slip overnight with wet barrels and they are rusty by morning. Do it regularly and serious pitting will develop and it will be impossible to clean the gun properly. The same is true of baize-lined motor cases and even gun cupboards.

You will need a roll of absorbent toilet tissue, a cleaning rod, a phosphor bronze brush, a wool mop, some clean rags, stock wax and gun oil such as WD40 from a spray can, fine quality grease, a tooth brush and a feather. With these basics you can do a good job. Clean the gun the moment you arrive home before you do anything else. There is an old code among game shooters which lists your after-shoot chores as dog, gun and self – in that order. The clay shot will not have a dog to worry about, so it is gun first. On a really wet day it is advisable to wipe down the gun with a dry cloth before putting it in the case to take it home. If you also give the barrels a quick pull through, so much the better.

Have a clear table top covered with newspaper on which to work. The really keen gun owner will have a special place such as an old table or cupboard top covered with a piece of carpet. The gun may be placed on this and worked on with no fear of damage or scratching either to the gun or to the furniture. Dismantle the gun into stock, barrels and fore-end.

I prefer to start on the barrels and squirt up each one with the WD40. Take a single sheet of tissue, roll it into a ball and push it through with the handle of the cleaning rod. Do this

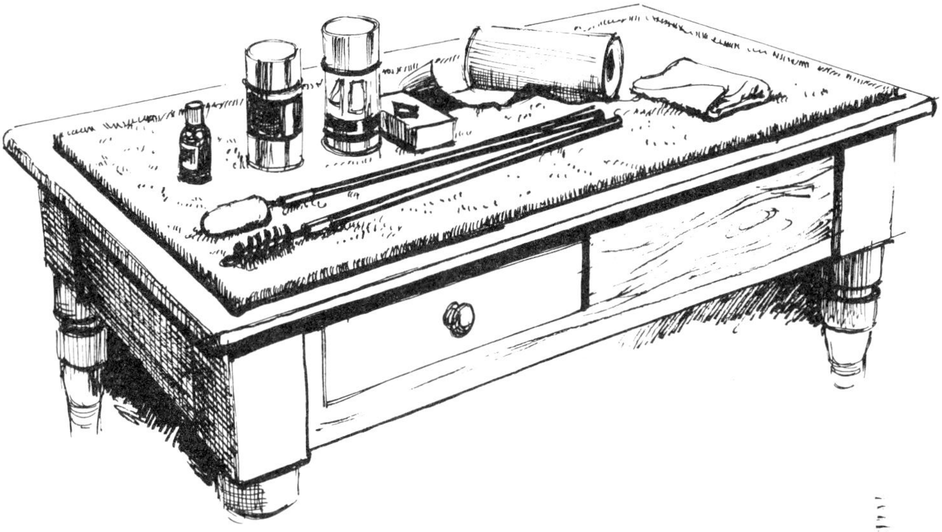

twice to each barrel and it will remove much of the powder deposits and wet. Some cartridges give a cleaner burn than others; while one will leave a barrel apparently unmarked another will leave a layer of what looks like soot inside.

Give another squirt and scrub each barrel with the phosphor bronze brush. This will remove any fouling under which pits can develop undetected until it is too late. Push more tissue through but do not use too much or make the wad too large. You should not have to force it through with any strength. Gun barrels are of soft metal and even a tight wad of paper hammered through can damage them. When the tissue comes out clean, give a final polish with a lightly oiled wool mop. Do not leave too much oil inside the barrels. A surplus can create an obstruction which causes severe damage to barrels known as a ring bulge next time the gun is fired.

Wipe down the lumps and hook until the tissue comes away clean. Lightly grease moving parts and the sharp edges of metal where movement against the action occurs. Clean the rib where it joins the barrels using a wooden toothpick and pay special attention to ventilated ribs, for moisture can collect in the holes. This is my main objection to such ribs. Each slot must be cleaned out individually with a feather or a tissue on the toothpick.

Finally wipe the barrels with a lightly oiled rag. There is a tendency to over-oil guns so that they are swimming in the stuff. The lightest application put on with a feather is all that you need. Too much oil will run off on to the woodwork when the gun is in the cupboard and swell and discolour the stock and fore-end.

Wipe the action clean of any deposits. Your rag will come away black for the first few wipes and then be clean. When thoroughly clean apply a light greasing to the flats, the face and the knuckle where most wear occurs. On no account squirt quantities of oil into the striker holes. This is a common error: they do not need it and oil building up in inaccessible places gathers dirt, creates pressure and will eventually result in a breakage. Wipe the outside of the action with the lightly oiled rag: you will be surprised at the amount of grime which has built up in just one day of use.

An oiled stock needs little maintenance, but remove all encrusted mud. If it is really

baked on, a soft sponge and soapy water may be needed. Make sure you dry it well afterwards. An oil-finished stock will need an occasional rub down with stock conditioning oil or even high-grade furniture polish will do. Buff it with the palm of your hand and finish with a clean duster to restore the lustre.

Varnished stocks require even less maintenance but varnish can chip and a damaged or old varnished stock does not look pretty. It is better to have the varnish removed and apply an oil finish instead. Clean grimy chequering with your toothbrush but do not fill the grooves with stock wax which can be difficult to remove. Wax only the unchequered parts of the woodwork. Note any scratches and bruises. It will be too much for you to remove them but a gunsmith can do wonders at taking out any marks.

The fore-end, which tends to be often neglected, needs the metalwork wiping down and the wood cleaning. Reassemble the gun and put it in your secure place under lock and key until you need it next. The whole cleaning operation should take no more than five minutes.

Once a year (some say once every two years) take your gun to a gunsmith for a strip and clean. He will strip down the action where you cannot see and clean it inside, check all timings and wear, lift bruises on the stock, identify potential sources of long-term damage and give everything a proper overhaul. This is well worth doing and it is a small price to pay to protect your valuable property.

A gun is designed and made to last more than one lifetime. Some game guns now in the field may be over a hundred years old and they are still in perfect condition. This is only because their owners took care of them; the few minutes it took to clean it plus the annual service being a worthy investment of time and money.

6

CARTRIDGES

Most clay shooting is done with a 12-bore gun and cartridges which have evolved over many years to a high standard of quality and consistency. Old cartridge cases were made with a paper cylinder but nowadays plastic is almost universal. The trouble with paper was that, while it produced better patterns in some guns, notably English game guns, the cases swelled and jammed when wet. In the clay shoot this was an insurmountable problem and there is one story of a foreign team competing on a wet day using paper cases while the team manager stood behind each shooter holding a screwdriver with which to lever out the swollen spent case after each shot.

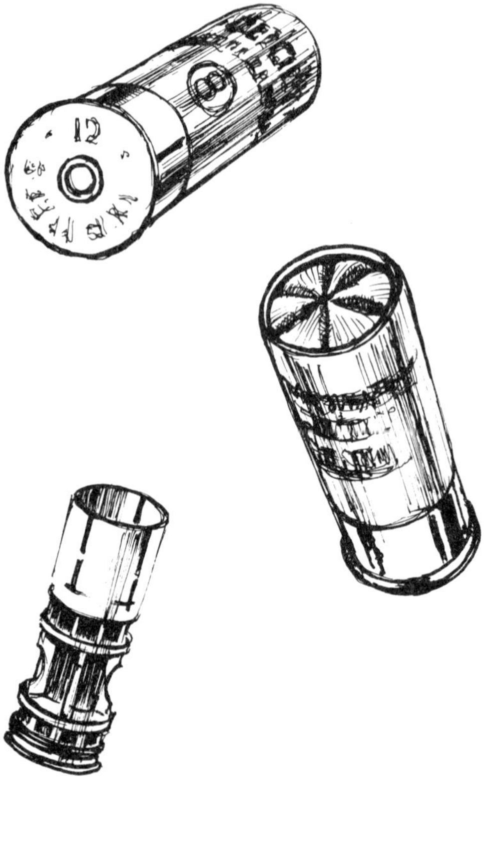

The open end of the case used to be closed with a roll turnover but today almost universally what is known as a crimp closure is used. This gives better patterns than the roll turnover, where the overshot wad would sometimes produce blown patterns.

The shot and powder are separated by a tightly fitting piston called the wad. This may be made of plastic and is specially designed to hold the shot together in a sort of envelope, allowing it to open and develop a pattern as it flies through the air. Some wads are made of compressed fibre and on some clay grounds fibre wads are compulsory to avoid littering the countryside with waste plastic. If you arrive not knowing this rule there are usually some fibre wad cartridges on sale at the ground. For down the line shooting, the plastic wad remains the most popular but for sporting or skeet the fibre wad is preferred.

In the centre of the metal head of the cartridge is the percussion cap. This contains a fulminate which ignites the powder, creating the expanding gases that move the shot up the barrel. Some caps are criticized as too hard and do not go off when lightly struck by the firing pin. On the other hand those deemed too soft are penetrated by the pin and detonate with damaging results to the face of the action. In most cases it will be found that a weak spring or worn firing pin are to blame rather than the cartridge.

Powder is carefully manufactured and exhaustively tested to assess the pressures and velocities involved before it is loaded into commercial ammunition. The powder is ignited by the firing of the cap: it emits a rapidly expanding gas which, having nowhere to go but up the barrel, propels the shot which lies in front of it up the tube. Modern powders are fast burning and will burn out within a short barrel. The old black powder of grandfather's day took longer to burn and the gases were given off more slowly. This meant that long barrels were required and even then a sprinkling of unburned powder grains might fall from the muzzle at the shot.

The shot comprises a measure of spherical lead pellets hardened with antimony. The pellets burst from the muzzle in an all but solid mass and spread out as they fly towards the target. The degree of spread and the density of the final pattern of shot is dependent on the amount of choke in the barrel.

There is currently a fierce debate about the introduction of non-lead shot for cartridges. The fear is that lead, being toxic, is harming the countryside. Whatever the rights of the matter (and no case of damage to the environment from this source in the UK has been proved beyond doubt), game shooters and wildfowlers might be affected by a compulsory ban in 1997 following a voluntary one beginning with the season of 1995. It is the writer's view that such a ban will eventually extend to all shotgun shooting. This would have grave repercussions on clay shooting for at present there is no substitute for lead in either price or performance. Experiments are under way to develop a replacement which is as good and possibly better than lead but as yet there is nothing to match it. The whole shooting community pins its hopes on such a substance appearing in time for the 1997 deadline.

When the cloud of shot is flying through the air, it is affected by what is known as stringing. Rather than flying in a dense pattern, some shot flies ahead of the rest so that, seen from the side, it would appear something like a squirt of water or puff of smoke in the wind. The conclusion is that any shooter at game or clay ought to aim to miss in front for the pellets at the back of the string will compensate for too generous a lead.

The tighter the choke the longer the string. Someone in the USA once fired at a moving train (under controlled conditions) and left a long trail of shot along the side, demonstrating better than any number of words what stringing means. An open bored gun would have left a shorter string.

The larger the shot size the thinner the pattern, but the greater the carrying range of each individual pellet. Shooting at edge-on clays presents a small target, so small shot is essential if the bird is not to pass between the pellets. Each clay discipline has its own recommended shot sizes, tried and tested, and the beginner is advised to stick to these.

- **For trap** use No 7 or No 7½ cartridges, which are the Italian and American equivalent of 7½ and 8 respectively.
- **For skeet** everyone seems to use No 9 which is 9½ Italian.
- **For sporting clays** No 7 or 7½ may be combined with No 9; the latter, which patterns well, is particularly useful for minis or the high tower. No 8 is especially popular.

An introductory book like this is not the place for a detailed scientific assessment of the combination of chokes and shot sizes and weights for each discipline. There are other places to find out such things later on. The main lesson is that the shot pattern should be centred on the target, that small shot is right for close range and heavier shot for longer range. The trick is to place the optimum pattern of shot at the place you expect to kill the bird and so eliminate the margin of error. A 1oz (28g) shot load is now used for all clay shooting disciplines except for FITASC where up to 32 g is allowed.

When buying cartridges find the best brand for your gun and stock up with 7s and 9s which will see you through most situations. The more you buy at once the cheaper they become so join a group of shooters for a bulk purchase or buy at least 1,000 at a time if you can afford it. Keep them in dry, safe conditions and you will find that they will last for many years before deteriorating.

A selection of the many types of cartridge available.

7

Clothing and Accessories

It is important that the clay shot should be comfortable when performing. The very smartest equipment is useless if the wearer cannot shoot in a relaxed way, free from binding coats or clumsy footwear. Weather permitting it is good advice to wear no top coat such as those used by game shots. The heavy waterproof or the tweed jacket with 'breathing' lining will not allow the swift gun mount and bedding the stock into the shoulder for the fast bird. The game shot can get away with it because there tends to be more time to seat the stock before addressing the bird. Also game shooting involves more standing around in all weathers and so there is little choice but to be well wrapped up.

If you are clay shooting and own a well-fitting gun, there is little point in suddenly introducing rucked up swathes of top coat between your body and the heel of your gun. The target is up and away from you in no time and you need the facility for an instant mount with the gun in exactly the right place. A lumpy top coat will prevent this.

• **Skeet vest** The clay shot needs a snug fitting skeet vest. There is a wide selection on the market and yours should be generous enough to take a light sweater underneath without being too loose. The side pockets should be big enough to take enough cartridges for one stand (15 is usually all you will need) and the holes for the arms must be big enough to allow free movement.

Do not buy one with a superfluous collar, flaps in front or pockets anywhere near where the stock of the gun should be. They can be dangerous as well as spoil your shooting. The skeet vest has a shoulder pad of leather or suede and this should extend from the shoulder seam down to the top of the pocket. Some vests have a shoulder pad on each side, but in any case the left hander will need to have a pad on the left hand side.

• **A top coat** is useful too, but only for wearing when you are awaiting your turn

and it may be slipped off when you step forward to shoot.

• **Waterproofs** Also handy is a set of lightweight waterproofs which will be essential on those really wet days. Waterproof trousers will protect the legs and the thin jacket will be worn under and not on top of the skeet vest. Nylon waterproofs take up little room, will not affect the fit of the gun and are loose enough to allow you to move easily.

• **Hat** The traditional headgear of the clay shot is a peaked cap. This has many proven advantages. It protects the head, keeps the wearer warm (for much body heat is lost through the head) and, most importantly, shields the eyes from the sun. The traditional cloth cap is popular but most often seen is the American style of baseball cap which has an extra long peak and offers good protection. There are still many clay shots who prefer to go bareheaded, seeing the hat as an unnecessary encumbrance. It is a matter of choice, but if anyone has ever suffered from a broken clay (or even worse an unbroken one) hitting them on the head they will quickly realize that a hat has its protective use, even on a dull day.

Hats with back peaks are awkward for taking overhead shots, for as you throw back your head the peak catches on your collar and pushes the hat forward. When choosing your hat, remember that you will be using ear muffs with it so it ought to have no side flaps.

• **Sunglasses** are another useful part of the kit. Some clay experts do not care to be encumbered in any way by too much extraneous gear but when shooting in bright glare or at clays against a difficult background, a good pair of glasses can make all the difference. Also there are some eyes still giving good service which would have been damaged by shattered clay fragments had their owners not been wearing specs. The lenses should be shatterproof and must be wide enough to allow for the peripheral vision which is so important in certain disciplines such as specialist trap shooting.

Glasses are most useful for skeet and sporting shooting and there are many colours

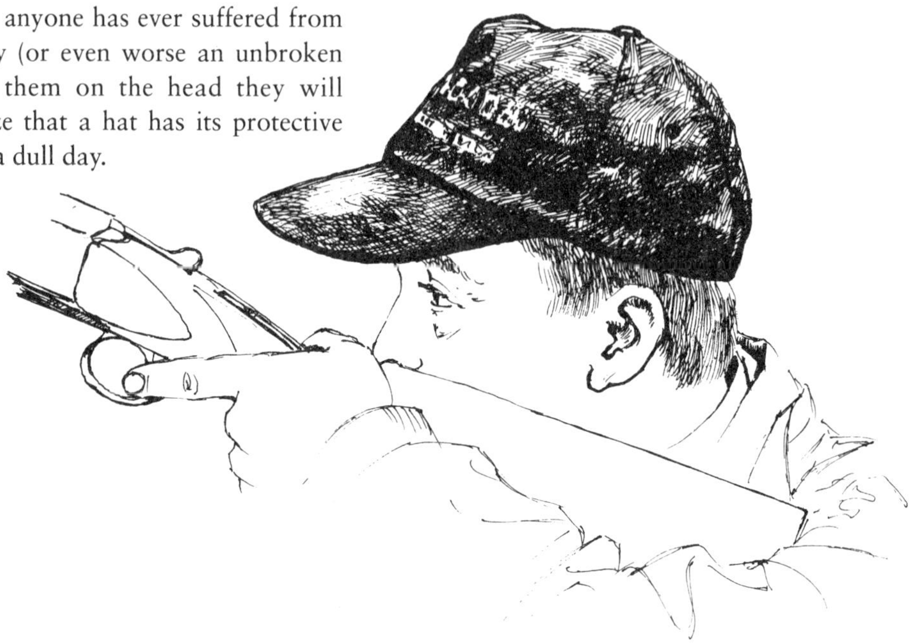

of lens available. The really keen shots take with them a selection of lens colours to suit any set of light conditions. Trial and error will show which pair suits you best, but they should be well fitting and rest well up the bridge of the nose.

- **Ear protection** There is no doubt that some form of ear protection is essential. Most clay grounds insist that all who shoot wear some protection, if only to guard against a costly law suit later on. There has been a revolution in this area in recent years, when it was realized that the shooting world was full of shooters becoming hard of hearing. The first damage always seems to appear in the ear opposite the shooter's gun shoulder. A right-hander suffers hearing loss first in the left ear.

Any protection is better than none (even a pinch of cotton wool or toilet tissue will do *in extremis*) but the serious clay shooter, indeed anyone who fires a shotgun regularly, should buy something more substantial. There is a wide range available, from the standard ear muffs as worn by chain-saw operators to a full stereo job with batteries which allows normal sounds to penetrate but cuts the blast of a shotgun. Hearing outside noises is less important to the clay shooter than to the game shooter who likes to hear the whistle of wings, birdsong and the cries of the beaters. The clay shot is in a private world and might find such noises distracting; the standard muffs are certainly popular and cheap.

A moulded ear plug which allows small sounds to pass freely is one made by Emtec Labs of Hadnall in Shropshire. Each individual is fitted with a set of uniquely tailored plugs. Others such as Lee Sonic come with a small valve, which is quite adequate. Make sure that whatever ear protection you buy does not interfere with smooth gun mounting and does not cause discomfort; any distraction is to be avoided. Put your name clearly on your ear muffs and do not lend them to anyone else.

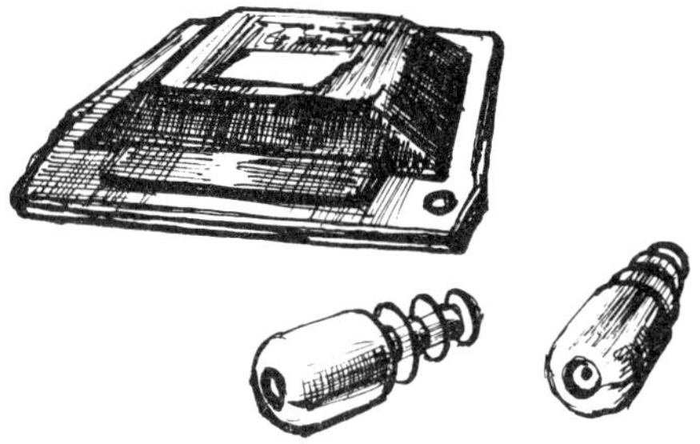

• **Footwear** On the feet, trainers seem to be a popular choice. These allow easy and fluent movement and are light to wear. You are on your feet for some hours, waiting your turn as well as shooting, and you need something which will be comfortable and help your stance and quick movements.

Permanent grounds have concrete pads on which the shooter will stand, but on wooded shoots and in sporting layouts you may find yourself in wet, wooded country. Wellingtons will do but are cumbersome and do not lend themselves to agility. Light hill boots with cleated soles will be comfortable and give a good grip in such cases.

A shoe flap is a piece of leather which is fixed by your shoe laces on to the top of one foot. This allows you to rest your gun muzzles (the gun being broken and unloaded at the time) on your toe without leaving marks on your shoe.

• **Gloves** On some days when it is cold or your barrels are likely to grow hot, a pair of gloves will be useful. The ones used by game shooters are good, made of fine leather, lined with silk and allowing sensitive touch. The trigger finger may be peeled back and fastened to the back of the glove with velcro. For left-handers, left-handed shooting gloves are available from the likes of William Powell. Alternatively mittens or ventilated driving gloves will do.

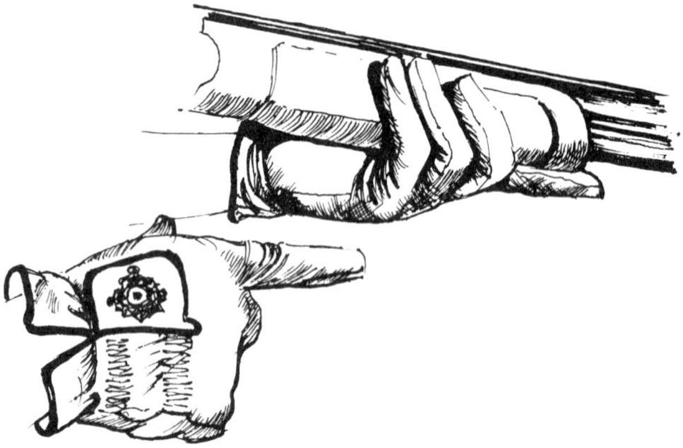

• **Gun accessories** The clay shot will need a light, nylon **kit bag** and many cartridge and gun makers produce one. They are rather more costly, though not necessarily any better than the one you might buy at the Saturday market, but you have the smart logo on the side. This will hold all your spare kit, glasses, light waterproofs, elementary first aid, ear protectors and so on. Have a check list at home and make sure you have everything with you before you leave. It is no good travelling 100 miles to shoot a round and find you have left your ear plugs at home.

Have with you a rudimentary **cleaning kit** and a roll of toilet tissue, enough to give the gun a quick wipe down at the end of the day or to run through the barrels if it has been wet. Keep this in your bag so you know it is always with you.

The gun may be carried in a leather or similar **gun slip**. This will keep it clean and dry between shooting and prevent superficial damage. While taking the gun to and from the clay ground in a vehicle you need a hard **motor case** made of leather on wood or crush-proof fibreglass, lined with dimple foam cushioning. In the event of an accident this will save your gun from severe damage in a way that a slip cannot do. It might have compartments for various bits of cleaning gear, but it is most important that the inside should be kept dry or the gun will rust in no time. If you happen, accidentally, to expose it to the rain, dry the case thoroughly as soon as you get home.

Cartridges should be carried in a conventional **cartridge bag** or a **magazine**. The bag will act as a reservoir from which you can fill your skeet vest pockets as required. The magazine has an advantage if you are using more than one shot size or type of cartridge for different disciplines. You can open it, assess the contents at a glance and take out the carton you need next. There is a plastic box made in the USA which takes four cartons of 25 and this has proved popular. For sporting shooting the cartridge bag is ideal and you will need one which takes 100 rounds. When you are in action the bag or magazine may be left on the ground behind your shooting station.

Jammed cartridge cases are rare with modern ammunition, but they do occur. A traditional **cartridge extractor** which will pull out a stuck case might be useful just once at a vital moment. Such a thing is light to carry and to have one with you is a wise precaution.

- **Finally there are two vital documents.** You must have with you your **shotgun certificate** at all times when you are in possession of your gun. The police can confiscate your gun at any time if you cannot produce on the spot documentation. You should also have with you your **CPSA membership card** which will show which shoots you have attended and the scores achieved as well as the bearer's classification.

8

Clays and Traps

Clays

The targets used for clay pigeon shooting are most often in the shape of an inverted saucer made from a blend of pitch and chalk strong enough to stand being thrown at high speed from the traps but also easily broken when struck by just one pellet from a gun. There are odd freak times when a single pellet will pass through a clay leaving a small hole unnoticeable by the judges so that a bird 'lost' is falsely recorded.

Most clay targets are black but coloured once are made, fluorescent orange, white or yellow being used in cases of a dark background. All clays are manufactured to exacting standards regarding weight and size and each one must conform to international specifications.

There are different types of target which have been referred to previously in this book. The so-called standard clay, 4⅓ in across, is used in all of the trap and skeet disciplines. Sporting shooting uses the full range of targets, so that the required variety of birds can be simulated.

- **Standard** is the most commonly used target. It must weigh within 5 g of 105 g (3.7 oz) and measure within 1mm of 100mm overall diameter and be 25–26 mm (1 in) deep.
- **Midi** is the same as the standard but with a diameter of 90 mm (3.5 in).
- **Mini** is the smallest and measures 60 mm (2.4 in) in diameter and is 20 mm (7.9 in) deep.
- **Battue** is a thin, flat target of about 100 mm (4 in) in diameter which flies fast at first but suddenly loses momentum and falls to the ground.
- **Rabbit** is a standard-sized but thicker target designed to run along the ground like a wheel and represent the running rabbit.
- **ZZ** is a plastic target of standard size attached to the centre of a propeller of a

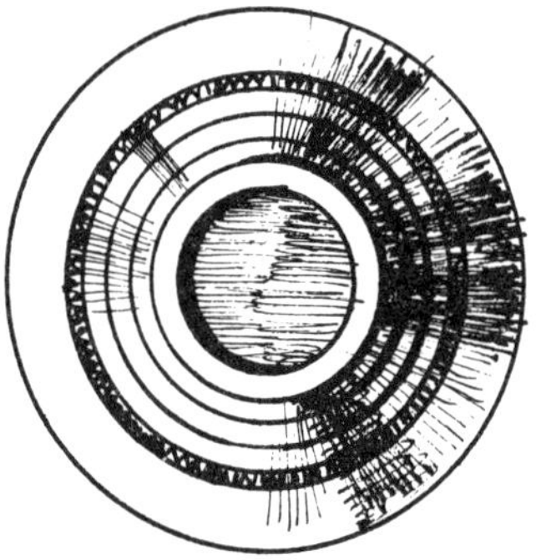

Standard

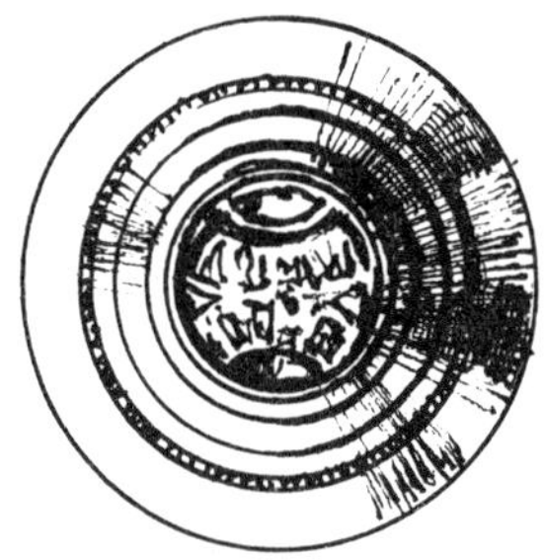

Midi

Mini

Battue

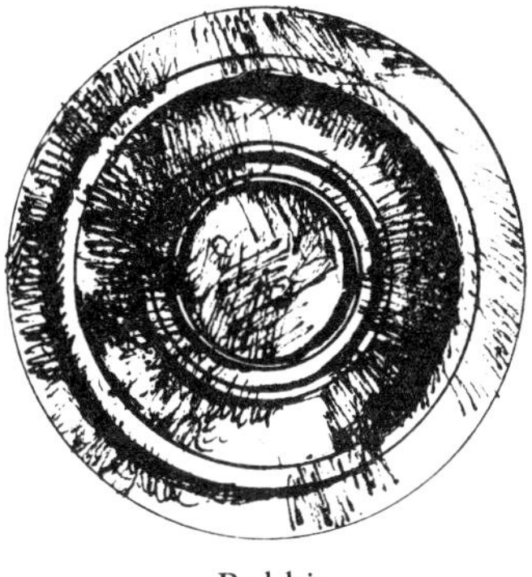

Rabbit

different colour, designed to zigzag in flight, a hit being registered by the knocking out of the plastic target in the centre.

Boxes of targets should be stored not more than six high and kept in a cool dry place. If you keep them in a damp shed where rain can destroy the boxes, the dampness will spoil enough targets to make them fly uncertainly and often break in the trap. On the box of targets often appears the instruction 'handle as eggs'. It is wise advice.

Traps

The traps used are purpose-made, spring loaded devices designed to launch the different types of target at high speeds and distances of up to 100 metres. There are a great variety of traps available, from the simple hand-cocked, hand-loaded and hand-released types to the highly sophisticated, fully automatic ones which can hold up to 400 targets in a magazine, are electrically operated and released by remote control either by a button or a system activated by the shooter's voice. Target speed and trajectory can be varied to suit the discipline and the type or standard of shooting.

The manually operated trap with its single or double arm is the most basic design apart from the hand flinger. The trapper pulls back the arm clockwise over centre, places the clay(s) on the arm against the retaining stop and, if the target is to be steeply rising (such as a springing teal), under a wire restraint which holds it in position. To release the trap the operator awaits the call to 'pull!' and gently pushes forward the arm which flies round and throws the target. Traps of this type such as those made by Bowman are cheap and popular but being manually operated are subject to operator error resulting in targets of varying trajectories. This may be cured by some basic coaching of the trapper.

The Farey trap is popular and slightly more sophisticated. There are various models

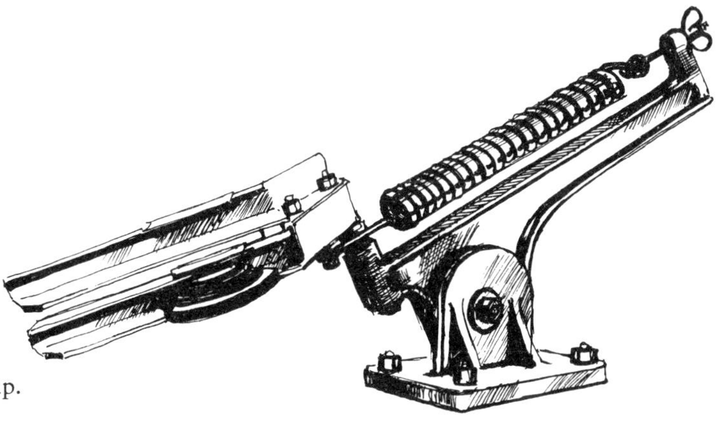

A basic clay trap.

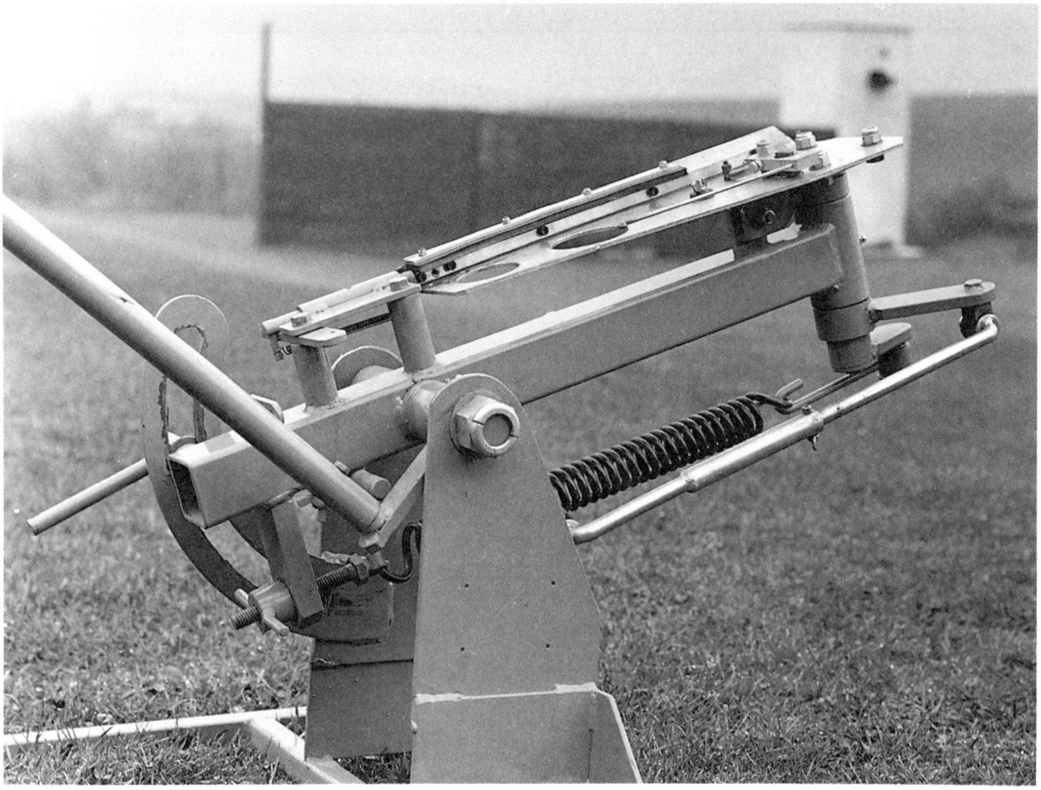

The Leslie Hewett sporting trap.

cocking either by the arm or by a levermatic system. When the clay is thrown the arm goes round automatically to the half cock position. Release is mechanical rather than manual. A sit-on model is available and includes built-in seat where the weight of the trapper is sufficient to hold the trap firmly in position.

The fully electronic and automatic traps are loaded in advance. The trap may be set in any position such as up a high tower or even on the jib of a mobile crane and can throw clays at any trajectory and rapidly. Farey and Sidewinder make electric magazine traps as do Winchester and Phoenix, both available in various forms and degrees of complexity. Spieth and Danlac are possibly the most sophisticated and can be used effectively for every discipline apart from ZZ.

Any clay trap suffers severe stress of its moving parts, for it is a powerful machine. Wear and tear occur and traps needs regular servicing and the replacement of worn or broken parts. The rubber target rails are vulnerable, as are the main springs. A rubber rail is reversible and turning it round will double its useful life. Main spring tension should be released after each session, nuts and bolts should be kept tight and a spanner should always be on hand for running repairs. Certain moving parts will need lubrication and this must be done regularly.

As with all your equipment, traps that are cared for will last longer and be less prone to breakdown. For serious matches spare traps and parts should be on hand. When not in use traps should be stored securely out of the weather and safe from theft. There has been a spate of trap thefts in recent years for such items are easily sold on and are expensive to replace.

A clay trap arm swings round at enormous speed. If it should catch the arm of the trapper it will result in serious injury. Never work on a trap with the spring under tension whether or not it has a clay in place. Keep all bystanders, especially children, well away and keep your body well back from the arm rotation when releasing a bird. Sometimes a clay will shatter on the trap arm, so goggles are useful. There is a curious assumption that everyone knows from birth how to operate a trap and the question is often asked, 'Whose turn is it to trap? Anyone fancy a go?' No one should operate a trap without having first received full instruction on how it works. The would-be trapper must not be ashamed to confess ignorance and ask for a lesson. Better that, than suffer a horrendous injury because you were too shy to enquire.

Traps that are operated by a trapper, as opposed to the automatic variety, need a trap house. The CPSA states that the house 'must

The great coach Ernie Johnson with a school team. Today, hearing protection would be compulsory.

Example of a dangerous trap house.

be large enough to comfortably house the trap, clays, trapper and that the trap house shall be fully protected from a full accidental discharge of shot or clay debris. The trap house should be adequately lit for trappers to operate in safety.'

The often-used and highly dangerous erection of straw bales or a rusty sheet of corrugated iron are unacceptable. Loaded guns are pointed in the direction of the trap house and one mistake could cost a life or cause serious injury. The CPSA recommends a sandwich of steel sheeting and straw bales, or a framed cladding of sheet steel. If there is any worry, double the thickness of the steel. Where the height of the house is lower than 6 ft a roof is recommended so that the trapper cannot stand up suddenly to stretch his legs and expose himself to danger.

In one of its excellent series of booklets, the CPSA has drawn up instructions to trappers which should be observed at all times even, perhaps especially, on the most modest little Sunday morning farm shoot.

1. Trappers must be fully briefed and understand the inherent dangers of traps and trapping

(**a**) They must be instructed and made aware of the 'safe' and 'danger' sides of the type of trap being used. (*Note*: Some traps throw on the opposite side to which they are cocked. Some throw on the same side.)

(**b**) They must be briefed as to the necessity of leaving a trap safe when unattended and made aware of the consequences of not doing so. Never leave a trap cocked with a clay on the arm.

(**c**) They must be shown the correct positioning of the clay target(s) on the arm and shown the safe side of the trap on which the clays can be stacked.
(**d**) Trappers should be aware of the intended flight paths of the clays and shown the remedial action required if the flight paths alter due to extreme conditions.
(**e**) Finally and most importantly, every trapper must be told that whatever the reason he must *not leave the trap until collected.* In the event of a trap breakdown he should safely raise the red flag provided for the purpose and remain with the trap until collected. (The STAY PUT rule.)

2. Organizer's responsibilities to trappers
(**a**) The shoot organizer should provide adequate hearing protection and any protective clothing necessary to the trappers such as gloves, goggles and helmet. Trappers should be instructed to wear all such protective equipment whilst shooting is in progress.
(**b**) Sufficient clays should be stacked next to the trap to last the duration of the competition.
(**c**) Trappers must be fully protected from shot and clay debris. *Remember out of sight is not necessarily out of shot.*
(**d**) Employed trappers should be a minimum of 16 years of age.
(**e**) The equipment provided must be in proper working order and safe to use.
(**f**) All trappers must be properly instructed as to safe and correct trapping procedures and should be made aware of the inherent dangers in failing to comply rigidly with these.
(**g**) Only one trapper per trap should be permitted at any trapping position.

All shooters should bear it in mind that trappers are human beings, often young ones, and not automatons. The labour of cocking and firing a clay trap all day is great as well as monotonous. Give the trapper time to reload and cock and see that there is a break for refreshment. Thank him at the end.

9

SAFE SHOOTING

A shotgun is lethal weapon. At close quarters it can decapitate or blow someone in half. At longer ranges a single pellet can take out an eye or even kill. I say this not to be sensational but to bring it home that, while you are shooting to have fun, the handling and use of your gun must be treated most seriously and responsibly at all times. To have an accident on your conscience is a terrible thing. While you will never eliminate them entirely, for acts of God and genuine misjudgements do occur, you can help to reduce them to a minimum. Remember at all times that any person or creature coming within range of a discharged shotgun, even if by accident, is at high risk of serious maiming or death.

A shotgun pellet can do serious damage at 100 yds, much further away than you would consider addressing a real bird or a clay target. The CPSA recommends that a safe zone of 300 yds is provided in every direction when shooting. It has been known for pellets to stick together and ball, in which case a lethal bunch of shot can travel great distances and hit an innocent bystander far away. Most grounds have a roped-off spectator area to prevent them inching forward until they are too close to the shooters for their safety.

You will have made sure that you have bought a gun which is safe. Having followed the instructions given earlier in this book, you know that your gun is sound, in proof and mechanically free from faults. You will have obtained hearing protection and spectacles as I have advised.

The old game shooting rules apply to clay targets and most of them hold good.

- **The basic one is that at no time and under no circumstances should the gun be pointed anywhere where, if it were to go off, damage to property or life would result.** Whether it is unloaded or not is an irrelevance for it is the 'unloaded' gun which kills. One cartridge left in by mistake once in a lifetime and a careless swing and there is your accident.

- **Carry the gun from place to place open and empty.** All can see that it is safe. Some prefer to carry their guns in a leather gunslip and

this is acceptable although the gun in the slip is not broken and not obviously safe. In the slip the gun will be over the shoulder and so pointing straight up or directly into the ground. The semi-auto should be carried with an 'unloaded' tag in the breech and with its muzzle pointing straight up or down.

• **Load the gun only when at your stand at the firing point and it is your turn.** You must be facing the safe direction where you expect to see the clay and not turning round to communicate with those behind you. Check the barrels for obstruction before you insert the cartridge. The smallest wisp of mud, snow or scrap of neglected cleaning material will result in a bulge at best and a burst at worst. A classic mistake is the accidental insertion of a 20-bore case into a 12-bore gun. The smaller shell will lodge forward of the chamber and so the gun will appear empty when you come to load it. If you then fire the gun it will certainly result in a burst

and possibly a lost hand to go with it. A glance down the barrels takes a mere second and should become a matter of habit.

• **The cartridges are inserted into the breech and the gun is closed firmly in a controlled way by closing the stock to the barrels and not vice versa.** To do it the wrong way round might bring the muzzles of the gun up to a dangerous angle. If you do it properly and there is an accidental discharge, the gun will fire harmlessly into the ground.

The so-called safety catch can itself be misleading to the inexperienced. Once the gun is closed the springs are fully compressed, the hammers poised to fall and the strikers to detonate the cartridge – and yet the flash on top of the gun reads 'safe'. All the safety catch does is to lock the trigger by means of a mere sliver of metal. If the loaded gun is dropped or even jarred it might go off even when the safety catch is on and shouts the word 'SAFE' to the world. In fact the gun is very far from safe!

• **When it is your turn to shoot, you take your shots from the stand having arrived there with an empty gun.** At the end of shooting you will turn and withdraw having with you again an empty and broken gun over your arm. Most clubs will have a safety officer who will advise the newcomer on any uncertainties and will be quick to point out any transgressions. The clay ground has much to teach the game shooting world in matters of rigid safety.

• **When you pass a gun from one to another for any reason, check that it is unloaded both when you give and when you receive it.** The gun ought to be broken already but it is not always so. This becomes a routine with experienced shooters and over the years will have saved many accidents.

• **Make sure that the cartridges you use in the gun are suitable for it.** They must correspond with the proof marks on the gun. The most common error is to slip a 2¾ in cartridge into a barrel proofed for 2 in ammunition. In this case, the gun will usually be an older one designed for game shooting, but one needs to be aware of the danger. The suitability of steel shot also needs to be cleared if you have an older gun. Your gunsmith will advise on both counts.

• **Organizers of even the most informal shoot are urged to take out third party liability insurance of at least one million pounds.** The CPSA expert will advise on this and all full members are covered by their annual subscription. No one should shoot unless properly covered.

To sum up here are the CPSA 'ten commandments':

1. Treat every gun as if it was loaded and with the utmost respect at all times.
2. When carrying a gun it should be open and empty at all times. Pump-action and semi-automatic guns should be carried with the bolts back and with chambers and magazines empty.
3. Avoid alcohol and horseplay when in possession of a gun.
4. When using a gun you should have on your person only those cartridges which are of the correct gauge and chamber length to match the gun (shot sizes 6, 7, 8 or 9 or intermediate half sizes).
5. All guns should be (a) nitro proofed, (b) in proof, (c) in safe and sound condition to shoot.
6. *Do not* point or fire your gun at anything other than a clay pigeon; i.e. do not point or fire your gun at any other animate or inanimate object. Failure to observe this rule can lead to disqualification and expulsion from the ground.
7. Before loading your gun with one or two cartridges check that the barrels are free from obstruction and that they are pointing up the range.
8. Keep the muzzles pointing up the range at all times until you have opened and emptied your gun. Then (and only then) you may turn round and walk off the firing point.
9. If there is any *gun malfunction*, keep the muzzles pointing up the range until the malfunction is identified and corrected. If upon firing the cartridge makes an unusual report, check the barrels before reloading and make sure they are free from obstruction.
10. *Remember* that you and only you are responsible for the safe handling of your gun at all times. You are also responsible for the behaviour and safety of your family, guests and animals when they are on the shooting ground.

10

Making a Start

It is possible to learn 'on the job' and a shooter with a grounding in game shooting can go straight to the clay ground and try his or her hand at a round of sporting. The fact is that the average clay shot tends to be better than the average game shot and to do well at the sport proper coaching is essential. Even those who try a few clays on a Sunday morning to sharpen up their game shooting can benefit from a lesson or two.

The cost of lessons may seem high but if you go to a reputable CPSA-qualified coach it will be money well spent. You will receive a grounding in the basics where all good shooting starts and learn how to deal with that tricky shot. The lessons need not be long, especially for youngsters, for the necessary concentration and physical effort are hard to maintain in the early stages. Half an hour is quite enough for a start.

Many youngsters make the mistake of starting with the little .410. The old myth that this is the beginner's gun is a hard one to dispel. The .410 is a hard gun to shoot with, a weapon used by professional keepers for bolting rabbits and sometimes by the best game shots in the land who test their mettle against high pheasants. It will kill well enough in experienced hands but the shot stringing and the little pinch of pellets create too many handicaps. The beginner wants it as easy as possible.

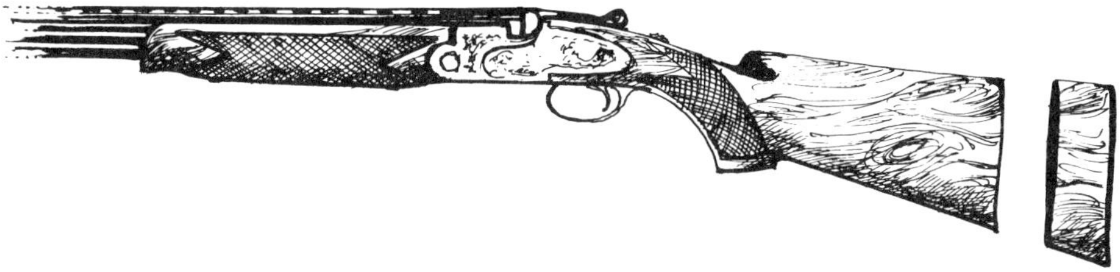

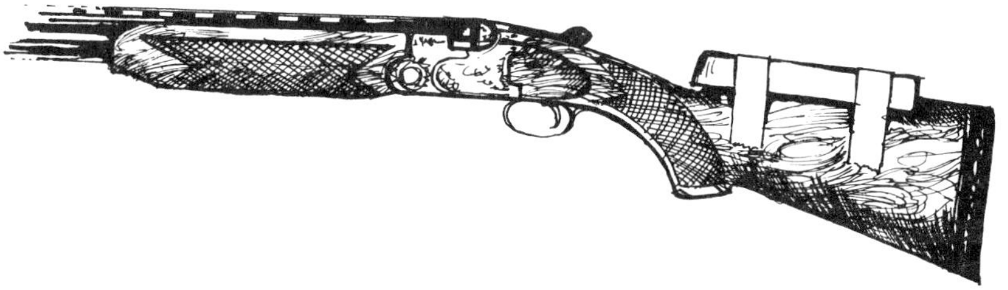

The smallest 'proper' shotgun for youngsters or those of light physique is the 28-bore but even better is the 20-bore with the light ⅞oz load. The recoil will be no problem so long as the gun fits and does not have the common fault of too long a stock. I have taught numerous children to shoot using a 20-bore with the stock shortened and rebalanced with every vestige of choke taken out. This gun is an ideal beginner's weapon with a good spread of shot giving instant success and a stock which does not cause bruising or incorrect stance at mounting.

When shortening a gun stock, which is an operation any gunsmith will carry out, keep the cut-off piece which can be replaced later when the pupil has grown. Similarly, the smaller facial dimensions of a child will make the comb too low and not allow the pupil to see down the barrels. This encourages the weaker eye to take over, so a right-hander would consistently miss to the left. It is possible to tape a comb raiser on to the top of the stock, so bringing the master eye level with the top rib.

Recoil can be a worry and this may be eliminated by starting with a semi-auto where the recoil is absorbed by working the action. It is a mistake to use a light gun with a heavy load, for the recoil will be unacceptable. It is far better to use the heavier 12-bore with a light load of ⅞oz than a 20-bore using a heavy 1oz load. The art is to match the gun to the pupil and if possible start with a 12-bore and a light load from the outset.

Early coaching is also the ideal time to drill the lessons of safety so that correct behaviour becomes automatic. Also start straight away with the rules about always wearing ear protection and spectacles and the correct and suitable clothing. The beginner may not have the proper kit but trainers and a close fitting sweater should be available to everyone.

Sam Grice, the excellent Cambridgeshire coach, who has made a special study of coaching young people, suggests that when the preliminaries are over and he has a pupil properly clothed, feeling relaxed and confident and holding a gun which fits, he slips in one cartridge, sees that the gun is placed properly in the shoulder and gives his three tips for success: 'See it, point at it, pull ahead and fire.' The pupil is delighted when the clay explodes into fragments and is hooked for life.

The progression is to get the pupil hitting that easy going-away bird every time, then to move round a few steps until the angle is increased and to hit that one too. When confidence is high, introduce gun mounting; this might cause a little setback for it adds another dimension to the shot. Keep instilling the three points until they become second nature. Once this has been mastered the pupil can progress to more difficult birds and can be called a fledgling clay pigeon shot.

Clay pigeon shooting is an ageless as well as a classless sport but there is a great advantage is starting when you are young. A young person comes without the baggage of wrong impressions and ingrained errors and is physically as well as mentally more malleable. The instinctive hand and eye co-ordination which brings success comes more easily to a child of 10 than an adult of 50 taking it up for the first time.

The CPSA has an excellent coaching scheme and provides a qualification only after a rigorous series of written and practical tests. Each coach might have his own individual teaching style, but any pupil who is willing and basically co-ordinated should

A youngster under tuition, but where is his ear protection?

be able to achieve his full potential. The coach has been trained to pace the pupil carefully and be alert for signs of staleness, tiredness or nervous tension.

In time the pupil will be able to manage the full hour which tends to be a standard unit at most coaching schools. It is important to arrive on time and have all with you that you will need. Time is money and while the coach will give you 100 per cent during the lesson, if you arrive late accompanied by unruly dogs or with the family in tow you will not be getting full value.

A coach will advise on gun fitting and have a try gun on site for taking measurements. It is hard to become a competent shot without a proper grounding at a shooting school.

11

Forming a Shooting Club

If your area lacks a handy shooting club and you think there is sufficient local interest you may well consider setting up your own club. This may be as modest or as ambitious as your funds will allow. You will need at least 20 committed people, ideally living locally, who would give their support to such a venture.

The club will stand or fall by the keenness of its members. A club should be not less than 20-strong and might be as many as 100. A membership of about 50 is a suggested CPSA guideline for viability. Limit membership to those you can handle; a waiting list helps to make those on it all the more keen.

Decide early on what sort of shooting you are to provide. Is it to be down the line, skeet or sporting or a mixture of them all? Look outside the known clay shooters and try to interest the game shots who might be looking for some out-of-season practice. Local businessmen might be shown the delights of clay shooting as an after-work relaxation. Many women are keen and good clay shots so they must not be overlooked in your recruitment.

Finding a suitable site can be important. If you have a ground in mind, and one of your number might well be a farmer with a suitable field to spare, hold an initial clay shoot with portable traps to generate interest. If no ground is available this must be top of your list of priorities. The ground you use should be flat and open with a clear background, free of trees and far from dwellings. Traps should be set so that the shooting takes place facing north or north-east to minimize the problems of blinding sunshine. The CPSA recommends 300 yds as a minimum distance in every direction from the point where shooting is to take place.

On no account should spent shot or unbroken clays fall on nearby property. You should be out of earshot of the nearest habitation, otherwise you might be obliged to build earth banks and baffles which can prove expensive. The CPSA has co-operated with the Department of the Environment on the preparation of a code of practice on noise from clay pigeon shooting relating to the Control of Pollution Act (1974). An update on this and information and advice concerning planning permission where needed and the frequency of shooting may be had direct from the CPSA whom you would be wise to consult at every stage of your planning.

As for planning your layout, this should be a long-term affair, not to be completed overnight, but no matter how humbly you may start you will have a picture and firm plan of what it will be like when completed. The size and shape of your ground will dictate just what you can achieve and, along with the wishes of the members, will

An unsuitable site.

determine which discipline you will be able to shoot. If, for example, you intend eventually to install four DTL trap positions and can only afford one, build it so that it will be part of the end product and avoid having to demolish and resite expensive work after a couple of years.

From the outset it is wise to involve your local gun dealer who will be in contact with many potential members and will be able to supply traps, clays and cartridges at competitive rates if you are buying in bulk. Apart from contributing useful expertise, a gun dealer is only too glad of any extra business that comes along.

The CPSA advises that the press should be informed of your plans. Clay shooting is a photogenic subject and local papers will be

This layout is designed to recreate a sporting scene. Two clays have been thrown at once.

pleased to have some colourful copy. The publicity will certainly attract new members which are the lifeblood of any club. National shooting magazines also will report your fixtures and any interesting developments. This will appear as part of the news service and will cost nothing. The cost of advertising nationally is prohibitive. The main magazines of interest will be *The Shooting Times*, *Sporting Gun*, *Shooting News* and *The Shooting Gazette*.

In time you will enhance your facilities to include a club house, resident coach, sophisticated electronic traps and purpose-built trap houses. Success breeds success and the better and more thriving your club the more people will want to come and shoot there. Your ground will also become, as many have done before, a sanctuary for all sorts of wildlife. The shooting seems not to disturb the wild creatures when they have become used to it and I know many clay shooting grounds which are havens for wild flowers not seen elsewhere as well as many insects, birds and small mammals.

To run the club properly you will need a set of rules and regulations and, of course, everything you do should follow CPSA guidelines. The CPSA has produced a set of rules which fit most clay shooting clubs and copies are available from them on request (for address see p. 74). Each club may insert its own elements, but to start with just the standard set of rules will save a great deal of time and hard work.

Organizing a shooting stand

A well-established club might be called upon to run a small shooting stand at a country show or fête. Clay shooting is one of the fastest growing participant sports in the UK.

As well as being testing enough to qualify for Olympic Games status, clays may be made easy enough for have-a-go visitors and novices. The CPSA has prepared a booklet to help those who are involved in organizing such an event.

The traps you use should be portable of the type mounted on a tripod or a sledge. Such a

Shooting from inside a cage which prevents unsafe shots.

trap will throw single targets at various angles and speeds and might even be able to throw a pair. As you will not be using an official clay ground where the safety parameters have been established, you will be starting from scratch. You will be dealing with beginners who are not trained in the safe use of a shotgun and you need to be ready for mishaps. Apply the usual CPSA guideline of 300 yds in any direction from the point of shooting.

Try to set the stand so that the shooter is not facing into the bright sunlight. Again the old rule of north to north-east holds good. If the background is dark such as a canopy of trees then the normal black clay will not show up. In such a case you will need orange fluorescent or white targets.

Be sure that your shooting is far from any livestock. Spent shot and missed clays should not rain down upon them and special care is needed where poultry are near, for they are especially susceptible to such disturbance. It is also good public relations and common sense not to set your shoot where neighbouring residents are going to have their weekend spoiled by the sound of continuous shooting.

One trap will do if it is used imaginatively and a suggested 10 birds might be right for a standard round. If you use more than one trap, a greater variety of targets is possible, but there must be a competent referee at each firing point. No one person can oversee more than one stand. Breaking one target with one or both barrels should count one point and a miss nil. To stimulate extra interest you might slip in a double to hit both of which scores three points, or a special bird of a different colour or size for which you get a bonus of an extra point.

For extra safety and peace of mind a cage for the shooter is advisable. This may be a simple wood structure built so that the shooter may not swing round and shoot behind and is obliged to lower his gun within the safe limits of the frame. Such a thing made of wooden spars or wire mesh is easily constructed and may be made portable for use at other shows.

The CPSA ten commandments for safe shooting should be rigorously applied (see p. 61).

Too often the safety of the trappers on such days can be neglected. If anything, even more stringent rules should apply than on the established clay ground. Trappers should be trained and provided with safe trap houses of straw bales and steel sheeting as explained earlier (see pp. 55–6).

There is often anxiety at little local shows that the experts will drop in at the last minute and scoop all the prizes. It is good that your event should be well supported and that no one is frozen out, so the answer is to provide non-cash prizes such as shields or plaques and to have three competitions. These might be an open competition available to all comers, a novice competition for those not CPSA affiliated or who have never won a competition and a six-mile competition for locals only. This ensures that everyone has a fair chance.

You need to charge an entry fee which should be a modest one so as not to discourage those who may not have shot before. You will, however, need to show a financial profit on the event and you will have your expenses.

It is most important that the organizers of all clay shooting events take out a third party liability insurance for at least one million pounds. Sometimes this will be arranged as part of a blanket policy by the fair organizers. The CPSA insurance specialist is the one to contact and will arrange all the cover you require.

12

The Role of the Referee

Sometimes referred to as the umpire, the referee is a key person on any clay shoot from the informal to international level. In this chapter I have found it more simple to write of the referee as if it were a man. These days, however, clay shooting is becoming increasingly popular with women and there are growing numbers of women referees.

The referee must be aware of the complexities of shotguns and ammunition, be confident in the interpretation of CPSA rules for the various disciplines, have sharp eyesight and be able to handle any situation or dispute firmly and fairly so as to earn the respect of the shooters.

The CPSA runs courses for referees. The main job of this official is to see that the competition runs smoothly, that everyone feels fairly treated, that guns and ammunition are properly handled and safe standards maintained. He should not be over-officious but remember that the event is for sport and enjoyment, no matter how seriously some may take it.

He must ensure that targets are released suitably, with no delay between the call and the bird. In the event of a target showing early due to the trapper being confused by a call from a neighbouring layout, he will quickly call 'no bird' whether or not the target is fired at and hit or missed. If he is quick enough he will call before the shot. A shooter presented with a slow or fast target has the right to refuse it, but the referee is the

final arbiter and should judge each case accordingly.

On a registered shoot each shooter may see a bird before scoring starts. This is the time to protest against irregular birds or those not shown in accordance with the requirements of that discipline. The referee will decide whether the target is irregular and if he decides it is not, the shooter is bound to accept it if he wishes to remain in the competition.

The referee must also be aware of distractions. Noisy spectators, dogs and children, or even an old newspaper blowing across the ground at the wrong moment, can all prove what are termed balks. If such a thing occurs as the shooter is firing the referee may decide to allow a 'no bird'. If the distraction occurs before the shooter calls for a bird and he fires in spite of it, the target should stand as good and the result will be scored.

The referee is the final judge of a bird killed or lost. He must concentrate, for sometimes the tiniest chip is knocked out of the target. He may not be overruled and all his decisions will stand. If a protest is to be made it should be done there and then.

In cases of a gun malfunction or a misfire, the shooter should hold position facing forward and not break the gun. The referee will examine it and decide whether or not the fault was the shooter's or a mechanical breakdown. If the shooter breaks the gun or moves the safety catch the bird is judged lost.

The referee should ensure that spectators keep a safe distance from the shooters and do not distract them. A quiet but firm word should be sufficient, for such behaviour is usually the result of thoughtlessness.

The referee should always be reasonable and in cases of a one-off disputed decision may decide to allow the shooter to repeat the target. There will be a jury on hand at all serious competitions and any serious disputes may be referred to them.

The referee must also be alert to the tricks of the trade. There will always be one shooter ready to try some old dodges. It is possible to induce what appears to be a misfire in the second barrel having missed the first shot and if the referee is fooled he may allow the target to be repeated. The referee should check the gun carefully in such cases. Sometimes a clay shooter will keep a misfired cartridge in his pocket and slip it into the chamber when faced with a difficult double. If he kills the first bird and successfully claims a misfire on his second, he has the double again and has only to shoot the second bird for which he now has more time since he can fire his first shot very quickly and miss. Such things are rare enough but an experienced referee will be on his guard.

The referee is there to help, his decisions are final and nine times out of ten he will make his judgement there and then and avoid disgruntled shooters. As that grand old master Chris Cradock says, 'Everyone will benefit from the actions of a fair and understanding referee whose whole aim is to interpret honestly the rules for the shooters without fear or favour.'

APPENDIX

FURTHER INFORMATION

THE CLAY PIGEON SHOOTING ASSOCIATION

The CPSA was formed in 1928 and succeeded the Inanimate Bird Shooting Association which had its roots back in 1892. The ban on live bird shooting in 1921 gave it an impetus. Today it has about 30,000 members and the numbers are growing as the sport becomes almost daily more popular.

The CPSA is the national governing body of the sport in England. It is recognized by the Sports Council, the Department of the Environment, the Home Office and the police. It is a constituent member of the International Clay Pigeon Shooting Council for Great Britain and Ireland.

Its main roles are to protect the sport from adverse legislation, to liaise with government departments and represent the interests of its members. It regulates and develops all aspects of the sport and promotes and organizes national competitions. It selects the English teams for major events, some of which are staged by the CPSA.

Membership is open to anyone and includes an extensive package of benefits such as insurance, information, magazine, advice, credit card, classification and badges. Anyone taking up the sport is urged to join the CPSA. It runs all the sport's major competitions, decides the way the various disciplines will be run and publishes the rules, some of which I have, with their permission, touched on.

Many competitions are registered events. This means that your score will be submitted by the shoot organizers to CPSA headquarters and you will be classified annually to shoot in a particular class in accordance with the level of ability, based on your scores. The CPSA publishes a book of members' averages for eight disciplines every year. Whenever you take part in an event you will be entered in the class against your name in the book. At first a shooter might be in the C class which means that if he enters a registered competition it will be to shoot against other C class competitors with similar ability.

It is difficult to see how anyone can enter this sport without becoming a full member. The CPSA may be contacted at 107 Epping New Road, Buckhurst Hill, Essex IG9 5TQ.

SHOTGUNS AND THE LAW

There are many pieces of legislation in the UK relating to the ownership of firearms, even for sporting purposes. Anyone entering a shooting sport, be it target pistol shooting, game shooting, deer stalking or clay pigeon shooting, should be well acquainted with current legislation. Ignorance of the law is no excuse for transgression and it is up to you to ensure that you are conducting yourself within the law. In almost every case, certification from your local chief constable is required if you wish to acquire, possess or use a shotgun under the Firearms (Amendment) Act of 1988. Shotguns will usually fall under Section 2 of the Act (Shotguns) but in certain cases may fall under Section 1 (Firearms) or Section 5 (Prohibited Weapons).

The following résumé is not comprehensive but contains the bones of current legislation. It is taken from the CPSA publication (No. 6), *Shotguns and the Law*.

1. Criteria for issuing a shotgun certificate

A chief officer of police will *not* grant a shotgun certificate if:

(**a**) he is not satisfied that the applicant can possess a shotgun without danger to the public safety or the peace,

(**b**) he is satisfied that the applicant does not have a good reason for possessing, purchasing or acquiring a gun. (Examples of good reasons are sporting or competition purposes, the shooting of vermin and some situations where the gun is not intended for use such as if it is an heirloom or part of a collection),

(**c**) he has reason to believe the applicant is prohibited from possessing a shotgun.

2. Section 1 – firearms certificate

This is required for:

(**a**) a smooth-bore gun with a bore of more than 2 in in diameter,

(**b**) a smooth-bore revolver (0.35 in) rim fire or muzzle loading only,

(**c**) a smooth-bore gun with a fixed magazine capable of holding more than two cartridges,

(**d**) a smooth-bore gun with a barrel length of less than 24 in.

You may not possess, purchase or obtain any of these weapons unless you have already obtained a firearm certificate from your local police. They will not issue a certificate unless they are satisfied that you have good reason for possessing a gun, that public safety is not endangered and that you are fit to be entrusted. The chief officer of police may impose conditions and may revoke the certificate.

- If you gain possession of any of these weapons without a certificate you are liable on conviction to imprisonment or a fine or both.
- You may not sell, lend or give any of these weapons to anyone who has not got a firearms certificate.
- You may not lend or make a gift of any of these weapons to a child under 14 and you may not sell them to anyone under 17.

Section 2 – shotgun certificate

This is required for:

(**a**) a smooth-bore gun with a bore not exceeding 2 in in diameter,

(**b**) a smooth-bore gun which is not a revolver,

(**c**) a smooth-bore gun with a fixed magazine capable of holding not more than two cartridges,

(**d**) a smooth-bore gun with a barrel of 24 in or more, not being an air gun.

Section 5 – prohibited weapons

You may not possess or acquire:

(**a**) a smooth-bore gun which is capable of

'burst firing', i.e. firing more than once for a single pull of the trigger,
(**b**) self-loading smooth-bore guns which have a barrel length of less than 24 in in length or an overall length of less than 40 in,
(**c**) pump-action, smooth-bore guns which have a barrel length of less than 24 in in length or an overall length of less than 40 in,
(**d**) a converted shotgun that has since become a prohibited weapon under the new laws.

3. Applying for a shotgun certificate
All shotgun certificates will bear a photograph of the holder. All first time and renewal applicants who apply will complete the post-1988 style application form.

The details contain a description of all guns held on the certificate, including any identification numbers. You will therefore need to provide this information on your application form.

A safekeeping condition appears on shotgun certificates. This creates two distinct levels of security to ensure safe custody of guns. These are:
(**a**) in the home where, although a steel security cabinet is not compulsory, the CPSA strongly recommends it,
(**b**) in the car in which case guns and ammunition should be locked out of sight in the boot or in a vehicle security cabinet. This is especially important if the owner is away from the vehicle.

If you already hold a shotgun certificate you do not need to apply to renew it until shortly before its expiry date.

A firearms certificate holder may apply to have the certificate issued with the same expiry date as the shotgun certificate. This will result in a slightly reduced fee.

4. Transfer and sale of shotguns
(**a**) A person transferring a shotgun must enter details of the gun on to the new holder's certificate. Within seven days of the transaction a note of the transaction must be sent to the chief officer of police who issued the shotgun certificate.
(**b**) Any person who acquires a shotgun must send a note of the transaction to the chief officer of police who issued their certificate.
(**c**) The notice sent to the chief officer of police must contain a description of the shotgun and its identification number, if any, and the name and address of the other person involved in the transaction.

5. Buying shotgun ammunition
You must produce your shotgun certificate when purchasing ammunition. If your gun is classed as a firearm you will need to produce your firearms certificate.

6. Young persons
If you are under 15 and have a shotgun certificate you may have with you an assembled shotgun provided you are supervised by a person over 21 or the shotgun is in a cover and securely fastened.

If you are 15 or over and have a shotgun certificate, you may be given a shotgun as a gift.

7. Exemptions
You do *not* need a shotgun certificate if:
(**a**) you borrow a shotgun from the occupier of private premises (including land) and use it thereon in his presence,
(**b**) you use someone else's shotgun on artificial targets at a place and time approved by the chief officer of police,

(**c**) you possess a Northern Ireland firearm certificate for a shotgun,
(**d**) you are in possession of a weapon for which someone else holds a certificate, in a theatrical or film production,
(**e**) your weapon is an antique firearm which has been sold, transferred, purchased, acquired or is possessed as a curiosity or ornament,
(**f**) you are under instruction from another person who owns a certificate and you are carrying a weapon for sporting purposes only,
(**g**) you are engaged in the business of a registered firearms dealer,
(**h**) you are in possession of a weapon in the course of the business of an auctioneer, carrier, warehouseman or a slaughterer of animals,
(**i**) you are in possession of a weapon on board a ship or as a signalling apparatus on board an aircraft or at an aerodrome.

8. Appeal
If the police refuse to grant, vary or renew a firearm or shotgun certificate in England and Wales you may appeal to the crown court on giving notice within 21 days to the administrator of the crown court and the chief officer of police. In Scotland you may appeal to the sheriff court.

9. Offences
It is an offence to infringe any of the Act's requirements. There are also the following specific offences created by the Firearms Act 1968:
(**a**) to trade in any way in shotguns without being registered with the police as a dealer,
(**b**) to shorten the barrel of a shotgun to less than 24 in in length,
(**c**) to convert in any way an imitation into a lethal weapon,
(**d**) to possess a shotgun and ammunition with intent to injure,
(**e**) to use a real or imitation shotgun to resist arrest,
(**f**) to carry a real or imitation shotgun with intent to commit a crime,
(**g**) to supply a shotgun to anyone who is prohibited from having one,
(**h**) to carry without lawful authority or reasonable excuse a loaded shotgun or air weapon or any other firearm whether loaded or not, together with suitable ammunition for that firearm,
(**i**) to sell, lend or give a shotgun to anyone who has not got a shotgun certificate (the penalty for doing so is a fine or imprisonment or both),
(**j**) to make a gift of a shotgun to anyone under 15 years of age (the penalty for doing so is a fine),
(**k**) to trespass without reasonable excuse with a shotgun in a building or on land,
(**l**) to acquire, possess or use any firearm or ammunition for five years after release from any detention or imprisonment of three months or more but less than three years. Anyone who has been sentenced for three years or more shall not at any time have a shotgun in his possession.
(**m**) The penalty for possession of a firearm without an appropriate authority is 6 months imprisonment or a fine of up to £2,000.

There is further advice on the subject of proof of shotguns, the use of guns by visitors from overseas, travelling abroad, the import and export of shotguns and guns in transit. It will prove useful in certain cases but is beyond the scope of an introductory book such as this.

Gun owners are urged to read the law in full and familiarize themselves with all current legislation. The law is changed from time to time and it is important that gun owners are familiar with new rules.

The CPSA has expert staff who can advise on all such matters. They repeat the suggestion that, although it is not compulsory, all who shoot ought to be insured for third party liability.

BIBLIOGRAPHY

I acknowledge gratefully the following publications to which I have referred when researching this book. Any clay shooter who intends to take the sport further should obtain copies in order to learn more of the subtleties of the sport.

Barnes, Mike (1993), *The Complete Clay Shot*, David and Charles.
Cradock, Chris (1983), *A Manual of Clay Shooting*, Batsford.
Hoare, Tony (1991), *Successful Clay Pigeon Shooting*, Crowood.
Reynolds, Mike with Barnes, Mike (1986), *Shooting Made Easy*, Crowood.
Ruffer, J.E.M. (1976), *Good Shooting*, David and Charles.

In addition I recommend the various informational and instructional publications from the CPSA, 107 Epping New Road, Buckhurst Hill, Essex IG9 5TQ.

INDEX

Life and Living

"I would like you to feel that I am not 'up here' talking to you 'down there', but that we are all part of a joint effort to bring about a contemporary understanding of God to planet Earth."

H-A

Life and Living

A Channelled Teaching of our Time

H-A

Channelled by
Tony Neate and Diane Furlong

PEGASUS FOUNDATION

First published in 1992
by PEGASUS FOUNDATION
Runnings Park
Croft Bank West Malvern
Worcs WR14 4BP

Printed on Recycled Paper and bound
in Great Britain by
The Longdunn Press Ltd. Bristol

Cover design by John Harlow

British Library Cataloguing in Publication Data
H-A (Spirit)
Life and Living

ISBN 0-9519827-1-0

CONTENTS

Foreword and Acknowledgements

LIFE AND LIVING is the first of a new series of books of H-A teachings, containing the original text, updated, of some twenty-seven lectures. These were given mostly during the 1960's and 1970's through my husband, Tony Neate, with additions from the 1980's, some of which were channelled through Diane Furlong.

Whether you consider H-A to be a discarnate entity, a thought/intelligence frequency or a spirit guide, his teachings have a clear message of inspiration for humanity today – a message that can be applied to practical living. Certainly, he has illuminated the understanding and lives of countless numbers of people, always honouring and respecting the freedom of each individual to choose and tread his or her own path. His message gives perspective, encouragement and clarity in these times of confusion and change.

Feeling such a close affinity to H-A and his philosophy, I have always enjoyed the subtle work of editing the teachings he speaks, just enough for them to be read as clearly as they can be heard. It has seemed to me that, on many occasions, his presence has helped me in this respect and I feel deeply privileged that this work has given me a unique opportunity to experience the limitless love, compassion and wisdom of a truly great spirit.

I would like to thank the following people for the various ways in which they have helped in the compilation and editing of this book: David Furlong, for initiating it originally; Anne MacEwen, Bill Deller, Anne Bassett and Muriel Kadwell; Mari Francis and Diana Morshead for their patient work on the word processor; and, finally, Lorna St Aubyn for her supportive Introduction.

Ann Neate – Runnings Park

Introduction

It is on the teachings of their guide Helio-Arcanophus, H-A, that Pegasus Foundation, originally The Atlanteans, has built its philosophy. Since 1957 his great wisdom has been channelled through Tony Neate and, in later years, also through Diane Furlong. A record of all these readings has been kept and it is from this rich treasure that the present volume has been selected.

Initially, the small group who founded the Society felt very diffident about proclaiming this new yet timeless outlook on the universe which had in such an unexpected and unsolicited way been presented to them. But as they began to absorb the philosophy, their attitude to life began to change; and in putting into being the suggestions made by H-A, they gradually found their lives turned upside down. More and more time was spent on matters concerned with the teachings; small meditation groups were founded; talks and workshops were given; a comprehensive system of healing was put together out of the knowledge gained from H-A. Slowly, organically, the Society grew. Finally, it seemed that the spiritual perspective had so taken over the lives of what had then become the core group, that this impulse could now only be satisfactorily expressed through the establishment of a Centre where it could be both lived and taught in a much more intensive way.

The purchase of Runnings Park on the Malvern Hills in 1981 by the four families most closely involved in the work, was the next step in the Society's development. Here a Conference Centre was established; an Esoteric School and the College of Healing were founded; and, inspired from here, yet more kindred groups formed both in England and abroad.

In 1986 further steps were taken in making H-A's outlook on life more public. Two books were published by Gateway

Books. The first was Annie Wilson's 'Where There's Love', a beautiful account of the emergence of H-A and the Society, leading to the Runnings Park venture. Secondly, Michael Dean, deeply inspired by this philosophy, gathered together a very interesting collection of H-A readings covering a wide variety of subjects. These were published by Gateway Books under the title 'The Guide Book'. The success of this volume, demonstrating as it has the wider interest now being shown in these spiritual, yet highly practical teachings, has encouraged the Society to publish this present volume. As only a small proportion of the 'readings' have as yet been published in book form, it is intended that this volume be one in a long line of future publications.

What is it in this teaching that makes it of such vital interest to us now? Why in these next ten critical years should we give special weight to H-A's words? The answer to these questions seems to lie in the blend of simplicity and great depth which comes through all his messages, whether in spontaneous talks or in answer to specific questions. His teaching covers, for instance, such fundamental human concerns as relationships, the education of children, ecology, money, material achievement and life-after-death. His guidance is always down-to-earth and of the greatest help in grounding our spiritual aspirations.

Although always eminently practical, H-A challenges many of our deep-seated assumptions, turning upside down what we had until now taken for granted. Relationships, for instance, when seen in the light of reincarnation, can date back many thousands of years and this must be taken into account once we start working from this new perspective. Our attitude towards children and their education must also be revised: they are not necessarily the new vessels we have imagined them to be. As experienced old souls they may well be bringing with them much wisdom from which their parents can learn. Paramount through all his teachings is the need to relate harmoniously to the Earth; for our disregard for our planet is leading us towards ecological disaster. The planet's future and mankind's well-being as a whole are the issues – not the fragmented bids for power that now occupy the minds of politicians.

Finance is another area in which H-A speaks of the need

for total re-assessment. Money is an energy, which is in itself neither good nor bad, but because it has now outgrown its original purpose, that of being a means of exchange, it has deteriorated into an instrument of power. As such, it has been abused and used to control rather than to nourish mankind.

It is perhaps when speaking on death that H-A so fundamentally reverses modern man's usual thinking that we realise how deep and complete is the turnabout needed if we are to achieve what he says is our task in order to accomplish a safe passage into the Aquarian Age. There is, he says, no death. There is only transformation. And transformation is the key word to everything. Once we know that we are on Earth in order to learn and to evolve, then we know that our life's work is to help transform ourselves and everything around us through the bringing of light into our every thought and action.

H-A's teaching on meditation, handling psychic energy, astral travel, healing and other spiritual disciplines give us very practical guidelines as to how these changes can be brought about. For those who are interested in the origins of the universe and its workings and many other fascinating aspects of life which have until very recently been considered esoteric – available only for the initiates – H-A also has wonderful insights to offer.

A note of urgency sounds throughout this book. There is no room for complacency in a world which has brought itself to such a crisis point. Yet at the same time H-A's great love for all human beings and, above all, his deep respect for their free will, prevents him from ever making us feel in any way coerced. For those who want to take their lives in their own hands and go forward with courage, H-A's teachings will be an invaluable inspiration and give them a profound sense of how to become in tune with the angelic forces who so want to help mankind.

This is a book which can be read on many different levels and which sets out from many different points of view. For those just starting on the Path there is much to be learned; for those who have considerable knowledge already, new ways of perceiving life can emerge on every page.

Lorna St. Aubyn
London

OVERVIEW

Global Metamorphosis

Thirty three years have elapsed since first I spoke through this sensitive and during that time a great deal has moved within the hearts, minds and wills of those who have felt a sympathy and an understanding for what I have said. The world was then recovering from a tremendous conflict, a conflict which we still need to look at personally; for the future of this planet depends not on hierarchical forces, but on each individual spirit incarnate on planet Earth NOW. It depends upon the will within you as an individual to change, to acknowledge your own imperfection, to acknowledge your own perfection and to feel that divine spark within you, linking you to the Godhead.

As we move into the Aquarian age it will become increasingly necessary for every human-being to take on the role of self-responsibility, for there is no other route to find that peace, the peace that has been talked about from time immemorial. Humankind has failed to grasp that the peace without can only be found through the peace within. The role that each one of you plays in this unfoldment is uniquely important. Each person needs to re-evaluate him or herself in light of that reality. What is happening all over the world at the present time is a metamorphosis, a deep change in which the door is being opened for humanity; and through that door is pouring spiritual energy, there for each one of you to take and use. It lies within the hearts and minds of every human-being to steer this planet, using these new energies positively, gently, for peace. You do not need me to remind you that these energies can be used for destruction as well as for construction and that it all starts within. You have to lift yourselves out of your own self-destruction, embracing the pure love that can warm, cherish and provide you with spiritual nourishment.

This move into the Aquarian age has a particular significance, for coinciding with the renewal and resurgence of energy lies the opportunity once again to re-establish the rightful spiritual guardianship of this planet. Remember, these new energies reflect the elements of air, fire, water and earth, not only as spiritual forces, but as characteristics of your own personalities, emphasising the need to blend these four qualities within you. For in the blending of those basic energies lies the warmth and balance of your own self, being not afraid of the light, being not afraid of the shadow, recognising the importance of seeing yourself as a whole, integrated being.

OUR EVOLUTIONARY JOURNEY

The Purpose of Life – Evolution

How many of you have at some time in your life asked the question: 'What is life really all about?' Is it possible to give a short answer to such a question, to sum it up in a nutshell? Let me try.

I look upon life as a schooling for the spirit, a wonderful opportunity for many different thoughts of God to undergo experience together on a physical plane, each learning and growing in understanding and wisdom along its individual path of evolution towards the Godhead.

Thought exists on all levels. In its fine state you cannot see it, although those of you who are sensitive may feel it; as it becomes more dense it eventually manifests as physical matter. So when we talk about spirit, subtle bodies, etheric bodies, physical bodies, we are really describing various densities of thought. Your spirit, a thought creation of God, links down to the physical through many other levels of thought, or subtle bodies, which gradually become more and more dense forming an alignment with the physical body.

Although the spirit, the real you, has no shape as you would understand shape, it is very important for it to be in a state of balance with the physical shell; if it is not, then it becomes more difficult for you to experience fully and, after all, you are in an Earth body to experience.

These thought levels emanating from the spirit extend even further, creating an aura that surrounds the body. This, as many of you know, is a form of protective barrier or forcefield that holds the spirit, the subtle bodies and the physical body in alignment and helps the whole to maintain a balance. One of the tasks facing any spirit that comes into incarnation is to try to establish this balance with the physical shell. You may very well think to yourself that a more evolved spirit would find it easier to achieve this balance, but this is not necessarily so. The more evolved a spirit becomes, the more difficult it can be for it to achieve a balanced relationship with the body.

A spirit will incarnate many times until it has gained sufficient experience of physical life to have learned the lessons of acceptance, love and wisdom, and to have found a balance and harmony within itself and in relation to all other physical life. Described very simply, evolution of the spirit means reaching a state of consciousness wherein you realise you no longer need to undergo a specific experience. I am sure that each one of you has gone through moments when you have been able to look at a circumstance and say to yourself 'I understand that now, I can see why it had to happen'.

One of the hardest things I have to say to you is that there are no short cuts in this process of evolving. Coming to this lecture or reading all the esoteric books that have ever been published will not help you one scrap unless you are really prepared within yourself to make the effort in your everyday living, in your relationships with other people and in the decisions you make that affect those around you. I might say, with a little humour, that the day you can sit in your car and smile when someone tries to hurry you on or flashes his lights at you with impatience will be the day you have learnt a lesson in acceptance!

When I dwell on this question of accepting other people and accepting experience, many people think 'Well, that is obvious, I know this'. But they are the very ones who do *not* know it. For those who truly appreciate it will recognize that they have a long way to go to achieve true acceptance. The process of evolving is recognizing experience and seeing it as something you can utilize and accept. There is no such thing as bad experience; the only thing that can be bad about it is your attitude towards it. This is why I have emphasized to you that God is a God of love, a God of understanding and compassion.

Life is a means of providing physical manifestation and experience for the spirit; it is then for you to handle that experience. There are those who believe that the path of spirituality lies in symbolism, in so called esoteric mysteries. Dear friends, all the esoteric mysteries in this universe are within you; each one of you has your tower of mysteries that can be as simple or as complex as you choose to make it.

In an ideal sense, physical life is beautiful because that beneficent Godhead has given you the freewill to make your own decisions. I know you are limited by your physical body; you are limited by the environmental conditions in which you live but, even allowing for those limitations, you have the freewill to move about inside that environment. You are the master of your own destiny.

Physical life is not only beautiful but is a unique experience for spirit. It is not always easy for a spirit to handle a physical body, especially in this day and age, but life is a form of experience it cannot undergo in any other way. Your physical bodies are a combination of chemicals that react to your thought; if something alarming happens and you feel a sense of fear then it means that various chemicals are reacting in your body to stimulate it; your senses are heightened and your reactions become faster to help you to cope with the emergency that has arisen. It is a very real experience. Yet I would suggest to you that fear is an illusion; it is an emotion of the body and not of the spirit. The closer the relationship of your spirit to your physical body, the more it will enable you to rise above such physical emotions. I am not suggesting that you should ignore physical emotions because they are a part of physical life and living, but it is important that you learn how to make the optimum use of those emotions, not allowing them to dissipate through negative reactions, but using them in a positive and beneficial way.

Your physical body will vary from life to life depending on the type of experience your spirit is looking for in any one particular incarnation. Experience is cumulative and everything your spirit undergoes, in or out of the physical body, is there for all time, so that each time you incarnate your spirit brings with it the sum total of all its prior experiences; you are what you have made yourself, at any given moment in time. That is why I always stress that you are each totally responsible for yourself, to God. You are making your own life pattern by your thoughts. Your actions and deeds are of course the product of your thoughts and your challenge in life is to cope with all the various problems and situations you meet. It is no good sitting back and saying to yourself 'I am what I am, this is how God made me, people must accept me as I am'. You cannot get away with that because God did not make you that way, you made yourself; you are fashioning your own future even now as you read this lecture.

You may very well argue to yourself, 'It is all very well for him to say these things; he doesn't have to handle my physical body!' That is true, that is why I said that there are no short cuts. Beings like myself try to help because we feel that by opening your mind to a broader understanding we can help you to come to terms with your life more easily. We are not here to live your lives for you because to do that would be denying you the very experience for which you have incarnated. So it is in your hands all the way. You cannot push responsibility on to anyone else, it is yours alone. In saying that, I would like to add that you should never be frightened of failure, because failure is only a state of mind. All experience is valuable and relevant and much can be learned from a mistake or a failure; in fact, what feels like a moment of failure may be a significant turning point on your evolutionary path.

Each one of you will experience in a different way from all other human beings; there are no two spirits that have ever experienced identically for all experience is unique, all thought is unique, every spirit is unique. The variation comes about in how each of you chooses to react or respond to similar information or in a similar situation; that is where the difference lies, for your choice arises from your own uniqueness.

Each one of you needs to become more objective in your understanding of yourself, to find a balance between, on the one hand, not negating or undervaluing yourself and, on the other hand, not over-expressing yourself in the belief that others may see you as a person of substance and that, without you, a situation will crumble! There is no such situation and it may be that, without you, events would take a different course that would be better for others involved. Ego is a trap for even the most wary; ego always inhibits evolution.

Dear friends, what others think of you is unimportant, it is their concern and not yours. Never at any time do something for effect, but do it only for a purpose; remember, God is not going to come down and say 'There's a good chap, you did that well!'. When it comes to the moment of reckoning the only judge will be yourself. It is you who will look at yourself and say 'My goodness, wasn't I a fool!'. See yourself for what you are, no more, no less. Try to see, in one sense, how insignificant you are in relation to the whole. Learn to understand your own relationship with those around you; learn to respect and love those around you and learn to extend this love and respect to animals, plants and all forms of life because all are thoughts of God and aspects of planet Earth experiencing in their own particular way. You are part of that whole experience.

Having just told you how *in*significant you are, I shall now tell you how *significant* you are! Each of you is playing a vital role in the evolution of this planet because everything you do, think and say is not only affecting the thoughts of everyone else around you, but it is affecting every being on this planet, in the solar system, in the galaxy, in the universe. All is one. You are here to find that oneness through harmony and balance, both within yourself and in your relationships in a physical universe.

You all know how easy it is to feel critical of somebody else, to feel that you could do better; or you may feel a sense of inferiority, that everyone else can do better than you. I am sure you can see with me that both those lines of thinking are false. You are forgetting that your thoughts are affecting that other person and may be causing him or her to do it 'wrong' in your eyes. You are also forgetting that you are unique and individual and that every other person is unique and individual. To compare is futile and hurtful – especially to yourself.

Some of you may feel that my words are too simple but believe me, dear friends, however deep or esoteric your approach, unless you can think and acquire knowledge in a simple balanced way, those deep esoteric considerations will be of more harm than good to you.

Evolution is not knowledge, it is understanding. This is what life is about: understanding, coming to terms with all the simple things you do in your life. Some of the greatest inspiration that has come to this planet has come not through reading books but through sitting in green fields, sitting under a tree, sitting on the side of a mountain.

In realising your responsibility and relating it to those around you, do not fall into the trap of worrying about other people. I could continue for another five hours looking at various attitudes of mind that can help and yet trap you because everything you do offers two alternatives. It is like the sword, isn't it? If you hold it one way you have the cross; if you hold it the other way it is a weapon of destruction. So every time you find yourself getting into a negative state such as over-worrying, ask yourself, 'Which way am I holding my sword? Am I using it as a cross or am I using it as a weapon? If as a weapon, am I using it against myself or against someone else, or both?'

So we come back to the beginning, that life is a schooling for the spirit through physical, material existence. Unfortunately, some of you have become so enmeshed in your material lives that you have lost sight of the real issues. Those issues are not how much you can fit into twenty-four hours but your attitudes of mind during those twenty-four hours. How do you react in the situations in which you find yourself? How do you react to others? Do you think generously or critically towards those whom you meet? It is a question of establishing priorities in your understanding. Do not become so enmeshed in material achievement that you neglect spiritual growth. What *is* achievement? As I see it, true achievement is evolution. It is a growth of understanding. It is appreciating the same situation from a wider perspective.

Dear friends, each one of you has within you the urge not only to advance yourself spiritually but, through your own experience, to help others. Take a long look at yourself and, through seeing yourself, you will more easily be able to see and understand others. As I said earlier, physical life can be a truly wonderful and beautiful experience and you can make it so by your own attitude of mind. You can obtain fulfilment from every second of your life and this is what you should be aiming for. This is why you are studying spiritually, so that you can make optimum use of this life and gain the widest possible experience from your every thought and action. Spiritual experiences are the hardest to handle. It is always much easier to go to a film or manipulate your box with the square eye and allow somebody else to do the thinking for you, to present you with a contrived experience without depth that will no doubt stimulate your emotions, causing certain chemicals to race around your body; that is always much easier to do and no doubt you will persuade yourself that it has helped you to relax as you sit there tense, watching that square eye.

You have chosen life at a very critical stage in the evolution of this planet. Humankind has advanced scientifically but has not carried spiritual thinking forward at the same speed. It has launched into technological experiences it does not fully understand. Many inventions are based on different types of radiation – radiations of different wave-lengths – and some of the wave-lengths come very close to the vibration of spirit. There is, in my opinion, a possibility – I'm not saying it will happen – but there is a danger that some of these experiments could affect the relationship of the spirit to the body. One always runs into this type of danger when one puts technology before spirituality; ideally these two aspects of life should advance in balance together.

You are abusing this planet in various ways, and have ignored the important lesson of having respect for all other beings. Man has become greedy because it has made life materially easier for him. You can touch a switch and the room becomes illuminated, the machine starts to turn, your vehicles transport you ever faster and faster. This is easy, isn't it? But gradually you are bleeding Earth and pushing the whole planet out of balance. Large areas have been turned into desert; you are polluting the sea and doing some terrible things to the air you breathe and to the various atmospheric layers that encircle the planet.

How humankind develops in the future depends on the thoughts and actions of those who are incarnate *now, today*, for it is the individual drops that make up the ocean.

Thank you for giving me this opportunity to share these thoughts with you and to help you to realise how important it is to take yourself in hand, to understand and learn to love yourself and others and to engender love and respect for all thoughts of God.

Making The Most Of Life On Earth

I have already explained how you incarnate on Earth to gain experience to further your evolution. In order to obtain the utmost from this experience it is necessary to proceed through life in balance and, to achieve that balance, the practical and material side of life must not be ignored.

You incarnated into a physical body, to obtain knowledge of the material world; for remember, this cannot be gained from any of the planes of spirit – if it could, then there would be no need for you to come to Earth at all. Let us, therefore, look at the best way you can approach this physical, material existence, so as to make the most of the experience it offers.

In looking at life, you will observe there are many moments of choice with roads leading in all directions – happy, indifferent, unhappy, good, bad. The life you have chosen is governed by the decision made by the free will of your spirit before entering incarnation. At any moment you have the free will to choose the path you wish to tread and not be fettered by past patterning. You should seek to lead your life in accordance with the dictates of your inner conscience; in other words, live to the best of your capability, always with an eye to growth and transformation. Remember, it would only be possible to evaluate evolutionary progress over a series of incarnations, not in any one particular lifetime. As you read through these lectures it is important to view them with an open mind, for if you do, I am sure you will find some answers to your problems, both spiritual and material. I consider it also important that you do not wholly accept what I say without carefully weighing my message on the scales of your own understanding, for I do not wish to force anyone to believe anything. God has given men and women free will to accept or reject anything and everything within the universe. How much a person accepts will be entirely in accordance with his or her own particular stage of evolution. Nowhere in my teachings will you find doctrines or dogmas for this very reason.

A fulfilled life does not mean mediocrity, nor does it mean living a narrow rut minding one's own business. People are inclined to think that a person who lives this kind of life must be a good person, but it does not necessarily follow. It has been said that it is the prerogative of each person to assert their individual ego in argument with their colleagues, stressing their uniqueness by constant differentiation. It is important that you express your own ideas, but always with tolerance towards those who differ from you, honouring *their* viewpoint. The balanced way is to use your ego as a *complement* to your fellow human beings. Perhaps if you did there would not be the wars and strife we find in the world today.

Thought plays a very important part in the living of one's life on Earth. To live at a superficial level is not sufficient; it is necessary to think harmoniously and to try to bring a balanced perspective to all that you do. You must have something deeper than mere outward show – a desire to progress, to find joy in what you do, to open your mind, and not close and shutter it against anything which you find unpleasant or undesirable. Remember, 'Seek and ye shall find', for God limits no one. It is *you* who create the limitations.

It is not necessary to attend a church or belong to a religious body in order to find God; but if you are a person who wishes to seek in a strictly orthodox way, then I would encourage you to continue to do so, for you will probably benefit more from such religious expression than from my teachings. To try to absorb other ideas may possibly destroy the very faith which you have found; and yet, to others, I say that additional teachings or philosophies will only serve to deepen your understanding and practice of orthodox religion. It is all a question of individual motivation. I have no desire to condemn the Church or orthodox bodies, for I am not concerned about what the Churches are, but rather what they are not.

Pacifism

Man is not perfect and should not even try to be, for you need to accept yourself for what you are; no more and no less. This remark is particularly relevant to the question of pacifism. Of course pacifism is right morally, but humanity will not attain this state until it has reached a level of evolution and understanding where differences can be worked out without aggression. You would not expect a child of six to lift a fifty kilogram weight and would consider such an idea ridiculous. It is equally as foolish to expect people to adopt a way of life before they are evolved enough to do so. Certainly there are many people in the world today whose stage of evolution is sufficiently advanced to attain and accept pacifism, but it is very much a question of the majority or general cross section of the world community upon which my remarks are based.

Pragmatic people on Earth often realise that it is sometimes painfully necessary to fight in order to preserve a hard-won order of free thought and expression. Those who strive for pacifism as an absolute before humanity as a whole is ready to take such a step, endanger the very ideals they are trying to achieve. Unfortunately, as history has shown, when an evolved nation or community comes up against one which, taken as a whole, is of lesser evolution, it is usually the unevolved people who win, for they do not have the same ethical limitations.

If it were possible to sum up how you should lead your life, I would say ... Always be ready to help and serve others; honour and respect God; understand and do not condemn your fellow men; be tolerant of all beliefs and observe humility; allow yourself that awareness which recognises and accepts that there are people in the world whose comparative standards are different from your own; and finally, seek evolution and the Greater Wisdom. If you are forced to fight, do so only to defend what is dear to you, for in the not too distant future, belligerence will become a thing of the past.

Know Thyself – A Meditation

Have you ever considered deeply the true meaning of 'Know Thyself'? Your life upon Earth is an experience and, through a succession of incarnations, that experience accumulates until the spirit acquires a state of realisation, of wisdom, which is the sum total of its understanding gained throughout all the incarnations and experiences it has undergone.

You can evolve as quickly as you choose, and so the question comes to mind – can I aid my own evolution? Yes, most definitely, and the first step towards doing so is to strive to know yourself as you truly are. Do not set yourself a standard of living which is hypocritical and which your mind, body and spirit are not capable of maintaining; but rather look at yourself and see yourself as you are, right now. Learn to recognise your shortcomings – physical, mental and spiritual. Learn to recognise your attributes – physical, mental and spiritual. See yourself as you are, no more, no less; for that recognition, that ability to strip yourself of all earthly emotions and face yourself honestly, is the first step to aid your own spiritual, mental and material evolution.

This is perhaps one of the most difficult tasks for human beings in a physical body. It requires a great deal of honesty, a great deal of humility and clear thinking, for to undervalue or overvalue yourself by assuming either an inferiority complex or a superiority complex will distort your viewpoint. You have to examine your very soul with love, tolerance and understanding; to realise when you have been intolerant and not shown understanding, and also to be aware of what you have done which has been valuable and may have benefitted other people. Learn to value and accept both your light and your shadow.

Look at yourself in the mirror, in the mirror of your soul,

and see yourself for what you are. Not until you achieve this state of mind can you consider how you are going to lead a spiritually progressive life.

'I am what I am, no more and no less'... Having learned truly to understand that remark, and having embarked on the path of 'knowing oneself' – what next?

It is from this point that you will feel you wish to open your mind to the esoteric wisdom of the universe. You can now begin to assimilate that spiritual knowledge for which you are thirsting. You may want to know how to do this and my answer is to do it in a way that is most natural to you. Choose your favourite armchair, sit back, relax, close your eyes, centre yourself within and allow yourself to be fully but firmly uplifted to the higher realms of spiritual understanding. Go to your favourite pew in your favourite church and do the selfsame thing. Sit in the corner seat of your morning train and, yet again, do the same thing. In other words, find the place where it is easiest and simplest for you to relax your body and mind.

> Having prepared yourself for meditation, relax your body from feet to head, becoming conscious of each part in turn and then mentally and physically letting go ... Allow the feeling of love and light from your heart centre to fill your whole being and radiate out from you ... Focus your mind on the infinity of the Ultimate ... Focus on the great wisdom and unconditional love of the Ultimate ... Consider for a moment the unique spark of God that resides within you ... Ponder on your relationship with that quality of unconditional love ... How do you express that to yourself? ... to others? ... to your environment? ... to your planet? ... Focus once again on the magnificence, the unequalled simplicity and beauty of God's universe ... Finally, return in thought to where you are sitting, centre and earth yourself.

Try it for just a short period at first and then perhaps a little longer, and you will find that upliftment which you so desire.

As you receive this unfolding of the works of the Ultimate you will find that it may tend to make your mind diverge from the material facts of life. I would remind you, however, that you are incarnate upon Earth to undertake a form of physical experience and, in allowing yourself to seek esoteric wisdom, do not exclude the material experience which is so very necessary for you to complete your evolution.

'Seek And Ye Shall Find'

Seek and ye shall find, for God limits no one, it is you who limit yourself. In this lecture I would like to explain more fully what I mean by this statement.

You incarnate on the Earth planet to undergo a series of evolutionary experiences which you are able to pursue by virtue of the gift of freewill. You can choose to seek or not to seek, to acknowledge the Godhead or not, as you wish. In fact, throughout your lives you always have the choice of saying yes or no, of doing or not doing; and through these continual decisions you experience and learn in the way you choose and at the speed you choose.

Were God to impose limits, your freewill would at once be destroyed and you would no longer be able to seek as you wish. You would become stereotyped and your life predestined; your way of life would be bounded on all sides by insurmountable walls. In other words, you would be turned into a negative being. Let us take the example of a very young child who is as yet unbound by environment or social laws. The natural instinct of children is to search unconditionally, asking questions without fear and with an open mind, which is surely a lesson in itself.

My friends, step forward without fear; search and, if your intentions are like those of the child, genuine, honest and without ego, then your seeking will be rewarded for you will be led to a spiritual understanding that is in sympathy with the needs of your spirit at this stage of your evolutionary journey.

Which Path?

Remember, there are many paths to God and which path you select is not of great importance since eventually they all reach the Godhead. Some take longer for their routes are winding, while others are more direct. You should follow that approach which helps you to feel in touch with your deepest inner promptings.

A word for those who participate in any form of orthodox church-going: it is useless unless you do so with a genuine desire to bring yourself nearer to God. If you are merely attending the services because you feel that it is the right thing to do, or because you think it might make things easier for you when you pass over, it is not only a waste of time but will in actual fact serve to hinder your progress and evolution when you leave your Earth body.

Ritual

In most religions certain forms of ritual are observed, some elaborate, some simple. Are these necessary? Since the spirit is essentially a thought state, the answer, broadly speaking, is no. But there are many people who find it easier to tune their minds to a devotional state with the aid of music and ritual and for whom a set form of prayer or discipline is helpful when raising their thoughts to God. Indeed, many minds thinking in harmony along a beam of thought as in a prayer multiplies the power of that thought.

Certain rituals do carry power which varies in efficacy according to their age, their use and the spiritual energies of their originators. But the power is limited to the ritual, whereas pure thought, if used correctly, has no limitations.

Perfection and Infallibility

One thing that all people on Earth should remember is that no one in an Earth body is perfect or infallible. If they were they would not be incarnate but with the Ultimate, the Father/Mother God. Some have reached a more advanced stage of understanding through many lives and have acquired greater wisdom, which in itself brings an increased responsibility towards others. But all spirits incarnate on Earth are here to experience, to learn and, in some cases, to teach, according to their individual karma.

To aim for perfection is a trap because it tries to deny the shadow and suppress it, thereby giving it energy; whereas acknowledging your wholeness, your light and your shadow, allows you to evolve in balance and accept yourself with awareness, love and understanding.

Spiritual Pitfalls and Initiations

Indeed, just as there are material and emotional traps in life, there are also spiritual traps and pitfalls. In reality, these challenges are the initiations of today.

In the civilisations of both East and West, there have been many routes to the 'I' within, to seeking that true spiritual Self. And it was known that as you 'walked the Path' you were tested; you hit the pitfalls, the stony way. In this day and age, many of you may not be so aware of 'walking the Path' unless you join a spiritual order. And yet, seeking for the 'I', the spark of God that brought you into being, is becoming more and more relevant for each individual on this planet and for planet Earth herself.

It is when the ego comes into play and, through the personality, wants to rule and prevent the true 'I' from shining forth, it is then that you have a spiritual dilemma. For the ego is very agile and crafty, very powerful and strong. Society is built on developing the ego states of each one of you and that part of the personality does not wish to give up its hold. The ego defends itself and issues become conditional rather than unconditional. Karma, the law of cause and effect, is used as an excuse, a reason for not doing or being in a certain way. The individual is challenged and confronted by the shadow side, by issues that have to be faced, with honesty. And, depending upon how he or she responds to these challenges, the Path progresses or is deflected.

Today, that negative pull is very strong; but so also are the spiritual energies, allowing you each a great opportunity to find and consciously explore your true spiritual Path.

Pre-Human Existence

Planet Earth provides expression for many different types of spirit through her varied forms of physical life. There are those spirits that inhabit the bodies of men, those of animals, those of fish, and those of plant life; there is even a type of spirit that inhabits the ground upon which you stand. These are all different forms of spirit life which together form a small part of the universe, all thought expressions of that Ultimate Creative Thought.

When a spirit is first created by the Ultimate, it finds itself on the plane of decision; there it passes through a series of experiences until it reaches a stage of realisation in which it knows it will enter either the body of a man or, for a different form of experience, the body of an animal, a plant or some other form of evolution.

Let us for the moment look at the spirit which leaves the plane of decision to enter the body of a man or a woman and experience human life on Earth.

When ascending from the plane of decision to the first plane of human existence a spirit will often enter an intermediary stage while trying to find its own level; such spirits occasionally manifest as elementary spirits or poltergeist phenomena. Sooner or later the necessity to incarnate will dawn upon the spirit and it will then enter a human body.

Spirits which have chosen to experience through animal evolution do not switch over to human experience as is taught by many schools of thought for, as I have said before, whilst all these forms of life blend together, the type of experience undergone by an animal is quite different to that experienced by a human. It is possible for there to be exceptions to this rule but it is very unusual, for each of these groups is going through a series of experiences quite independently, thus adding to the Ultimate in a different way.

Body and Spirit
– Do They Evolve Together?

It is no exaggeration to say that an understanding of the true meaning of evolution is a key to the appreciation of what your life means and how it can, will or should unfold. The evolution of homo sapiens has two facets, one being the evolution of the physical body and the other the evolution of the spirit. As you know, the spirit is the 'I', the essence within you, that spark which gives you beingness and which causes you to initiate thoughts and ideas. It began its existence as a thought created by the Ultimate Thought or Godhead and entered a universe of infinite experience as pure, fresh thought, an embryo having neither depth, vision, understanding nor wisdom.

Every moment of your physical life you are learning. Every action, every decision that you make is helping to mould you in your present incarnation. Life itself is basically simple and consists of a series of challenges which have to be met; all the time you are having to make decisions which can affect your entire future life. Some of these decisions can be made easily and readily for they are part of the routine of everyday existence; but there are those decisions which are difficult because they involve other people around you, those dear to you, those with whom you work. Your challenge is to accept each situation as it arises, deal with it separately and really handle it. You cannot expect to make the right decision every time but to make a decision, even if it is wrong, is better than making none at all. At the same time, you need to think carefully because you are not only moulding your present incarnation, you are also moulding your future incarnations.

As the young spirit enters the universe it begins to grow. After a period it reaches a stage in its growth where it begins to see and understand and, as it looks around it, so its vision becomes broader and its understanding wider. It will then find itself in a state where it feels ready to take on physical experience and this it will do through the medium of a physical body. Your spirit has complete freewill which means it can make whatever decision it wishes, and here we meet one of the most interesting paradoxes of physical incarnation. Although your spirit has this complete freewill, in a physical body its freewill is somewhat curtailed by the physical limitations of genetics, environment and by the actions of other spirits and people around it. So one of the first things a spirit has to do in incarnation is to come to terms with its physical shell. This is not always easy and will depend upon the relationship between the ego and its vehicle. Let me explain a little further.

Over the centuries the physical shell of man has evolved and developed in a particular direction; your spirit does not only take on one body and one life, it may incarnate many times, each incarnation being complementary to the one before. As you experience and grow, so you choose in your subsequent incarnations a physical body which you feel will give you the type of experience for which your spirit is ready. The spirit itself will contain the sum total of all its past lives and pre-human experiences; so in each incarnation it is able to choose a different body. If, for example, it desires an incarnation where it wishes to use the intellect, then it must select a physical body in which the brain has intellectual capacity.

It is very difficult to be categoric in a lecture such as this because there are always exceptions and deviations but, generally speaking, a spirit will seek a physical shell which is complementary to its stage of evolution at that time. However, not all spirits make the right decision in their choice of body, just as you do not always make the right decisions in your everyday life, for your spirit, like your body is not perfect. There is only one state of perfection and that is within the Godhead itself. So while you are evolving towards this Ultimate Thought you are liable to error and your spirit may choose a body which it cannot handle. When this happens conflict ensues. I am sure you can all appreciate how it is possible for a physical body to have a brain with brilliant capacity and yet somehow there is something lacking in the entire beingness of that individual. The personality has fallen short because the spirit in charge of the physical shell has not sufficient wisdom and finds itself unable to cope with a high-powered body; it is rather like putting a novice driver at the wheel of a high-powered racing car and it can be equally as dangerous.

Let us take the case of Mr. B, a shoemaker, who passes over. He has spent a great portion of his life playing darts and partaking of the artificial forms of entertainment available today. He has led a 'good' life, attending church on Sunday mornings and the 'pub' in the evenings. He is not a particularly wise soul but, on the other hand, has not done anyone much harm, except perhaps to cheat a little in business matters and use a few words not in the English dictionary. So as not to complicate matters we will say he is a single man.

Upon passing over, his spirit will dwell on the second plane until it reaches a state of realisation in which it is able to assess its own standing. It realises that in its last existence it neither learned much nor did much good, so it elects to come back in a learned capacity and chooses to incarnate into a body which will in due course become a professor of science.

The body is born and grows up. He studies and becomes a very brilliant professor. In time a war comes along; as he has a very clever brain but not a great deal of wisdom to go with it he uses his brilliance to invent weapons that will cause destruction and suffering: some poison gas, perhaps, and later on a few atom and hydrogen bombs.

In due course his spirit passes over and, because of the things he invented with his brain while in an Earth body, it descends down the scale a little; for, my friends, the path of evolution is not always a straight one, it sometimes doubles back on itself before taking a step forward. His spirit amuses itself in a mental state, still thinking of its unpleasant devices and instilling thoughts into the minds of others on Earth to do likewise.

Eventually, our Mr. B's spirit reaches a state where it

again becomes aware of itself and what it is and, with the assistance of spirit helpers, it is able to draw itself out of the mire of sadistic thought. It realises that it has again made a mess of things and will need further Earth experience. This time, however, it elects to return as someone who will suffer greatly, as it realises that it has caused suffering before and must now take the place of the sufferer. It therefore chooses to enter the body of, say, a woman who will be ill-treated by her husband.

However, Mr. B's spirit will not lose the experience it has gained in previous incarnations although, when limited by an Earth body, it will probably be unable to bring it forward to the conscious mind. Nothing is lost, for all experience and lessons learnt stay with the spirit, determining its level of understanding and thereby its evolution.

Conversely, a spirit of much more understanding may choose a body which is too heavy, dense and cumbersome for it and this, too, presents difficulties. The vibration of the spirit will be somewhat fast for that of the body and it may have difficulty in synchronising with it.

Here again one is trying to single out particular cases, but the point to bear in mind is that wisdom is a strange thing for it is not bound in any way to intelligence. A person's brain capacity can be quite limited and yet that physical shell can house a thought or spirit of great wisdom and beauty. One of the greatest traps into which man can fall in his seeking is to think that intellectualism and academic prowess are synonymous with evolution and wisdom. True wisdom is simplicity and it takes a great person to be able to view a complex problem in a simple way. The ability not to become enmeshed in intellectual detail or over involved in petty problems is the hallmark of true wisdom.

Physical appearance is to a certain extent governed by the state of evolution of the spirit. A highly evolved spirit would not incarnate into the unevolved physical body of, say, Neanderthal man, through which it could not express itself. This does not mean that people of handsome physical stature are necessarily evolved, for it is not the good looks but the wise words which portray evolution. Nevertheless, spiritual and somatic evolution do run side by side and a serious lack of this evolutionary alignment can cause genetic deformities.

Some of you may wonder whether it is possible for spirits of a similar type to *homo sapiens* to incarnate into Earth bodies from other planets, in order to gain experience on a different sphere. The answer is yes, this does happen and, similarly, some Earth spirits choose to incarnate on other planets in the universe. Also, if the general stage of evolution on one planet is too high to enable a specific spirit to undergo the experiences it requires, it may go to another lesser evolved sphere to incarnate; and the same applies where the evolution of the planet in question is not advanced enough for the requirements of a particular spirit. But these are rare exceptions and not the general rule.

Each person and each spirit is in its own individual stage of understanding; therefore no two people can possibly see exactly the same picture. Each one of you is forming your own individual idea, your own interpretation of the whole. This, of course, is as it should be, for such is the nature of the universe which, in its inifinity, has room for infinite facets of thought. As you grow in each individual life, so you begin to mould the physical shell which you inhabit. It may well be that an advanced spirit of wisdom will come to terms with its physical body, lightening it and refining it as it matures. Equally, a spirit of humbler evolution will normally house itself in a body with which it can harmonise and live in balance. But it is those spirits that are out of tune with their physical bodies and are unable to handle them in balance that will experience great difficulty. This applies at both ends of the scale. Much of the trouble that arises in the world stems from 'fringe' cases such as these and this is where the overall guiding influence on a planet begins to take effect. Let me explain further.

You live on a planet, which is part of a solar system, which in turn is part of a galaxy. You as an individual are surrounded by other spirits; you are part of this infinite cosmic scheme in which all forms of intelligence are interconnected. The whole of nature works this way; in fact, your body is made up of millions of atoms, each of which could be likened to a solar system within itself. In a sense, spirit evolution follows a similar path and, as you go through your own individual cycle of evolution, you will at all times be affected by other forms of spirit from all dimensions around you: those on a similar path to your own and those that may seem far removed from you such as the devic spirits that guide your own and other planets.

All spirits are subject to error and can be out of balance until they have evolved to the state of perfection known as the Godhead. All have freewill and are capable of the state of imbalance known as 'evil' wherein they no longer acknowledge God but set themselves up as gods. If this should happen to a devic spirit that has reached the stage of guiding a planet, its influence will have very far-reaching consequences. Planet Earth is at present suffering from an 'evil' influence of this nature. You do not have to look far to see the results around you and it is those 'fringe' spirits I mentioned earlier that will be particularly affected by such an influence. A person leading a balanced life with the spirit nicely in tune with the physical body, who is able to express himself in a comfortable way, will rise above temptation and the little nudges which urge one to do things that can only bring distress and upset the balance of existence. The balanced spirit can cope, but those spirits which are out of adjustment with their physical bodies cannot and it is these people who will be affected by the evil influence around your planet. If you look anywhere in the world you will find that most of the trouble and unhappiness is caused by the minority, not the majority; unfortunately, the majority are inclined to consider that they are able to see the problem in greater depth and can therefore detach themselves from it, sit back and do nothing. I would hope that this does not apply to people such as yourselves, for if you were not prepared to do anything with your thoughts and ideas you would not be reading this. You are part of a pattern which is emerging.

The thing to remember about the universe in which you exist is that it is forever expanding, for there is no end to experience and therefore no end to what you can achieve in understanding. Through the type of experience you are having and will have in future incarnations, you will eventually reach a stage of evolution in which you will find a complete acceptance of the universe around you, a state of balance and perfection, an at-one-ment with the Godhead.

And the achievement of this at-one-ment with the Godhead means being part of that supreme state whilst all the time retaining your individual thought and expansion within it. This is an expanding universe, a physical manifestation of an expanding Godhead. That is why it is necessary for there to be a system of reincarnation. It is necessary to go through a number of lives because in each one you are gaining experience, you are evolving. You will notice that I very carefully used the word 'experience' rather than 'wisdom', for the path of evolution is rather like a meandering stream; sometimes it doubles back on itself but in an overall sense it is going forward. Your spirit gains wisdom according to how it learns from experience.

This is a very deep subject, one which has many aspects and one which I would like you to think about, for I have tried to give you stimulus for further thought. It is not necessary to think identically to others; but it is necessary, if you are to grow in wisdom, to learn to harmonise your thoughts with those around you. The difference is important. To become at one with other people does not mean that you are in complete unison with them but that you are individuals in harmony. The key to peaceful co-existence is not unison but tolerance and harmony. Whenever the 'absolute' ideology is thrust upon you, then you will have people as individuals becoming dissatisfied and feeling guilty. This is because they are naturally incomplete, they would not be incarnate in a physical body if their spirit had attained 'perfection', and yet they are not being afforded the opportunity to find a proper means of self-expression. How can any spirit fulfil itself without the right to choose its own individual beliefs and, having chosen, to express them in harmony, freedom and love?

Spirit and Genetic Evolution

The Complement

The universe in its magnificence is entirely composed of thought, thought on varying degrees and levels. The Ultimate or Godhead is thought at its 'highest', thought at its finest, its lightest; it is supreme, creative, all-wise. As one descends to the lower paths of evolution, thought becomes less fine, narrower and less wise. The denser it is the more limited it becomes. Thus you see that thought only achieves a complete infinity of expression when it reaches the Ultimate, in total harmony with all other thought.

The spirit which is evolving in your Earth body at this very moment is utilising another form of thought, a physical body which provides both a shelter for it and a vehicle through which it can express itself. The physical body itself is thought on a very low, dense vibration and, as such, is performing the kind of evolution suitable to the physical conditions which surround it and from which it has evolved.

An appreciation of life in the sphere of dense matter or physical existence is essential to a spirit passing through an evolutionary cycle such as that of *homo sapiens*, as this path demands experience *through* the material, but not *as* the material. By this I mean that your spirit expresses itself through your physical shell in order to appreciate such material experiences as are available to it in any one particular incarnation, but that the actual physical body in which you have incarnated is of a different form of evolution from that of your spirit.

The molecular atoms of which your physical body is composed move at a frequency of vibration which is much slower than that of your psyche or spirit. These atoms are part of the spheres of the four elements of which a physical planet is composed – air, fire, earth and water. When your spirit leaves your body, as in death, by cosmic law the four elements reclaim those parts of the body that are 'lent' it for its existence. Fire and air are the faster elements and they are the first to leave the body in the form of warmth and breath. Next comes the drying process when water in the form of all moisture evaporates; finally, the decaying of the denser tissues comes under the jurisdiction of the element of earth. In Atlantis of old the whole process could be achieved in a few seconds by the power of thought, when the priest commanded the four elements to reclaim instantly those parts of the physical body which were from their domains. The result was disintegration without a trace.

Perhaps I could illustrate the relationship between spirit and genetic evolution by comparing it with your electric heaters. The element alone produces nothing, but when the electric current is turned on, warmth is produced. Without the element through which to express its vibration the electricity is nothing and imperceptible, just as the element is but a piece of cold metal until ignited.

If the connections between the current and the element are faulty there will be an irregularity in the expression, or even no heat at all. So it is with the human body and the spirit: if the connecting link between the two is faulty, illnesses and all forms of imbalance may result, even to total unconsciousness.

When an electrical implement is wired to take only a certain amount of current and this is overloaded, a blown fuse will result. The human body is the same with regard to vibrations; it can only take those vibrations to which it is attuned at any one time. Exceed this load and mental trouble will ensue. That is why higher and wiser spirits deem it unwise to grant requests for a display of power or phenomena, the close proximity of which could prove too great for those present. The body needs to be carefully schooled by self-discipline, rest and diet before it can lighten its vibrations sufficiently to accept the very powerful 'currents' from the higher spheres of thought.

Physical evolution moves at a speed relative to the planet upon which it exists; thus the body's shape, height, weight etc. change and adjust according to the physical conditions prevailing. An evolved body does not necessarily house an evolved spirit, as in the case of a person who is academically clever but without wisdom. Equally, an evolved spirit may choose a body of humble evolution in which to incarnate, although in this case the body would never be one of extremely low evolution with a very limited capacity, as an evolved spirit would be unable to express itself through such a body. The ideal state for physical expression is when the evolution of the body is complementary to that of the spirit. Consequently, as the human race evolves genetically, more evolved spirits are able to use bodies as vehicles through which to express their wisdom.

Many people do not realise that spirit evolution is entirely separate from physical evolution and much confusion has arisen as a result of this misunderstanding. Darwin's 'missing link' was, in fact, a spirit transference, where the bodies available were taken on by a different form of *spirit* evolution which refined them according to needs. So, although spirit and physical evolution run along separately, they have a strong influence on each other, especially the spirit on the physical body. Indeed, the resident spirit influences its physical vehicle far more than is generally supposed and can even alter the shape and appearance of a body, as in the 'missing link' between ape and man. I should like to examine this influence of the spirit on the body in a little more detail.

When you make a decision, the elements of which your body is composed will receive certain experiences of action; these are derived from the decision of the spirit through the impulses of the brain. Remember, your spirit has the freewill to make the best or the worst of its physical body, to accentuate its strengths or its weaknesses by the decisions it makes; and the results of these decisions will gradually become imprinted on the physical. In fact, your physical form carries the whole of your story up to date. Each of you has your own own private story written plainly in your body for those who can read; what you think and do between the cradle and the grave impresses the material of the form with its habits. The sum total, the essence, is assembled after the grave, condensed, converted, you might say, into basic principles within your spirit; and that is what you start with next time.

It does matter what you do and how you think in this life because it is fashioning your form, your circumstances and your abilities, and your spirit is learning and benefitting, or otherwise, from the experience. The glands of the body secrete chemicals, the formulae of which are created by habits; you created the habit and you stipulated the figures in the formula. When you see a face lined with pain, the result of ulcers, growths or other illness, you see a person who has by long and persistent effort created the chemical formulae in the glands which in turn have imposed their programme upon the physical body.

The tragedy is that even when suffering greatly, many people do not have a clue as to how the illness came about; their negative attitude to circumstances blocks the flow of wisdom from their spirit, with the result that they continue their unsuitable habits, not realising the significant effect they are having on their health. Thus you have psychosomatic illnesses which are frequently the most difficult form of suffering to dispel.

From this you can begin to see how the type of life-matter which is evolving as your physical shell is influenced by and dependent upon the spirit which it is housing. It is also a perfect example of the way in which two different forms of evolution complement each other.

Materialisation

I would like to clear up one or two points on the subject of materialisation and spirit communication. Many people ask 'Is there such a thing as materialisation? And, if so, how is it achieved?'.

Materialisation does exist. As to how it is achieved, let me first of all make the following statement. Ectoplasm, the substance through which materialisation is formed, is something physical. It is not, I repeat, *not* spiritual.

Let us picture a room containing seven people. Six of them are seated round a table while the seventh is a medium sitting for, or shall we say hoping for, a materialisation. What takes place? Picture now your own human body, bearing in mind the vibrations on many levels of which it is composed. Try not to think of your spirit, physical shell and aura as entirely separate entities, for they are all functioning as a complete unit. Think of it as a colour, the colour blue; the higher the vibration the lighter the blue would be, so that a very light blue would represent the spirit; as the vibration descended to the various denser tissues of the body it would tend to become a deeper blue; in fact, you would see many different shades. The aura, which is the link between the spirit and the outside world, would appear again as a pale shade of blue.

Now let us return to the seance room where everyone is hoping to see a materialised form. 'Look,' somebody cries, 'ectoplasm is forming!'. The medium has found that, by relaxing the body and inducing a certain mental condition, ectoplasm will appear. What is not generally understood is that each of those six people present has put out a thought to encourage that ectoplasm to appear.

Why is it, then, that when the chemical composition of your body is analysed you cannot find this strange substance called ectoplasm? Man is not, as yet, familiar with every chemical substance on his own planet and ectoplasm is of a much finer composition than could at present be distinguished by your Earth instruments; it stems from the central regions of the body and, since it is actually a part of the physical body, you can see how dangerous it can be if it is damaged or cut.

Now a spirit can manifest itself, utilising the ectoplasm. You could say that ectoplasm is a semi-physical substance providing a form of vibrational link between the physical body and the spirit. A spirit is able to control the ectoplasm into a shape by the power of its thought; this it can do by projecting a thought form from its own sphere of evolution. It is not essential for that thought or spirit actually to visit the ectoplasm in its etheric body.

The reason I have given you this little example is because I am trying to bring home to you the oneness of the universe. Those seven people, the materialising spirit in the ectoplasm and all the spirits in that room are all one in varying stages of density. I am sure that if you can have a strong realisation of this it will help you greatly with your future studies.

If a group of people were to come together and will a spirit to appear before them, so long as they harmonise their thoughts along similar lines and put out a similar amount of power, there is little doubt that a manifestation would appear in one form or another. The level of vibration upon which this manifestation would occur depends, of course, on the harmony, purity and intention of the sitters.

When a spirit from the higher planes materialises it does not need ectoplasm; for it can transcend the ectoplasmic vibration – which is a material one – and create a thought form from its own power and the power generated by the harmony of those present. This is a quite different process from the one I have just described when, by a transference of thought from another sphere, a spirit fashions the ectoplasm provided by the medium. Non-ectoplasmic materialisation was the form perceived by the apostles after the death of Jesus. These higher forms of materialisation only take place where there is great spirituality and harmony; holy people who have seen such forms often prove their vibrations later with feats of healing etc. In Roman Catholicism they sometimes receive recognition for these 'miracles' in the form of canonisation; sanctity, however, is not limited to any one creed and many 'saints' have passed unnoticed.

Spirits who communicate from those planes nearest to the Earth plane, the second and third planes,* do not necessarily remove themselves from these planes in order to make their presence felt or convey their messages; instead, the communicating entity projects a thought-form, using ectoplasm, whereby it may be recognised. The intensity of this projection may vary but its recognition will depend on the fineness of the vibration to which the medium can attune. This form of communication is quite different from that used by devic spirits or those from the higher planes that communicate either by using an aspect of themselves to negotiate the lesser spheres or by using, say, third plane spirits through which to transmit, these spirits providing

---

* The varying levels of thought in the universe can be broadly divided into seven planes: Earth physical experience is the first plane; the nearest spirit plane to the physical is the second plane, and the Ultimate is the seventh plane.

a sort of transformer or filtering-down device for their power.

In certain altered states of consciousness, you may be able to perceive some of these other planes of existence. As your spiritual sight widens you will notice not only those of your own form of evolution upon each plane, but also some of the other infinite varieties of thought-expression which exist within this universe and which are evolving side by side with your own form of life. You may be able to bring back some of these experiences with your conscious mind, which will help you considerably in understanding all things around you.

Discarding the Physical Body

Physical death is something which seems to cause a great deal of worry to people. If I can clarify this transition of the spirit I feel it will help each one of you to look at death from a more balanced perspective.

A physical body is discarded by the spirit at that moment when it is right, from the spirit's point of view, that this should happen; and this applies whatever age the physical body may have reached for many spirits choose to incarnate for only a short period. Remember that from the moment a spirit enters the embryo of a human being at conception, it is experiencing; it may have chosen to experience for one month, one year, thirty years or eighty years.

Speaking generally, when a person has just died the spirit has the full experiences of its life still with it and, consequently, there are many cases of spirits that do not realise what has happened. Whenever possible, if a spirit should so wish, it will be helped by those who have already passed over and have given themselves the task of assisting other spirits still in their physical bodies to encompass this step more easily.

It takes anything from a few minutes to a few days before the spirit finally leaves the body and the cord is cut; this is often done by those who have come to help. According to the evolution, the understanding of the spirit passing over, the helpers will enlighten it as to what has happened, as this is often necessary because of the state of mind in which the person died.

Very often, if a physical body has met an abrupt death such as in a war or an accident, the spirit is in need of great help when it leaves the body, for it may have been catapulted away from the physical shell with great velocity, thus causing much confusion of thought. A spirit in this condition needs more time to recover and, in fact, the longer it has the better; if it reincarnates too quickly some form of mutation, physical, mental or even spiritual will most probably result. Many of these spirits are Earthbound and very often have no realisation of the death of their physical bodies; they are helped by other discarnate spirits to realise what has taken place and then they pass on their way.

Many well meaning people endeavour to assist these lost spirits from the Earth plane and although I realise that this is done with the best of intentions it is, in fact, superfluous and sometimes confusing, as the problem is normally, in such circumstances, dealt with very adequately in the spirit world. There are, of course, instances of truly Earthbound spirits that continue to affect places and people long after their demise. These may need to be released from their mental state by exorcism, which is a specialised form of healing.

Death, far from being a tragic thing, is actually a step forward in any spirit's evolution. It is an initiation into the next phase of its learning experience. It would be much better for people if they were able to look at it in this way, instead of regarding death from the point of view of personal loss, without any real thought of the upliftment that the spirit has possibly experienced in passing. It is understandable that the death of a close friend will cause sadness but, if it were realised that for the spirit in question it is the right time to pass, and that it is even now furthering its evolution by new experiences, it would enable people to go forward in their own lives in acceptance and without fear. Unfortunately, there are many people who dwell morbidly on the past, thereby not only halting their own progress but also holding back the progress of their loved one by their possessive thoughts. The time is long overdue for death to be regarded from a broader perspective.

Further Aspects of Life After Death

The 'Summerland'

When a spirit first adjusts itself to the realisation that the physical shell is dead, it has a whole new existence before it which it must try to comprehend. Remember, a spirit is thought and as such is unencumbered by physical limitations; and yet it has other limitations, the limitations of its own experience and understanding.

A spirit finds that it is freed from the fetters of a physical body. What happens? Because it is purely in a state of thought it is able to create all manner of situations merely by thinking them. It is like a 'pipe dream' with no interruptions but, of course, it is limited by the spirit's own experience, knowledge and evolution. This is why, when you hear reports of life after death coming from this level which is so close to the Earth plane, they tend to sound like a garden of paradise or an idyllic desert island! This thought state is called by many the 'Summerland'.

Life after death is something far greater and quite different, and all spirits realise after a while that this state of 'pipe dreaming' is static and leads nowhere. Having come to this realisation they then pass on to further experience.

The Unbeliever

Let us consider the unbeliever, the man who does not believe in any life after death. What happens when his spirit passes over? It may remain Earthbound for some considerable time. This happens because it refuses to accept that it no longer has a physical body and so it creates one by its own thought power. There are many spirits wandering through the ether today that imagine themselves to be incarnate when they are not; this definitely has a retarding effect on their evolution and can cause trouble and inconvenience to others at times. They are usually helped sooner or later to realise their mistake and to pass on their way.

In the case of a person who dies slowly, knowing they are dying and expecting nothing when they are dead, the spirit may remain in a state of coma after leaving the body. Because it is expecting nothing it will receive nothing, until other spirits manage to awaken it to a state of awareness.

Failure to believe in life after death is one of the factors which is holding back the evolution of your planet considerably at the present time as it causes a number of almost blind reincarnations, in which many spirits come back into physical bodies without fully understanding why they have done so.

Self-Judgement and Hell

Life after death is feared by many people because they envisage an hour of reckoning with God. I do not particularly wish to destroy anyone's pet illusions, but I must emphasise that this is an illusion. God does not judge; in fact, the more evolved spirit is, the less inclined it is to judge. It is only Earth people in their foolishness who try to pass judgement.

When you leave your present incarnation you will sooner or later come to a realisation of yourself and, because you will no longer be limited by the physical, your vision will be wider than when you are in the body. You will see yourself for what you really are and for what you might have been. Believe me, you will be a far harsher judge of yourself than God would ever be, if that state of Being were ever to judge.

This knowledge and self-realisation is in itself a form of initiation and for many spirits it can be a state of hell. I have been asked if the hell of Dante, the hell described by certain religions, really exists. My answer is that it exists for those who believe it exists. Many spirits choose of their own volition to torture themselves to atone for what they have done; it is possible to rise above this self-punishment by a complete realisation and understanding of the error made; but there are few spirits who are able to achieve this.

Ghosts

When you speak of ghosts you are referring to basically three types of spirit. Firstly, those that have left Earth bodies but, through lack of realisation of what has happened to them, cannot leave their old Earth surroundings; they may have been killed or have died suddenly and been shocked out of life. Secondly, those that have died in an unresolved emotional state and become Earthbound to a certain house, room or place through the intensity of their emotions. And thirdly, those elementary spirits that are in a stage of pre-human existence, as explained in an earlier chapter. These should not, however, be confused with the spirits of the elements, elemental spirits which belong to a form of evolution outside *homo sapiens.*

A poltergeist is a mischievous spirit that is trying to attract attention to itself for some reason. It moves physical objects by drawing energy from an incarnate person. It is trying to say something which may relate to the incarnate person it is disturbing.

All disturbed and Earthbound spirits can be helped and healed and sent on their way by a person with the necessary awareness, healing ability and knowledge.

How a Spirit Selects a Body for Reincarnation

Most of you who read these teachings will be reasonably open-minded in your ideas and, I hope, always ready to listen to new ones. Others of you may secretly be quite determined that what you believe is correct (which may be this philosophy or another) and that anything different must be discarded. If you are to succeed in your present incarnation your mind should always be open to other points of view, because you are here to learn and the results of that learning will determine your spiritual future.

It is rather like going to school but on a grander scale. The great difference is that when you are at school and you do not learn your lessons you may be reprimanded; but in the school of life there is only one person to reprimand you, and in a very much more severe way than would your school teacher, and that is yourself. You will eventually reach a point in your evolution when the past catches up with you and you become aware of what you are and where you have succeeded and failed. This realisation can have an overwhelming spiritual impact.

We have discussed how the spirit has freewill and that you are here in your physical body because of that freewill, because of the decisions you have made. Experience involves constantly making decisions: what you do, why you do it, when you do it and how you do it. At an early stage in its evolution your spirit made a decision to experience through the homo sapiens stream of evolution and then, after a period of preparation, you reached a moment when you were ready to enter your first incarnation on a physical planet.

Entering into one's first Earth body is not a form of spiritual bingo, nor is it decided by sticking a pin in a map. You would incarnate as part of a group soul and when you came to take on this first incarnation you would find many others from your group already there waiting to help you.

How does a spirit know when it is ready to take the next step? If you look back, even over your present life, you will realise that there were certain moments when you suddenly became aware of something, of the sky, of food, of your mother or your father. These were early discoveries in your present incarnation, but they were important to you. A spirit becomes aware in exactly the same way; but there is also another aspect.

You walk along the street and decide to cross the road; you have made a decision. Have you made the right decision or the wrong decision? You step into the road but it is not a pedestrian crossing and a car comes along, so you step back very quickly and realise you have made a wrong decision. If you have absorbed that lesson you then walk along the pavement until you reach a pedestrian crossing where you cross in safety; but perhaps you have not learnt your lesson so well and you try to cross again making the same mistake. This time the result is less fortunate and you are involved in an accident.

Some people make the same mistakes again and again; others learn the first time. This is evolution. This is growing within because, if you do not make the same mistake again, you have not only learnt but have understood what you have learnt, and it is this understanding which is important. It is no good knowing that this or that has happened unless you understand why, for a true understanding can only come from an open mind and one that acknowledges its own mistakes.

No two people in the universe are in identical stages of evolution. Each person sees things in a slightly different way and so you all make your decisions and understand problems in ways which are individual to yourselves. I believe that an understanding of this unique individuality is one of the most fundamental and important aspects of any teaching, philosophy or religion.

Many 'isms' and sects follow a detailed concept and their

followers accept each one of the details gladly, because this gives them a psychological security upon which they can lean back and forgo many individual responsibilities of choice and decision making. They do not have to think for themselves because someone has presented them with a set of ideas with each detail neatly ticked and filed in the right place. Very nice, but how limiting! All you will learn from it will be somebody else's concept.

The only true way to advance spiritually is to be open-minded and ready to experience within yourself. This is the way you choose a body for reincarnation.

Before you entered your present body you made your choice in conjunction with other spirits or guides from your group. You were able to see the broad outline of the life which lay ahead of you, the general pattern it presented, the karma. The view from the world of spirit is very rarely detailed in the way that incarnate people see the minor facets of existence. A spirit decides that, in the stage of evolution it has attained and in order to complement all its previous existence, it will need a certain set of experiences; and it is the overall pattern to which it is drawn, not the tiny incidents which assume so much importance once it is in the body.

Let us say that a spirit wishes to enter a body which is going to give it male experience. This man grows up and marries when he is twenty-one, he has three children, he works on a farm; the spirit chooses to work close to nature in this life and the body in question is suited to such an occupation. One of his children suffers from Down's Syndrome and from this he learns much tolerance and understanding. His wife dies before he does and he experiences his last years alone, reading and meditating and learning many things.

When spirits are young they tend to incarnate with the group, following the general impulse which can be generated by a group of spirits moving together along their path of evolution. Young souls do not like to separate from the group and will gravitate back to it once in incarnation if they should, by chance, incarnate amongst those who are not of their own type. Evidence of group spirits can be seen anywhere in life when people act together en masse rather than as individuals.

But as a spirit grows in stature, so it individualises and eventually leaves its group, branching out on its own. This can be a mentally painful period as it means leaving the security of the group and perhaps the religion to which the group originally affiliated itself. In such an incarnation a spirit would have to accept new ideas and carry out much soul searching. After spirits have individualised away from the original group soul, they may later choose to work in small groups for specific purposes, together with other spirits with whom they are in sympathy.

Some of you may be wondering whether choosing the karma of your life amounts to predestination once you are incarnate. Remember, fate in its truest sense is not what lies ahead of you; it is the result of how you handle your life. If somebody predicts what is going to happen to you next week it is not because your action is written down but because they have seen the results of certain decisions you are going to make.

This is the reason why when some people have visited clairvoyants, it has changed their lives because they have made decisions to fit what they have been told. This may be a good or a bad thing and I do not intend to enlarge upon it as I have only used this example to illustrate a principle. However, when the next week comes the person might think to himself: 'Well, I don't want to do what has been predicted, I will do the alternative'. In so doing he changes the shape of that particular incarnation.

Let us take an example whom we shall call Kate. At the age of twenty-one Kate meets a young man, but she does not feel ready to marry although it is part of her karma to do so at that time. In ten years' time she meets somebody else and marries him. Kate has changed her karma and, when she finishes that life and leaves the physical shell, her spirit will look back and see that when it entered that body it had planned to travel to certain milestones. It sees that it did not achieve all the milestones it aimed for, but it achieved certain other results which were not planned. It can see how it handled the troubles and problems of that incarnation and it may or may not be pleased with what it has gained from the experience.

On the other hand, another spirit that has left its Earth

body may be filled with remorse for what it has done. Perhaps it was born into a male body named Fred which lived during the war and committed some atrocities. No longer fettered by the emotions of a physical body, it feels badly about this and creates its own hell. As I have explained elsewhere, hell is not the mythical state of fire and brimstone. It is a mental condition which spirits create for themselves when they are faced with the truth about the evil deeds and misdemeanours they have carried out during their lifetimes. Each one of you is totally responsible to yourself; it is your *own* true conscience you will have to face when you leave your physical existence and I am sure that if people realised this it would make a great difference to their outlook.

When Fred's spirit has gone through its own hell and emerged from it, it may feel that, although it gained much from its previous life, it still has a great deal to learn from physical experience. The spirit will see itself for what it is; it will experience a realisation of the lessons it has learnt, the lessons it has failed to learn and the type of experience it needs to undergo next in order to complement that which it has already experienced.

Fred's spirit does not come to these decisions on its own for there are other spirits around to help it; and it is not forced to take on another life although the idea may be suggested to it by wiser souls. The ultimate decision to reincarnate will come by virtue of its own thought processes.

If it does decide to reincarnate, Fred's spirit, again with the help of others more experienced, will have the opportunity to choose the type of life that would be most suitable to help it to go forward in its evolution at this particular stage. Being in a state of thought, with no physical body to make it want to take the easiest path, it may well choose a difficult life, either as an atonement for past misdeeds or purely as an experience from which to learn. It may choose the life of a cripple or one fraught with emotional problems. It will be shown the milestones along such a life and the challenges they represent.

Hence the importance of accepting your life, of coming to terms with it, however arduous it may seem, for your own spirit has chosen it and it is your own spirit that you will have to face when you leave it.

Fred's spirit will continue to incarnate into a physical body until it reaches a stage of realisation, a point in its evolution, in which it has a complete understanding of the lessons to be learnt through physical existence. It is then ready to progress further along its own ladder of evolution through other realms of experience. But this is no sudden process; it will not jump through a door or merge with a mystical cloud. It will simply reach a stage of understanding in which its whole vibration becomes lighter and it ascends. When I use the word 'ascend' I mean that the vibration, the essence of the spirit, becomes finer, enabling it to penetrate the purer regions of the higher planes. It is a natural, filtering process as the soul or spirit rises above its denser, self-orientated thoughts and reactions.

Knowledge and wisdom are not synonymous. You cannot gain wisdom from books or classes; you can only gain it through an understanding of what you have learnt from this life and previous lives. It is possible to have wisdom without worldly knowledge, but a knowledgeable person is not necessarily a wise one for knowledge does not endow a person with wisdom. However, both attributes may go hand in hand; it is entirely a question of the consciousness of the individual. You all know the old saying that there are many paths to the centre of the city. Take which path you will; your path is an individual one and let me assure you that no one else will ever tread it.

Life is not something to fear or to dread; it is something to enjoy, to make the most of, because it is enabling your spirit to partake of physical and material experience; it is helping your spirit to temper its freewill. Remember that, although your spirit has freewill, your physical body does not have it to the same degree for, while you are incarnate, your freewill is conditioned by the body's limitations. Your physical mind is limited by the capacity of the brain. Your eyes are limited in their range of vision, the speed at which you can move your body is governed by natural laws and your environment rules over all these things.

You have social and personal limitations. You may live in a tribe in the Andes or in Vietnam. You may live in New

York, Iceland or in Central Africa. Wherever you live, the shape of your life is influenced by the prevailing conditions. Are you poor? Are you wealthy? Are your parents kind and helpful? Are they resentful? What are your neighbours like? What are your friends like? Do you find it easy to give to other people? I speak not of money but of yourself. Do you enjoy extending warmth and comfort to your fellow men or do you find it difficult to communicate? Do you want to withdraw, to isolate yourself on top of a mountain in a little hut, or do you want to live in a market place in the centre of a city?

Life is full of conditioning factors, some of which you may have chosen consciously, while others may be the choice of your spirit before incarnating; and these are things which prevent you from having complete freewill whilst incarnate. But, of course, there is still plenty of scope for freewill. If you do not want to live in a certain place you can move on; you can even emigrate to another country. If you do not like your job you can find another. If you are a shy, retiring person and you make positive efforts to overcome this by extending warmth and friendship to your fellow beings, you will find that your efforts will be rewarded.

The conditions in which you find yourself are factors which need to be put into perspective, for some of them you have attracted to yourself and others are your self-chosen challenge. It is my belief that if you face yourself honestly and take greater responsibility for how your life is, you will be very close to finding the reason for your incarnation and the lessons you have come to learn. Whereas if you blame others or 'life' for your circumstances and problems, you are shutting yourself off, both from the inspiration of your higher Self and from the natural flow of life.

It is very important to realise that every thought, and every action which is the result of thought, is not only affecting your present life now, but determining your future. After all, is not your life one series of 'nows'? What has gone before must influence what follows. To live in the past, in some period when, in retrospect, all seemed very rosy, can be a real trap. It is equally important not to create castles in the air about the future, expecting certain things to happen which will solve all present difficulties. If you are living in the past you are living with past mistakes. Learn from past mistakes, but do not live with them or you will surely make them again. As for the future, this you can consider but always with an open mind, prepared to accept and adapt yourself to the unexpected turns life takes.

When your spirit enters a physical body it brings with it all the experience it has ever had in the past, stored in the unconscious mind. A spirit which has learnt much in previous lives will, upon incarnating enter, perhaps, the fourth form in the school of life. On the other hand, a younger spirit will choose a body or environment which will give it a first form experience. Many lives later these spirits may return straight into the fifth or sixth form.

Remember, the broad outline of your life has been chosen by the freewill of your spirit to provide the necessary lessons of experience it wishes to learn. Do not be depressed or indulge in feelings of inferiority, but think positively and acquire the ability to assess yourself for what you are, no more and no less; and to treat life for what it is, no more and no less. It is an adventure which can bring you great rewards, mental, spiritual and material. Keep one foot firmly on the ground and with the other seek and you will find the purpose of your life.

Do Humans Evolve From Animals

Animal evolution is another of the many physical forms of evolution which can be experienced on Earth. There have been many questions and many theories regarding the lives of animals. Some people believe that the spirits of men inhabit the bodies of animals during an earlier stage of their evolution, while others reject such an idea. I would like to give you the picture of animal evolution as I see and understand it.

The evolutionary experiences undergone by animals are entirely different from those undergone by human beings. When a spirit is on the plane of decision, as I mentioned earlier, it has the choice of which evolutionary stream it will enter. A spirit which chooses to experience as an animal does not subsequently enter into the body of a man, but progresses through the animal kingdom to the spirit planes and then ascends those planes in the same way as a spirit of man evolves in *its* particular cycle of evolution.*

Spirits which have chosen animal incarnations and those which have chosen human experiences belong to two quite different branches of spirit evolution; just as the spirits of the elements, which are part of the deva kingdom, are again different. There are an infinite number of different forms of evolution throughout the universe; and although all spirits are as one in the sense that they are all 'children' or 'thoughts' of the Ultimate, the forms of evolutionary experiences they elect to undergo give them that certain individuality which distinguishes for instance, the spirit of

---

* It is not *impossible* for one form of spirit evolution to experience through another form of physical vehicle, but it is very rare and would only be undertaken for a very specific purpose.

a cat from the spirit of a plant or the spirit of a human being. They are like the branches of a tree, the tree of life, each branch representing a different form of evolution and contributing its share of experience to the whole.

It is not necessary for a spirit to undergo every form of physical experience which exists and, if you think about it, the reasons are quite obvious. As the universe is infinite and there are an infinite number of forms of evolution at every level, you would need to be of the Godhead itself to be part of them all. As you evolve, your spirit takes in the conscious understanding of different forms of life and energy until it finally reaches the Ultimate, in which state it has a complete knowledge of all infinity and timelessness.

When we begin to look at the various forms of evolution, particularly those of animals and human beings, we have to think in two directions. First of all there is the physical aspect, the physical body, the somatic evolution. To this the answer is quite simple and straightforward: human beings and animals have undoubtedly evolved from the same life cells; the actual brain capacity of an animal is restricted compared with that of a human being and its form of experience is on the whole of a very much more disciplined nature. But when it comes to the evolution of the spirit it is quite a different story.

The theory of somatic evolution as expounded by Darwin is correct in as far as it goes, but it fails to take into account the evolution of the spirit. In all physical evolution there is a fusion of two types of evolution: that of the spirit and that of the physical body. The spirit experiences through the medium of physical matter. When at death the body disintegrates and returns to its component elements, the spirit, being eternal, continues its own growth, its own evolution, by further incarnations into the physical world. Eventually it ceases to need this type of expression and it then moves on to other realms.

Somatically, then, men and animals did originate in the same life cell but, from the spirit point of view, *homo sapiens* is a form of evolution entire unto itself. What was the 'missing link', you may ask, and when did the transitional stage occur?

The true beginning of the existence of *homo sapiens* spirits on Earth was when a different type of spirit entered the bodies of apes. These spirits influenced the growth and size of the physical brains of the bodies they entered, causing them gradually to develop the faculties of discernment and creativity. Early progress was slow but, as the somatic development advanced and the brain capacity increased, a more evolved human spirit was able to enter. And so it went on until the pattern of *homo sapiens* emerged, branching off, as it were, from the main stream of animal evolution.

People normally do not like to consider that animal evolution, from a spiritual point of view, is as great as their own, because this is a blow to the ego. But I can assure you that if a cat walked into a gathering of people, it could have a spirit of much greater evolution than the spirits of any of those present. And that is no insult to anyone.

I want you to appreciate that all the time you are going through various forms of physical experience in many varied incarnations, your spirit is growing in understanding. Whether a spirit chooses to experience through the cat family, the horse family or the human family, there comes a stage in its evolution, its understanding, when it has no further need of experience through the medium of a physical body; the spirit has become finer, lighter and wiser and it has begun to ascend further up the ladder of spiritual evolution.

No two spirits evolve at the same rate. Each spirit or thought ever created by the Godhead is in its own entirely individual and unique stage of understanding and wisdom and, from that point of view, has no relationship with or similar standards of evolution to any other creative thought. You will appreciate also that when a spirit reaches a stage where it has no further need for physical evolution it has not reached the Godhead by any means; in fact it still has a long way to go. It would be wrong to say that a spirit is only a quarter of the way or an eighth of the way along its evolutionary path, because these terms do not mean anything where spirit evolution is concerned. These stages are not comparative and this makes them difficult to understand. On Earth you are apt to judge everything by your own standards: 'he is almost as good as so-and-so', 'he is a better leader than that one' or 'that cake is better than this cake'. When you come to understand things of the spirit you cannot use these yardsticks because everything is individual. You are individual, every animal is individual, every flower is individual.

I may seem to have digressed a little, but I have tried to outline to you why animal evolution is a direction, a form of evolution quite different from *homo sapiens*. Nevertheless, these two forms of evolution exist side by side and have a close relationship with one another.

Animal Evolution

Now let us take a look at the many types of animal. Do they change their type during successive incarnations? How many incarnations do they have? Are some animals more evolved than others? I would like to answer the latter question first by saying that some forms of animal experience are of a less evolved state, although I would prefer to use the expression 'enjoy a lower state of consciousness'. The fish is an example of this, its conscious expression being limited far more than that of a cow or a pig; and yet, even so, within the fish family there are different levels of evolution.

Animals do not change their type. For example, a spirit which chooses to experience as a cat would not return after two incarnations as a horse or a dog, but could experience within the many different branches of the cat family. Your little cat may have been a lion or a tiger before, or even a panther; if you look at it closely you will probably observe a likeness to one special branch of the cat family. The same applies to the domestic dog, whose spirit may have experienced as a wolf or a jackal before becoming the docile pet who sleeps so peacefully by your fireside. The number of incarnations an animal may have can no more be assessed than the number which a human undergoes; in other words, there are no hard and fast rules as each spirit advances at its own speed.

Do animals have freewill? is the next question which will come to your minds. Yes, to a point, but not in the same way as you experience it. The freewill of an animal is limited to the choice the spirit makes when it is discarnate; as soon as it enters the body it has chosen it is subject to the natural conditions and limitations of that body and is obliged to accept them.

The spirits of animals can appear from the planes of spirit

in exactly the same way as human spirits, and clairvoyants often 'see' them. Your deceased pet may stay with you for a long time and may try and help you from the world of spirit. Some animals are excellent guards against the lower astral, especially cats; ancient civilisations knew of these powers and used them. Animals which have become very attached to a human may follow his or her evolution, being together both in the world of spirit and the material world. You may have known your pet on many occasions.

Which animals are the more evolved? Cats, dogs, horses or even elephants? I have heard many suggestions made and would like to say that the domestic animals such as the cat or dog are more or less in a similar stage of evolution. They express themselves differently; the cat, for example, represents the passive receptive instinct and the dog the active. Some animals within each group are more evolved than their fellows, just as men and women are. You cannot make judgements about the evolutionary status of your pets or about animals in the wild, any more than you can about your friends and fellow human beings.

There is one thing you must bear in mind in relation to animals. Each animal is individual just as each of you is an individual. They have their own traits of personality or character and will serve you in the way best suited. Treat your animals gently yet firmly and try to *understand* them. To feed them and turn them out occasionally is not enough; they need to give and receive affection, as do humans; for although they cannot answer you in the way you would like, or even earn money for their keep, they can give you sympathy and that certain harmony which you sometimes find difficult to achieve with your fellow human beings. There were times in the past history of planet Earth when animals were the friends of man and did not attack him, but in those days man knew how to communicate with his animal brothers in a way that has been lost through centuries of cruelty and callousness. We can, however, look forward to the future when such times will return and the spirits from all forms of evolution on Earth will harmonise once again.

In countries where animals are treated with great brutality and as very inferior beings, would some sort of karma be built up by these actions?

Where karma is concerned, each case is individual. If people who are young in spirit do not understand the position of an animal, can you condemn them for not treating it with respect? Yet if their treatment reaches that stage where it is barbaric, with deliberate cruelty, then of course this will rebound on them. Any form of deliberate cruelty must karmically rebound on the perpetrators at sometime or other, whether in their present or some future life, and this can apply to nations and races of people as well as to individuals.

I agree with you completely that there has been a great deal of abuse of the animal kingdom and one can only hope that, as a deeper sense of spirituality emerges amongst people, such abuse will gradually be replaced by a much more tolerant and kindly attitude. Unfortunately, some of the great religions have not helped to foster this understanding. Some teachings given in the past, especially those that place stress on the superiority of *homo sapiens*, have caused a lot of misunderstanding and abuse of the animal kingdoms. This is one of the reasons why spirits such as myself are trying to bring through a truer concept of the role of animals, because if this were fully understood and appreciated it would alleviate a lot of unnecessary suffering on both sides.

When you say 'in certain countries' I hope you are including your own because, whilst it may not be so evident in the average home, it can still take place in many other ways; and even in the home we all know of the indulgent mistress or master who overfeeds an animal! Think of the suffering which this can cause. Then there are the experiments that are carried out on animals, supposedly in the name of humanity. These cannot be condoned if one looks at it from a spiritual point of view.

Surely man is sometimes born with less understanding than that of an animal. Man has the freewill to choose his circumstances; yet the terrible crimes which we read of in newspapers are worse than anything an animal could do because they are done deliberately.

Man is an evolving creature, as is the animal, and man is not perfect any more than the animal. Looking at the two forms of evolution as a whole, I find it very difficult to draw any form of comparison. If you take individual cases then, yes, perhaps you can. But if you think back to the earlier part of my talk you will remember I said that, in any gathering, a spirit inhabiting the body of an animal might be of greater evolution than any of those human spirits present and vice versa; it is all a question of individuals, human or animal.

Do you consider that plants and other forms of life such as animals are here only to provide food or do they have another role in the scheme of evolution as you see it?

All forms of evolution are inter-dependent. Do not forget that the human mind is conditioned to think in terms of life and death mainly because people regard death as a bad thing. I am not suggesting that life should be held cheap, but I do say: take another look at it and consider whether the human race has a balanced perspective on life and death. Are they not both gateways to further experience?

All forms of experience on this planet are here for a purpose. The universe is an orderly well directed affair, for if it were not it could not progress; and all forms of experience are part of the scheme of things. The important thing is to find a balance in one's understanding. People say it is wrong to eat an animal and that one should be vegetarian. But, then, is it not wrong to cut a lettuce? It may sound funny to you but if one is going to extend the argument, then why not?

This is why I have always been extremely careful about what I have said on the subject of vegetarianism. Certainly vegetarianism is an ideal; a good ideal, because if man can avoid eating animal meat then he is refining his physical shell and this can assist him spiritually. But on the other hand, you could find an individual who experiences spiritually in a very beautiful and wonderful manner and yet is not a vegetarian. It is all a question of the individual outlook. If you ask me as a generalisation to say which is better, to be a vegetarian or to be a non-vegetarian, then I must say to be a vegetarian; but when you bring it down to the individual it is quite another question.

The state of evolution of your planet is such that the majority of people are carnivorous. Whether they were originally intended to be so is quite another story; the fact is that they are.

If animals can be spiritually superior to men, how is it that men can reason, think, build and understand mathematics, while animals cannot?

Each stream of evolution which involves incarnation into dense matter accepts the level of intelligence at which that matter operates. On a planet such as Earth, in order that cosmic law shall be fulfilled and things operate in a state of balance, it is necessary for different streams of evolution to accept different roles. The bodies into which their spirits enter will be equipped to fulfil these roles and no other. The role of man on Earth was to construct, to reason, to create in matter; and to use those gifts in order to assist the growth of the planet generally.

The role of animals is an entirely different one for which a physical reasoning brain is not required. They are more concerned with the psychic forces around the planet, acting as a go-between for man and the elemental kingdoms. The psychic faculty is often much more highly developed in animals than in man, for all the latter's ability to write his experiences down in a book. Had an animal the brain capacity to enable it to write it could say far more than many men! When the forces within Earth prepare to move, as with an earthquake, man is totally unaware of what is happening unless he employs some form of technology. But animals and birds know well beforehand because they are in tune with planet Earth and her elementals.

For the one who feels spiritually superior to his or her animal brothers, the time of reckoning will come when they will meet face to face in the world of spirit, unfettered by the limitations and advantages of brain and body. There will be some shocks in store for the ego of some people, for God is not in the image and likeness of man; in fact, God has many faces and many names, and within the infinity of the Godhead are *all* forms of existence.

Some animals display spiritual or moral gifts such as fidelity, love, devotion and will even give their lives to save those they love. Are these indications of a more evolved spirit?

Yes, indeed, and from this you can understand how illogical it is to assume that the spirit of an animal which has displayed such highly evolved traits would suddenly forget the knowledge of such things if it were to enter a human body in a succeeding incarnation. Yet many who subscribe to the idea that the evolved animal becomes the unevolved man do not seem to see this. Lessons once learned and spiritual qualities absorbed are not forgotten from body to body. This is how the wiser spirits who brought about the bridge in the evolution of *homo sapiens* achieved their end: they influenced the development of the brain through the evolution of the spirit, thus bringing forward certain qualities which gave primitive man the impulse to use his brain capacity to a fuller extent. This type of evolutionary mutation always originates from the world of spirit or from spirits which have evolved on other more advanced spheres.

Could you tell us something about the role of dolphins on our planet?

Dolphin spirits are very advanced souls who have incarnated on this planet to experience through the physical and water realms. You could say that at one level they are guardians, one of the guardians of the seas, and what is happening to them at this moment in time is tragic; for if humankind were to recognise, harmoniously, the rightful place of dolphins in the scheme of things, they would learn an enormous amount from them.

Your awareness of how they can do tricks and find a rapport with *homo sapiens* is just an infinitesimal aspect of the dolphin nature. If you were able to work truly with the dolphins, they would take you into areas of this planet, into worlds that you haven't yet discovered. In your ignorance you are missing a wonderful opportunity for the dolphin spirits are truly compassionate souls; they recognise and understand the frailty of men and women who do not understand what they are doing. They are trying in their way to heal the planet; just as you in your way are trying to heal it too. They are wonderful healers, as mankind is just beginning to discover, and advanced spiritual beings, but they also need your help. So if you have any spare healing thoughts, send them to your brothers and sisters, the dolphins.

But then, the same applies to all the animal kingdoms, the plant kingdoms, the jungles, the trees, the air you breathe and the earth on which you stand, the water you drink and the food you eat – all need your healing thoughts. It does not matter whether you are training to be a healer or not. It does not matter if you feel you have insight or not. Each thought that any one of you sends out, whether it be in the form of a golden beam of light, a prayer, a blessing, a compassionate feeling or, indeed, when you commune with your plants in your own garden and allow a harmony to be found in that place; all such thoughts are helping the planet to find a balance which it so sorely needs.

For when you send out your healing thoughts, it enables us from our level to add our thoughts to yours. We cannot slow right down to your vibratory level because we do not exist within the space/time continuum of physical life. We need you to communicate so that we can add our healing energy to yours.

All of you have an important part to play; *all* of you can help if you choose to do so.

COSMIC LAW

Laws of the Cosmos

Infinity

The Universe is infinite. Everything in the universe is also infinite, in that the Godhead is infinite, the spirit planes are infinite, the number of planes similar to Earth is infinite, the many forms of spirit life which descend from the Ultimate are infinite; and yet each form of expression differs from all others in its own individual way.

The following lectures aim to present a mental picture of cosmic laws in action and to show how their principles apply on the varying levels of existence.

Basic Principles

Cosmic law is that principle of nature that holds the universe in a state of balance and is responsible for the perpetual motion of all evolution.

There are many basic universal or cosmic laws that can be translated into terms acceptable to the human mind. Some of these are obvious, such as the law of gravity and those laws of physics that govern the relative speed, density and interpenetrative qualities of atoms. But there are also cosmic laws manifesting on all levels from pure thought downwards and a lack of co-operation with these principles is the cause of many of the problems facing human beings today, in their relationships to each other, to the planet itself and to the universe beyond.

The forms of life and evolution you encounter on your planet are by no means the only forms of intelligent or sentient life. In your own type of physical evolution there are infinite variations throughout the universe that obey the cosmic laws of adaptation to prevailing physical conditions, just as your genetic forebears adapted their bodies to the rapidly changing face of the planet in the early stage of its evolution. Nor does this principle apply only to somatic evolution, for intelligences existing on other levels – from a pure thought state downwards – also obey similar patterns.

Each branch of universal existence is a separate form of evolution, yet is a perfect complement to the whole. Most of these are quite beyond the scope of man's imagination while incarnate in a physical body, but they all stem from the Ultimate Thought and are bound by the directional impulses of cosmic law. Any movements against the principle can only result in disharmony, both for the offender and for those it encounters on its backward slide.

The forward directional impulses of cosmic law are harmonious and therefore they are the generators of the love principle. This love principle is the key to the cosmos, for with love comes harmony and with harmony comes progress and freedom from pain. Evolutionary progress through love broadens the wisdom and understanding and completes the perfect pattern of life on all levels.

What is the Cosmos?

As you stand on your Earth planet and gaze upwards into the vast expanse of sky, how often you must have wondered where it all begins and where it ends. The answer is that there is no beginning and no end to this infinite magnitude of thought. As all thought stems from and is part of the Ultimate, so *you* are part of the Ultimate. The clothes you are wearing, the ground you walk on, everything on your Earth planet, the solar system, the galaxy of which you are a part, everything in the infinite universe is of the Ultimate. Accordingly, the power of the Ultimate is infinite and in that infinity lies wisdom, understanding and creativity such as would be incomprehensible to the human mind.

Thought flows out from this infinity of greater wisdom, it flows to every corner of the universe. As it leaves the Ultimate it follows a pattern; in other words, it is orderly. I leave you to decide for yourselves what would happen if those thought-patterns were not orderly. This orderliness stems from the Ultimate and it is not until thought reaches the great infinity of the cosmos that it begins to lose its direction of purpose.

There are spirits or thoughts in the universe that might be described as 'evil entities'. I would prefer to describe them as 'disorderly thoughts'. These are either spirits of lower evolution or thoughts from the higher spheres that have strayed off their forward path and descended to the paths of lower evolution. Although a spirit has freewill and can follow many paths it has an overall pattern or 'directional impulse'. If, in its evolution and by virtue of its freewill, it decrees that it should experience *outside* the breadth of that impulse, then it has lost purpose.

Every step of its personal evolutionary ladder serves to broaden a spirit's vision, because every rung affords a greater view and therefore a greater understanding of the universe. So, in order to reach towards that infinite wisdom of the Ultimate beyond the limits of the rational human mind, it is necessary for a spirit to direct its thought forward along its directional impulse. This may sound as though there is limitation to one path of expression in order to reach for the Ultimate which is unlimiting; but the limitation is in the *overall* directional impulse and not in the many varied approaches towards that goal. Here is an example of the law of the cosmos that decrees that a spirit in its evolution has to be both rational and irrational in order to gain wisdom. It is an aspect of cosmic law that tends to confuse the logical mind of reasoning Earth man or woman.

We see then that thought in the universe has a directional impulse and that, in order to obtain the utmost evolution, it has to keep that direction orderly and purposeful. It is only when a thought becomes disorderly and without purpose or direction that it actually narrows itself, for the lower a spirit descends the narrower is its comprehension.

There, my friends, you have lesson number one, which is perhaps the greatest lesson of all. If you have understood this most important law of the cosmos quite fully and simply, then you are helping yourself in your own evolutionary progress and, by that, helping others in theirs.

The Cone of Evolution

The plan of the universe is *evolution* with the Godhead as the Ultimate. This is another fundamental cosmic law that presents a simple and straightforward picture of the universe that allows for infinite possibilities; and understanding it enables you to have a balanced perspective of your present stage of experience.

Let us look a little deeper into this law of evolution. When a thought leaves the Ultimate it descends to a plane lower than your Earth plane. I want you to picture an inverted hollow cone; the top of this cone – in appearance like a cup – continues upwards to such a height that the lip is inconceivable to the human mind for it represents a universe that is infinite.

When a new thought leaves the Ultimate it descends to the bottom of that cone. At this point it has no evolution and only a limited realization; when it views its position it can only see where it is in relation to the stage of its advancement within the cone. As realization comes upon it, it takes the next step forward and begins to rise up the cone; the higher it rises, the finer it becomes, and the more its vision of understanding and wisdom increases and broadens for the less it is narrowed down by its surroundings.

The scope of this cone is infinite and, because it reaches into infinity, the possibilities of experience that a spirit can choose – the different ways in which it can evolve – are infinite. It can start ascending the cone and then move across, or even descend again if it so wishes, for the Ultimate has given every spirit the freewill to choose. Indeed, that is another cosmic law in itself.

You will know what I mean when I refer to the striving of a spirit, that innermost conviction and desire of a spirit to uplift its evolution. In the language of the cosmos, it is a desire to think itself on to an orderly path or along its own directional impulse of movement. If it starts to stray down the cone again, it will not only be working against its own directional impulse but it will be failing in what it has set out to do because it will be narrowing its evolution and wisdom. That is why I have spoken against narrow-mindedness, as it is one of humanity's biggest pitfalls. Let us also not forget that narrow-mindedness has two extremes, for is not the fanatic as limited as the sceptic?

To help you to understand the movement of these directional impulses and what takes place when a spirit moves against them, picture a large crowd of people all moving in one direction. One man in the crowd is trying to push through them in the opposite direction. His movements, varying in violence from a gentle push to a heavy thrust, affect not only his own path but also those people he is obliged to push aside in order to achieve his objective. Many may be hurt or misplaced as a result of his actions.

As a thought or spirit ascends the cone on its unique directional impulse, its wisdom increases. It has more to see and more to find out as the cone becomes wider. So you can see that the higher a spirit evolves the broader its evolution becomes; it is an ever-widening and ever-ascending spiral, a spiral that is infinite. With each stage it succeeds in attaining, it gains in an infinite number of ways. Should it at any time lose its cosmic orderliness and directional impulse, the higher/finer it has reached the further will it descend, so that spirits that have reached the fifth plane of thought, or even in certain cases the sixth plane, *can* drop right down to the bottom, the densest level.

It is true to say that if a spirit reaches an advanced point in its evolution, retrogresses and then by spiritual endeavour regains its former state, it in fact experiences more fully than its fellow spirit whose evolution has followed a fairly even path. But in the process it will have caused itself great suffering and lived through many 'hells' of its own making.

God Becoming

Every thought of God has no beginning and no end. Each has come from and eventually returns to the Godhead, which is infinite. Each of you is a part of infinity itself, if indeed it is possible to have such a part. Each one who reads this lecture is God in that he is part of God. Your whole Earth planet and everything therein and thereon is God to a greater or lesser degree; therefore, all the laws of the cosmos and all the wisdom of evolution are available to each one of you. But you have closed all this off from yourselves by the state of unknowing to which your spirit has 'descended' in order to experience.

As you evolve and ascend the ladder of evolution, learning through the lessons of many lifetimes, you open your understanding and regain your rightful heritage. That is why, when those with an evolved spirit study the universe, they find that it comes to them very easily. Many people begin to lose interest when they have reached a certain stage of understanding, declaring that there is no need for them to go any further. They should never be criticised for this for they are all thoughts of God experiencing in their own individual way, but they have not yet mounted that next rung of the ladder that gives them a further sight into the cosmos.

Each one of you has a subconscious knowledge of what has been and will be. This has probably brought to your mind the following question: 'If my spirit knows all these things, then why am I here?' The answer is that you are here because the Godhead, in its infinity, is ever expanding its infinite wisdom and thought; it is an infinity without limit. The purpose of your being here is to add to the infinity that is already within the Godhead; and each form of evolution, whatsoever it might be, is adding to that infinity by the experiences it is undergoing.

I must now further explain to you that there is no such thing as time or space in the universe, for the experience you are undergoing has already taken place. Furthermore, everything you have done previously is still to happen in the future and everything that is to happen in the future has already happened in the past and is happening in the present. The Ultimate can see what it has experienced in the past, the present and the future; it can see all experience as the Eternal Now. Such is the power of thought. Such is the nature of the universe.

If you have followed this, then indeed you are managing to get a glimpse of what is meant by time and space, another fundamental law of the cosmos. I have always said to you 'Seek and ye shall find', for in so doing your experience will be enriched and your understanding and evolution will broaden.

The nature of the universe is simple. God the Ultimate does not make complicated laws; it is the human mind that introduces the multitudinous details, those small details of time that are so much a part of limited human reasoning. Beware of these traps. Rise above them, rise through them and uplift yourselves to the higher thoughts of God's universe.

Masters and Archangels

Let us together consider the cause and effect of a spirit from the finer realms of thought incarnating into a physical body, a spirit that has reached a fineness and breadth whence it is able to see and comprehend many wonders of the universe.

This spirit returns to a lower plane of thought, such as an experience upon your Earth planet, bringing with it the conscious realization of the wisdom, breadth of vision and near infinity of comprehension it has gained. This not only *can* be done but *is* done, as may be evidenced by many of the great teachings the world has received. Such a step is not achieved by contravening the laws of the cosmos, but rather by developing the cosmic plan one stage further.

You will remember what I said about thought being orderly and flowing in a directional impulse. Thought that has reached a high degree of existence has done so by being able to control the directional flow of its creative powers. In other words, it has exercised its freewill in a direction that has enabled it to overcome the negative pulls of the lower levels of thought. You will understand from this how essential it is, from the evolutionary point of view, to maintain harmony.

Now this thought is able to return to Earth, not by negating what it has achieved – which is what would happen if it slid back down the sides of the cone – but by developing its thought into a progressive direction and lifting itself outside the limits of its own sphere of evolution. It can then return down the cone on another dimension, as it were, where it is in no way limited by the narrowness of the cone.

These spirits or thoughts that return to Earth planet from the very high planes are conforming to an entirely different evolutionary pattern; they are what you would term in orthodoxy 'masters' or 'archangels'. By following this process, they are able to ascend directly to that stage of wisdom whence they came, once they have finished the task for which they have returned.

Contained within these lectures is the basic understanding of cosmic law. They give you the broad framework for understanding the reason for all existence; why you are here and how best you can progress along your own evolutionary ladder. Think about it so that you understand its fullest implications; by doing so you will be broadening your vision of the universe and ascending that infinite cone of evolution.

A Spirit Hierarchy?

I am very proud of the question mark after the title of this lecture and, as I proceed, I hope you will begin to see why! The type of hierarchy we are going to consider in this lecture bears no relationship to the governmental departments of the various nations on your planet, for it has a different nature and a very different *raison d'etre*.

A spirit hierarchy exists because certain forms of intelligence have reached a stage of understanding whereby they are able to pass on what they have learnt towards the guidance of others. This statement, in itself, barely does justice to such a mighty title, yet most great things are rather disappointing when one actually comes to them, unless one understands what lies behind.

As I stated in my previous lecture, the universe is orderly. When a 'thought' or 'spark' is created, it carries two facets: one positive and one negative. You are the product of a thought, a thought in which either the positive or the negative predominates. The whole universe is made up of positive and negative thought. Should you consider that too simple, you might ponder on the fact that positive thought can be negative and negative thought can be positive! Solar systems are predominantly positive or negative; thus each system within the galaxy acts as a complement to the next. This solar system falls into the positive category and therefore its Sun is predominantly negative.

The universe in its infinity contains evolution on all levels and as each individual thought evolves it constantly changes. This is not quite as simple as putting one foot on the next rung of a ladder; it is more like passing through a series of filters. As the wisdom and understanding of a spirit grows, so it becomes finer and passes through the next filter; and so on. Eventually that spirit reaches a stage of complete understanding and is in complete harmony with all other existence in the universe. It has then passed through the finest filter of all and has rejoined the Godhead whence it was first created.

As some of you who read this lecture are aware, planet Earth is at present under the influence of a devic spirit that has fallen on to the wrong path, that no longer accepts God as an Ultimate Force but rather considers itself as a god in its own right. Because of this, the type of influence which it impresses on your planet is not as it should be. Yet the blame for this state of imbalance cannot be laid wholly on the wrongful devic influence, for the power of the rightful deva of Earth could not have been usurped by Lucifer had the actions and reactions of those evolving on your planet been different. The amount of influence or power any deva has over a planet is a reflection of the evolution on the planet itself. For example, if for some inexplicable reason humanity were suddenly to pull together, dispense with all ideas of belligerence, war and suffering and fearlessly set forth to bring understanding and love to Earth, then Lucifer could no longer hold its influence over the planet. It can only retain its control by your permission, collectively.

The understanding I am trying to convey here is of equal responsibility because, often in the past when I have spoken on these subjects, people have questioned the responsibility of humanity for the fate of the planet. Yet, as I see it, you have a real responsibility which is very plain and very important. The thoughts and actions of each of you *do* matter. You each send out an influence which has an effect upon the whole, for good or for evil.

My task in this lecture is a difficult one in that I must try to break through the barriers which have been created by thought throughout the ages. Your understanding of any form of hierarchy will be influenced greatly by what you have learnt through your studies. It does not matter whether you started off in a religious vein or a scientific vein, for whichever way it was must have led you into a conditioned way of thinking.

If you were suddenly capable of transporting yourself on to what, from an orthodox point of view, would be regarded as the fifth plane, you would not meet a series of spirits answering to the names of Metatron, Samael, Beelzebub etc. You would encounter states of thought or beingness of quite a different nature. These entities have their own individual sound or vibration, but they could hardly be translated into such limited terms as many esoteric schools would have you believe. Try, first, to understand this state of beingness or thought existence, for such comprehension is essential before the hierarchical picture falls into place.

I have explained to you how Lucifer, the deva whose influence is at present affecting this planet, has rejected the Godhead. The Godhead gives you freewill with which to accept or reject it and Lucifer has chosen to reject God. But, as you will realise, it is more than just a case of Lucifer saying 'Well, I don't believe in God, I think I'll make myself into a god'. This spirit in its seeking discovered what it thought was an easier way to expand, it found it could gain power for its own ego by feeding off others. Thought builds and this type of thought grows by appealing to other spirits of an egotistical nature; it doubles up on itself until it becomes difficult for those caught in its mesh to look both ways. When that happens they are in difficulties.

Now I am not suggesting that all your seeking should be conducted in a reflective vein, nor that you should sit back and wait for something to happen. The process of understanding is something which can only grow slowly within you. It is like Lucifer's power in that it builds, but its growth is *not* one which boosts the ego! It may, for instance, build up in a way that gives you contentment in one respect, but fires you to help humanity in another.

To return to our subject matter: a spirit hierarchy does exist in this solar system. The Sun, being the physical core of this solar system, is also its spirit fountainhead. The force which comes from this orb not only gives life but inspires life. After all, is not the Sun the source of all life on your planet? If your planet operated in spiritual balance many things would be quite different; but, because it is out of step, the forces which come to it from the Sun lose a certain amount of power. This is a process which continues up the hierarchical tree. What you are doing here and now is affecting every other person on this planet and, because of this, the way they react to you will cause them to react to other people in a certain way, and so forth; until eventually every other person, animal, flower or form of life on this planet is affected. You, in your individual way, are affecting the planet's destiny which, in turn, affects the destiny of the solar system, the Sun, the galaxy and the universe. Every facet of existence in the universe affects all other facets, from the humblest to the greatest and from the finest to the densest.

Perhaps now I dare mention again that question mark after the title of the lecture and you will begin to understand how important it is. There can be no ending to this lecture and no conclusion to the subject. In fact, I can only leave you half way, because it is something for each of you to go on thinking about for yourself.

Consider also the Godhead, that Ultimate Thought which is the creative force behind the expansion of the universe. It is continually creating new thought which goes forth, adding to all previous experience. This Ultimate Force, which is the head of the hierarchy, has no ego in the sense that its eternal power is purely a force of love, understanding and wisdom. You can see from this why I have so often referred to it as being a passive force. It is man who has tried to make God a power of vengeance that demands an eye for an eye, a tooth for a tooth; all very judicial and convenient, but it is time that man grew out of this way of thinking and moved forward in his understanding.

When you consider the various governments of the world, the attitudes of their members and the levels of thought upon which they exist, does it not make you reflect on the evolution of the planet? Does it not raise a tremendous question mark in your mind? I am not concerned with politics and these remarks are not meant in any way to imply that I favour one party or one regime more than another. I merely want you to relate governments all over the world to the universe and the Godhead, because I think that such a simple exercise would bring home to you very forcibly how far humanity has to go in its understanding. How often can you say that the wisest person has the greatest influence?

Over the past few years man's practical knowledge has

gone forward in leaps and bounds, but my concern is that his understanding has not. Therefore, I feel that people like yourselves, people who are prepared to try to understand, are the people who can help; because, unless knowledge is matched by understanding and wisdom, you will be letting yourselves in for even greater troubles than you have at present. Understanding the hierarchy of the universe does not mean knowing names, rituals or symbols; it means something which cannot be put into words except metaphorically. Let me end with this thought: water finds its own level, wisdom finds its own level, evolution finds its own level. It is the growing within you that is important and I beseech you to consider it very carefully. Your world is in a very precarious state and it needs understanding and action!

The Positive and Negative Aspects of Creation

The Godhead is not a triplicity as many people think. It is a duplicity, having a positive and negative aspect which together form a whole. By using terms like positive and negative I do not mean good and bad, but a flow of energy which is both outgoing, creative and expansive, and passive, receptive and harmonious, yang and yin in eastern terms. It is a state of beingness which is constantly evolving within itself and, as a part of that evolutionary expansion, it creates a continuous stream of new thought. This new thought leaves the Godhead from either its positive or its negative aspect and, once created, it seeks expression through a series of experiences in one form of evolution or another, gradually gaining in wisdom until eventually it reaches a breadth of understanding comparable to the Ultimate Thought from which it has stemmed. And so it rejoins the Godhead, adding its own individual experience to that which is already there.

Now when a spirit is created it also has a dual nature, a positive and a negative aspect, but only one part of this duality goes out to experience while the other part remains in the background. By this I do not mean, metaphorically speaking, that every spirit is attached by a long piece of elastic to the Godhead! Although, having been created by God, all spirit is in essence part of that Ultimate Thought. What I mean is that whatever stage you have reached as a spirit and whether your spirit is positive or negative it has in the universe its counterpart, the opposite polarity. The factor which determines whether a spirit is predominantly positive or negative is the aspect of the Godhead from which it is created. A spirit leaving from the negative half of the Godhead is predominantly positive and, conversely, those spirits which are created from the positive aspect are predominantly negative.

Let us say that yours is a positive spirit; somewhere you have a negative half. Now that other half will always remain in the background, but it is not strictly true to say that it is still with the Godhead because it is, in fact, with you, experiencing with you. Let us put it this way: if you are incarnate as a positive spirit the negative part of your spirit will be discarnate. When you are discarnate that negative part will be with you as a complement. Now, as you ascend the planes towards the Godhead, the negative and positive aspects of your spirit become more definite; they become more accentuated or individualised and in doing so they also become more at one with each other.

Many of you may wonder whether twin souls are the positive and negative aspects of the same spirit? The answer is no, they are not. It is possible for two spirits of similar evolution to choose to evolve together for much of their evolutionary cycle and, because of this, a close affinity grows between them; they may then choose to enter into the bodies of twins. But these are two individual spirits and *not* the positive and negative aspects of the same spirit.

In the higher stages of evolution where the two aspects, negative and positive, have become very marked, a certain kind of transcending force takes place and they then begin to experience as separate entities; from the fifth and sixth planes and the Ultimate itself, *but from these stages and these stages only*, it is possible for both sides of the polarity to incarnate at the same time. If such a spirit deemed it necessary to incarnate in this manner it would do so because it had a certain task to accomplish; both aspects would be engaged on that task in one way or another.

When the spirit of the Ultimate which looks after this particular solar system – the Solar Logos as it is sometimes termed – manifested itself through the medium of the physical body of Jesus, another spirit representing the negative or polarising aspect should have incarnated in a different part of the world at the same time. Interference from the powers of evil prevented this happening so that Jesus the man was denied a living polarity. However, due to the complete understanding between the two aspects, the positive half was still able to continue and, when Jesus reached manhood, the negative aspect brought its balancing influence to bear from the world of spirit. It was from that time that Jesus was able to reach a point of fulfillment in his initiations which allowed him to perform his many miracles and feats of healing. This is often referred to as 'the over-shadowing of the Christ spirit'. The Gnostics and early Christians were perfectly aware of this polarity and descriptions of the dual nature of the Christ spirit can be found throughout their literature, referring to the negative aspect of the Godhead as the 'Sophia' or 'Wisdom'. For any advanced teacher or healer to function to full capacity a polarity of equal evolution is needed, otherwise imbalances can occur. Indeed, in Jesus's case, had he been a spirit from the fifth or sixth plane, it would have been far more difficult for him to continue his mission without his other polarity.

Only in the Godhead itself is a state of perfect balance achieved, but it is nevertheless important that, at all times throughout an evolutionary cycle, the two aspects of a spirit should strive towards this state of balance. If, at a comparatively advanced stage of evolution, the negative and positive aspects of a spirit become seriously out of balance the resulting influence may become evil or bent. Some of the disruptive influences which are so malignant around your planet at the present time are caused by the spirit Lucifer that I mentioned earlier, which has a serious imbalance between its positive and negative aspects; unfortunately for those involved with this planet this is basically a negative spirit. I say unfortunately because, when it is a predominantly negative spirit creating the force of evil, it is sometimes far more difficult to shift precisely because it *is* negative and receptive: all representations to bring light to your planet are just received and accepted but seldom acted upon! Where a positive spirit is creating the evil there would be a tendency to try to push back the representations of light and this would bring the matter to a head very much more speedily.

I mention this spirit with no ill-will, but with understanding and compassion.

One important question which comes to mind is how this dual aspect of the spirit affects the work of advanced healers (positive) and those who are mediumistic (negative) and whether they need to be polarised at their own level. In following such a path the student is accentuating one aspect of him or herself; there then arises a real danger of an imbalance with their inner opposite polarity. This is one of the reasons why a person practising psychism can so easily become out of balance; and why I have always stressed the importance of finding a working partner on the other polarity and, also, of switching polarity occasionally so as to experience the opposite psychic flow.

The effects of the dual nature of a spirit are simple and basic yet it also requires a degree of understanding and study to fully appreciate these ideas. As time goes on you will begin to see how important this subject is when considering the picture as a whole.

Man, Woman and the Law of Polarity

Following my previous lecture on the positive and negative aspects of the spirit I would like now to examine this principle as it relates to man and woman incarnate on Earth. But, first, let us look at the way humanity has developed socially.

The brain, physically speaking, of both man and woman is identical; therefore, given similar conditions, they can be of equal mental ability upon attaining adulthood. Many thousands of years ago, man had to stand in front of the cave with a club to protect his wife from animals, human and otherwise, while she bore his children; and as humanity progressed he took advantage of his dominant position and kept woman in the background.

The twentieth century has brought a significant change and women today are taking far more prominent positions in the affairs of society and government than ever before. This is a good thing so long as they do not take more than a 50-50 position with men. There could be a danger in the future of women becoming more dominant than men, which would be equally as unbalancing as having men in that position. This is a very broad generalisation and, as such, cannot be applied to the individual, for there will always be men who will dominate women and women who will dominate men.

On another level, the spirits which enter your physical bodies are sexless in your understanding of the meaning; in fact, they are androgynous. In one incarnation a spirit may choose to experience through a male body and in the next a female. Nevertheless, that spirit is a duality and so it follows that a man may have either a positive spirit with a discarnate negative aspect, or a negative spirit with a discarnate positive aspect; and a woman likewise. Although it is predominantly positive or negative, a spirit should always strive to be in balance within itself as a duplicity, in order to achieve harmony and an understanding of God.

If a spirit becomes seriously out of balance one of two fundamental things can happen. It can either over-emphasise its ego and see itself as a master in its own eyes; or it can become apathetic and lose its evolutionary desire to advance. An over- emphasised ego can therefore be taken as a spiritual danger signal, both in oneself and in others, as can also an introverted rejection of life's continual flow. So you will see from this that, when you are in physical incarnation, not only is it necessary for you to strive to maintain a balance between your spirit and your physical body, but your spirit must endeavour to maintain a balance between the two facets of itself.

I would now like to associate this question of polarity with men and women incarnate on the Earth planet. You may well ask what happens when a man and woman union, or marry, as you would say. Should this be necessary, apart from the procreation point of view? Let us take a spirit that comes into a male body. A man tends to be the more head-orientated of the two, analytical and rational, which can make him less in touch, intuitively, with his own deeper nature. This is another reason why men tend to be more dominant in earthly affairs than women and why, from an evolutionary point of view, the male incarnation can push the spirit back a little, unless the mind is open enough to counteract the tendency.

Conversely, a woman tends to be more heart-orientated, emphasised by the maternal instinct and there is an easier acceptance of so-called 'irrational', intuitive feelings, that allows for a closer link with the spirit. Of course, both men and women have male *and* female qualities and there are many instances in which the reverse orientation is true. Knowing yourself and finding the balance between the rational and the irrational, the head and heart aspects of yourself, is a fundamental challenge to any spirit experiencing in a physical body. It helps you to be in touch with your own spirit and that, in turn, creates a better balance between the incarnate aspect of your spirit and that which is discarnate.

Let us now consider a good marriage or partnership, a good union between two people. I use the word union after the word marriage because marriage by either civil or religious rites on your planet is not necessarily a spiritual union in the eyes of God. When two people are unioned together and they love and understand each other spiritually, mentally, emotionally and physically, thus finding happiness and relaxation on all these levels, they are in fact aiding the evolutionary balance of their spirits. In such a state of union the predominance of the various facets in both sexes becomes balanced out. This not only helps them in their physical lives on the planet but it can considerably advance the evolution of their spirits. That is why, when you find a couple who are partnered in such a way, you will be able to observe that they have a broad outlook on life and an understanding and tolerance, not only between themselves, but of humanity as a whole.

For those who do not find a true partner during a particular incarnation, it can be a little more difficult to achieve this evolutionary balance between the two facets of the spirit. Nevertheless, remaining single is infinitely preferable to being enmeshed in an inharmonious marriage or partnership; and those who remain single throughout their lives may have a greater opportunity to find that *inner* marriage which is the most fundamental partnershp of all: knowing and loving yourself, your strengths and your vulnerabilities, with true acceptance.

The moral for all is to keep a reasonable balance and not allow one side of your character to become over-exaggerated. As I have said many times: know yourself for what you are, know your virtues and your failings and you will thereby aid your own evolutionary progress.

PERSONAL ISSUES

Fear, Competition and Discipline

Fear

The most destructive negative quality that humankind needs to overcome is fear, for fear is a powerful energy that can push you into all kinds of critical situations. It leads to the lust for power, the lust for greed, the lust for trying to make yourself greater than your fellow beings. Fear prevents change; it is that which keeps your feet in the mud and prevents you from going forward. And fear of change itself is fear of the unknown; it is a trap that prevents growth and fulfilment.

So there are many different forms of fear, some of which are purely instinctive. In the natural course of evolution many of these are overcome and man reaches a state of understanding and acceptance of conditions around him; this alleviates unnecessary fears with their accompanying mental distress and physiological side-effects. One of the most widespread of human fears is the fear of death, especially in the western hemisphere where an understanding of the law of reincarnation has been rejected by the principal religions. A greater understanding of both the evolution of the spirit and its role in the universe would alleviate much unnecessary suffering and fear in this respect, for your present life's journey is only a small part of the overall journey of your soul.

Then there is the type of fear, again brought about by ignorance, that makes its appearance when people are confronted by something they do not understand. They become frightened and adopt an attitude of either blind acceptance or fanatical opposition. Such people are difficult to help because their fear usually stems from a lack of wisdom or experience; in other words, their spirits are young and not yet ready to rationalise the emotion they are experiencing. Patience and understanding are needed in helping these people; also the knowledge that they will eventually reach the stage when they will be able to view these things in their correct perspective.

But where the dark forces really make use of the emotion of fear is in the overwhelming insecurity that abounds on this planet, which has reared its ugly head in one form or another in every generation. Fear for survival, fear for the safety of loved ones, racial fears, fear of disease, fear of standing by what you believe to be right, fears wrought by political and ideological systems, by religious dogmas and persecution, fear of the atom bomb.... one could go on. Even on an emotional level men and women fear to seek the security of an inner connection with their own spirit and look, instead, to material possessions, money or the love of another person in a possessive sense. You fear to be yourself and, rather than seeking to find what lies within, you have to rely upon other means, other people to provide this sense of security; for without these props things seem to go wrong.

There is something corrupt in a system that creates such fears, many of which are quite genuine and not simply the manifestation of psychological illness. Insecurity is sometimes fostered for economic reasons; perhaps a man fears to lose his job, to be made redundant, so he works just that much harder than his body will allow, with the result that his health breaks up. Nor do many of the religious creeds, including Christianity, help in this matter. For centuries religions have followed a bible full of stories of God's wrath, a God that is feared, a God that must be obeyed under penalty of being struck down or condemned to everlasting tortures. Let me assure you, my friends, such words do not stem from God; that all encompassing state of wisdom has nothing but love and understanding to offer you.

Fear is alien to the Godhead – that state of pure love and forgiveness that does not wish any of its children be made to suffer in its name. Fear is a manifestation of negative forces working through the blinkered minds of men, usually for purposes of power. The old story: 'My God is better than your God and to prove it he will knock you down' may be a tale which is laughed at by rationalists of the twentieth century but, remember, for centuries it was and, even amongst some people today, still is believed implicitly and followed. The maxim is 'might is right' and, in a world where force has held sway for so long, this blatant heresy against the love of God has ruled unchallenged, except by the occasional saint or mystic who has incarnated.

You need to come to terms with fear and with the fact that you do not need your fear, for you can find all the security, all the love, all the peace that you need, within. And the freewill that each one of you possesses can be the enabler that can carry this planet into the 21st century, overcoming the need for fear.

Competition

Much of the fear referred to in my previous lecture results from the great emphasis that is placed on competition. The spirit of competition is considered by many to be advantageous and healthy, but I do not agree with these sentiments.

When mankind was given this planet upon which to undergo a cycle of evolution it was not intended that he should do so in a state of constant competition. Games that are played in healthy competition for pure enjoyment and for their own value, are a great aid to human development; but as soon as the element of fierce competition enters the game, tension builds up both in the players and the audience which is of use to neither. People become emotionally identified to such an exaggerated extent that the 'other side' can become the object of violent feelings approaching enmity.

We see this in everyday living. If each individual were to contribute to life the type of work to which his or her talents were best suited the world would be a happy and more balanced place in which to live. But false values have escalated with the result that competition has become fiercer and only the more ruthless people succeed under such conditions. A man may teach himself and find inner fulfilment in creating a fine work of art which he lovingly fashions, yet he may spend the other half of his life chained to a job which he hates, fearing to be sacked in case he no longer earns the money to support himself or his family. It is the birthright of every individual to be able to express himself or herself without fear or competition, yet within a self-disciplined framework.

Now I am not for one moment suggesting that a type of state should be set up where there are no rules and everybody does exactly as he or she wishes. Anarchy and cosmic law are arch-opposites. But let me recall the story that Jesus told of the talents. The man with many talents used them, as did the next man and so on; but the man with only one talent became resentful and, rather than use that one to make two, he buried it in anger declaring that if he could not have as many as the next man then no one should reap the benefit of his one talent. What he did not realise was that the only person who would suffer as the result of his action was himself, because to double his one talent would have given him the same fulfilment as the person who doubled his ten. In other words, use the talent you have and what you give out you will receive back with added blessings, as did the men in the story.

Discipline

In contrast to fear and the spirit of competition, discipline is an essential part of cosmic law. It is right that each one of us should come under some form of discipline, rules or laws, until such time as we are able to discipline ourselves without these aids. This was the design for *homo sapiens*, but few have attained to this state of maturity so that it has been necessary to create civil laws as guides to the general discipline of living in a society.

From the spiritual point of view, the 'powers that be' have found it necessary to visit the planet from time to time to remind humankind of the path it should be taking and the self-disciplines required in so doing.

Is Business Immoral?

The title of this lecture is quite inadequate for, taken as a straightforward question, it can be answered in a matter of words. Business is not immoral. The immorality arises in the way in which it is carried out. However, I suggested this title because it brings a number of other issues to the fore and encompasses the psychological difficulties people meet in their everyday lives, a few of which I shall deal with in this lecture.

Is not life itself a business? Surely life is the most difficult business of all, because you are the director, you are the staff, the employer and the employee, and you have to manage all these facets of your own business. From the point of view of your own progression it is a very important business, because your future life will be affected according to how you handle the present.

How I wish I could see each one of you shake away the cobwebs, the inhibitions that chain you to your very selves! If only you could stand aside from your physical shell, have a true examination and then start again, keeping an open mind and not allowing your ego (and here I mean the egotistical side of human nature) to become the dominant part of your personality! When an ego becomes predominant, the personality becomes something false, trivial and petty – the first step to a meanness of nature and a limitation of spiritual advancement.

The world has grown up and developed and each one of you is a part of that development. Because of the way in which this growth has taken place, a situation has come about in which a great many people suffer from some form of inferiority complex and consequently they seek means to bolster their ego. They say to themselves, 'I can do this better than most people!'

How many people have you met in life, at home or at work, who feel they know the *right* way of doing something? You suggest a different way to them and what is the answer? Maybe they retire hurt because they feel you cannot accept what they have said. Perhaps they are hurt because they feel you are rather better than they are, because they feel a little inadequate. Yet they say bravely, 'No one is going to push me around!' and promptly dig their proverbial heels firmly into the ground. Some call it obstinacy, others may refer to it as awkwardness but, whichever way you look at it, there are few of you who would not fall into this category somewhere or somehow.

Let us take another example of the way in which people like to feel they are superior to others. Mr. X attends a meeting of a hypothetical society. He disagrees with their beliefs, and as he walks away he says to himself, 'They don't know what they are talking about – its all a lot of rubbish!' What a pity he is unable to adopt a more sympathetic and tolerant attitude and say, 'Well, they have their point of view and I respect them for it, but it isn't mine for my own experience has taught me to see things differently.' To respect another person's point of view is a most essential ingredient for living a balanced life.

Then there are those people who are unable to channel their lives in a particular direction. They know not which way to turn, nor what to do. 'Shall I leave the country, leave my job, shall I leave home, change my flat, change this, change that? I must have change! Must make a fresh start!' And so they go on. What are they trying to do? From whom are they trying to run? Do they honestly think deep down within themselves that these changes are going to make such a difference?

A change must start from within oneself, with an adjusting of the mind and a simplifying of life. Life is not really complicated at all, and it is for this reason that I speak on what may appear to many of you to be an elementary level, because from this level one can obtain a true understanding of wisdom. True wisdom does not lie in a mysticism which is like a maze – a maze of language, a conglomeration of words sounding highly intellectual. True wisdom lies in simplicity and understanding – understanding which can be applied to every thought and action in everyday life.

Look at some of the music and art of today! Is that not direct evidence of the mental turmoil from which your world is suffering? You have only to look at the various forms of expression and you will see how they have tended to become more complicated, more extreme. Man constantly feels he must find a fresh answer, something new, a new form of expression. The local church tells him to seek within, but that does not seem to help him much. And yet they are absolutely right.

It is all a question of equilibrium . . . What is your equilibrium? Have you found it? The first thing to remember is not to be afraid of life but to accept it; and this applies not only to life around you but to your own particular life. Accept yourself for what you are, no more and no less, and then you and your life will begin to move forward. Secondly, do not be afraid of people. By this I do not mean that you should be rude and objectionable to others, because those who go around in this manner are the very ones who *are* afraid, because they are not sure of themselves. I do not mind a person being sure of himself, provided that surety brings with it balance and understanding.

All this, you may say, is a far cry from the subject of this lecture. And yet is it? I would say to you: is your business, is your life honest? Are you honest with yourself? Are you honest with your fellow men? And here I am talking of the honesty between mind and spirit. If you have done something wrong, are you able to admit it, to accept it and face up to it? If so, you are being honest with yourself and you will learn a valuable lesson from your experience. You cannot run away from life or its problems.

I realise that in this lecture I have brought the whole question down to the personal, which is really the only way I could handle such a subject. You see, morality or immorality is a personal thing and your views on it will depend entirely on your own individual stage of evolution or spiritual development.

The world today is in that stage of evolution where business is carried out, and where unscrupulous methods are sometimes employed in the transaction of such business. Most of the people employed in this capacity are not yet ready to understand the true ethics of what they are perpetrating, nor its ultimate effects upon mankind. But many of you who read this lecture will be capable of this understanding, so I can but stir your individual consciences and hope that time will gradually produce the dawn of truth. Where business is concerned, and taking into account your modern economy, the dividing line between morality and immorality is often a very fine one and must therefore be definable to the eyes of the beholder alone. Of course, what seems ethical today will cease to be so in years to come when man has evolved further and comparative standards have changed; similarly, today you do not condemn a man to the stocks for a minor offence, whereas past generations considered themselves perfectly within their ethical rights to do so.

Lastly, I will make a request that you take a look at yourselves without fear or favour – without pride or prejudice and with open hearts and minds. It will take some courage but it will give you a fairer chance; and in giving yourself such a chance, you will be helping the rest of mankind in your own individual way.

Sexual Energy and Celibacy

Sexual energy is an energy like any other within your psyche. It is as important as your spiritual energy and is not just for the procreation of life on this planet. If you lead a celibate life it is through choice, albeit not always conscious, for your circumstances always reflect that which is within you at some level. I acknowledge that this is a very difficult concept for some people to accept, for circumstances can be very difficult and occasionally horrendous. But from the way I see it there is always, deeply buried within a person, a decision on the path he or she leads.

As part of certain spiritual disciplines established in the past, it was thought that by repressing sexual energy and transmuting it through the chakras[1] onto a spiritual level, you would become a better person and assist the evolution of your spirit. From my perspective this is quite a distorted view, for it is based on a misunderstanding of the natural flow of this energy. In other schools the whole ethos was based upon manipulating sexual energy to control people. That I do not agree with at all for it is evil practice.

Each of your chakras expresses a particular quality of energy which is necessary for you as a spirit in incarnation. Sexual energy is a vital force that needs to be expressed in balance and harmony with all your other energies. Indeed, because of the fact that it has been suppressed over recent periods in history for many different reasons, of which religion is but one, the natural expression of that energy has become distorted. This has resulted, in today's culture, in a swing of the pendulum from suppression to perversion

---

[1]Energy centres within the body that act as transformers of both cosmic and physical energy.

and between those two extremes you have a wide range of variation.

So let us look at what that sexual energy, which resides within each one of you, is all about. It is about creativity; first and foremost, about the procreation of your species. When two people come together to re-create themselves there is a great interplay of energy on many levels. Ideally, this uniting should begin at a spiritual level for, from that point of oneness and harmony, an impulse will be created which will attract to the couple a spirit of similar evolution. The sexual energy working in harmony with the spiritual can provide a vehicle for soul expression in a truly beautiful way. Is that not a wonderful gift, to be able to create a situation which allows another spirit of uniqueness to come into a physical body to experience life on this planet? But of course that is not what usually takes place, for the sexual energy is more frequently used for physical pleasure alone with very little consciousness of other levels of energy whatsoever, thereby missing the unique power of its creativity.

There is also a deep rooted fear around sexuality that lies buried within the psyche of the planet, which gives rise to many painful experiences for most of you. Yet, if you were able to allow the dynamic of that energy to flow harmoniously, you would have the potential to be truly creative in the material world through music, art, the written word, organisation, physical structure and so on, for everything that you create is part of your sexual energy in its broadest sense. All human beings need a creative outlet through which to express their uniqueness. They do not have to be great artists, writers or composers but simply to be able to create something that expresses themselves.

What the sages of the past failed to see is that you do not need to sublimate sexual energy consciously, you just need to allow it to flow and immense creativity will come from it. When I say allow it to flow, I do not mean that you need to have sex frequently, nor do I mean that if you are not in a sexual relationship your energy cannot flow, because it is an energy – it is flowing all the time. It is how you balance and handle that flow that is in question, for sexual energy has many different levels of expression. In this sense it is no different to the energies of your heart or your head for it is all part of the uniqueness that is you.

Marriage and Divorce

What is marriage? In the distant past when the various religions and faiths sprang up, the priests found it necessary to hand out religious beliefs and rules on a plate. When people desired to live together and have the blessing of God upon their union, they went to the priests. In such a manner ceremonies were built up, which in due course became the marriage ceremony as you know it today.

But I say again – what is marriage? If two people live together and offer their prayers and minds to God, they will be showered with blessings, for a true marriage in the eyes of God takes place on the level of the spirit. All such matters of relationship are the dictates of one's own conscience, and conscience is unique to individuals and to different ethnic and religious groups.

God does not condemn what you call divorce. The Godhead is all merciful, wise and understanding, therefore how can it condemn? If two people make a mistake or grow apart and realise that they have done so, it is of no use to themselves or to God if they continue to live in misery. Divorce is only a sin in so far as man himself sees it as such. The attitude of some Churches in this matter is lamentable; many of their rules and dogmas are archaic and entirely unsuitable for the people of today.

The Church teaches: 'Those whom God hath joined together let no man put asunder.' Let us then distinguish between a marriage which is truly joined by God and one which is joined by man. The Divine Sanction could only fall upon a union in which there is a true affinity on all levels.

Prostitution

This is a subject which causes embarrassment to governments, religions and to most people generally – the query that is uppermost in people's minds being, 'Is it right or wrong?'

I say to you, surely the answer lies in the number of prostitutes who are at present operating in your own country. Of course morally it is wrong – there is no doubt about that. The sex organs were given to men and women for the purpose of procreation and for the expression of deep love, not for the purpose of earning a living. But let us not forget that it is the oldest profession in the world. It is a mark of the evolution of this planet and not until man has achieved much greater harmony in both his spiritual and his material life will you be able to dispense with this unfortunately necessary profession.

I say to you, peoples of the world, stop fighting shy of this! See it for what it is, no more and no less. Instead of making half-hearted attempts to try and stamp it out, be honest with yourselves and admit that at the moment you will be unable to do so. Face up to it and acknowledge that at the present stage of the world's evolution, it is a necessary 'evil'. Treat it as such and let it not be thrown into the squalor, filth and disease of the back streets. Stop hiding it, let it be cleansed and brought into the open, for soon you will enter into that stage of evolutionary development when it will no longer be necessary.

Do not forget that as long as there are men whose emotions and sexual life are in a state of imbalance and whose social conditions are such that they feel compelled to consort with prostitutes to save their own mental balance, there will always be prostitutes to meet that demand. I put it to you as to what would happen if you took away these prostitutes?

The way to treat this problem is not to remove the prostitutes, but to help those people who visit them; for if you were able to help those who keep the prostitutes in business to be true to themselves and find a balance in their lives, there would be no need for prostitution. So I say to you, be sensible, it is the cause you must strike at, not the effect; for by removing the effect you will only force the cause to go elsewhere and that could have and is already having the most unfortunate results. You have only to observe the rise in crimes of a violent sexual nature against women and children.

Many of you will find great difficulty in accepting the above, for it will be contrary to what you have always been taught, but you must realise that this is a very deep problem which has given rise to much suffering. So I beg of you to read this lecture carefully, for I am not asking you to condone prostitution, but to regard it in a balanced perspective.

Man needs first to accept himself for what he is, his strengths *and* his weaknesses; only then will he begin to become what he truly is. To try it any other way is only narrowing his concepts and blinding himself to the truth. This is why he is filled with so many unnecessary fears, prejudices and misunderstandings.

Homosexuality and Lesbianism

There are many people in the world today in a state of abnormality whereby they release their sexual emotions upon their own sex. Why? you will ask. The answer in many cases, from the point of view of the spirit, is simple. It is caused by the aggregate influence of past incarnations.

People are evolving and as they do so the personality of the spirit grows also, accumulating experience from the different lives it undergoes. Let us suppose that a spirit has three female incarnations consecutively, the last one being a very dominant one, and that the following incarnation is in a male body. As a consequence, this male would tend to have female characteristics and be sexually more attracted towards members of his own sex. The opposite conditions would apply, of course, in the case of lesbianism.

Let us now look at the problem on a psychological and physical level. You are a spirit in a physical body, experiencing physical life through your particular vehicle. In this life you have entered a body which is either male or female, but you are aware of being to some extent a mixture of both masculine and feminine, for no person is entirely masculine or entirely feminine. The way your physical body is constructed and the way in which your mind triggers that body, with its particular evolutionary history, are two factors that come together to create a set of circumstances that maintain the particular sex of the body in which you are experiencing. This in itself is a delicate thing, for if any one person, let us say a woman, is subjected to certain influences through psychological pressures, she could very quickly start to incline towards the masculine; and if she were to be stimulated by certain drugs the inclination could even manifest physically. So it is quite a delicate balance that helps you to maintain your masculinity or your femininity.

It seems that there is today a considerable increase of this type of imbalance and I would say that it is a reflection of both the overall imbalance that is influencing Earth at present and the stage of evolution of your present civilisation, particularly in the so-called civilised areas of the planet. Homosexuality is a psychological and sometimes physical state that needs to be handled with great care and has become more prevalent since mankind's fight for survival has become less pronounced. He no longer has to hunt for his food, to grow his own crops or even to pick berries off a bush. He goes to the supermarket and buys them out of a freezer. I do not think the same set of circumstances would apply if you were living in Vietnam or Central Africa. It is allied to the type of life you are living.

One should not condemn homosexuality and lesbianism but, at the same time let me make it quite clear, they are not natural relationships from a cosmic point of view. Those who make your laws tend to get themselves into a confused and complex state of mind over this issue; everyone tries to bend over backwards to ease the situation for those concerned. Whether they are men or women, they need understanding and acceptance, certainly; but if homosexuality is too easily condoned it will spread and very quickly provide one of the elements for the breakdown of your civilisation, as has happened before in previous civilisations.

Having made that statement, may I reiterate that I am not against any man or woman having this type of sexual affection for another man or another woman. Nevertheless, it represents a polarity imbalance. When you get an almost fashionable interest in it as there is at the moment and, taking into account the delicate balance I mentioned earlier, those who are closer to the centre can very quickly be pulled across the line if influence is exerted on them.

The Effects of Smoking

In the world today you have a great deal of tension with which to contend. Every way you turn you find circumstances which play on your nerves; you find it more and more difficult to achieve that necessary relaxation which helps you to maintain a balance, a harmony of living, so you seek means to enable you to relax. One of the ways in which many people imagine they are achieving this is by smoking.

Let us first of all look at the physical aspects of smoking. If you inhale too much smoke from a burning bonfire of wood and leaves, you know very well what happens. When you inhale tobacco you are inhaling smoke from a burning leaf. It may not be the same volume of smoke in the same given time, but I think you can well imagine the effect that this smoke has upon your breathing organs and, to a lesser extent, those of others around you. There has been a great deal said on the question of cigarette and pipe smoke causing lung cancer.

On a subtle level, cancer is caused by the maladjustment of the physical and etheric bodies. The etheric body is a non-physical counterpart of the physical body, often referred to as the etheric double as it is an exact reflection of the body. In order to maintain good health, the two aspects, the physical and etheric, need to harmonise together in perfect alignment. It follows quite logically, therefore, that anything that can contribute to the maladjustment of the physical and etheric bodies can help to cause cancer. Heavy and continuous inhalation of tobacco fumes can undoubtedly contribute to this effect, but not in the way that is generally supposed.

I said earlier that people 'imagine' that smoking helps them to relax. In fact, smoking stimulates rather than relaxes. This stimulation is caused by the nicotine fumes acting as an irritant on a certain portion of the brain, which in turn affects the nervous system throughout the body causing corresponding tensions in the body and in the mind. These tensions serve to irritate the balance between the physical and etheric bodies, causing a friction which weakens the etheric web that links all parts of the body. This friction also weakens the aura, rendering it unable to cope with the natural protection of the body which it normally provides. Hence the smoker becomes a sitting target for diseases such as cancer, which are unable to exist inside a healthy aura and which need this frictional weakness between the physical and etheric bodies in which to thrive.[1]

I would like to digress here for a moment to say that one of the best ways in which you can maintain good health is by not allowing yourself to indulge in worry and tension. I know this is difficult for many of you and I consider that one of the contributing factors is the rate of material advancement in the world today. The mind is unable to keep pace and adjust itself to the ever-increasing rate of progress. If people were only able to accept their own lives and the lives of those around them, they would soon find that their tensions and worries would disappear. Most problems from which human beings suffer are only problems inasmuch as they make them so.

Finally, having looked at the physical and mental effects of smoking, I would like to comment briefly on its psychic effects. There is no doubt that over a period of time continuous smoking would stem the development of a sensitive worker such as a healer and have a detrimental effect on his or her own advancement.

Now I would not say to you, 'You must not smoke', because it is something which lies within the dictates of your own freewill. As with all things, you will not come to much harm if you smoke in moderation. But weigh up for yourselves the advantages and disadvantages of smoking, and I hope that in some small way I have helped you to clarify the subject for yourselves.

---

[1]For a pregnant woman, this balance is doubly important and strong advice to any couple would be to think of the needs of the unborn child in its delicate state of formation. Ideally, both parents of an intended child should cease to smoke at least one year before conceiving.

The Effects of Alcohol

Those of you who have had several drinks at a time will know precisely what I mean when I say that alcohol has a most peculiar effect on the physical body! You feel a little lighter and slightly dissociated from yourself. This is because alcohol quickens the vibrations of the body.

To an incarnate person a physical body appears as a solid mass, but in fact it is not really so. It is a collection of atoms blending together to create the result which you see as a physical body. The particles of these atoms revolve at a certain vibration which results in a reasonable functioning under normal conditions. The imbibing of alcohol causes a slight quickening which, whilst it affects the physical body, does *not* affect the spirit and thus a lack of balance results.

The spirit, remember, is the 'I' or 'Ego' which sparks your mind and body and which causes you to react and live in your own particular way. If for some reason an imbalance is caused between the spirit and its physical counterpart, all manner of weaknesses result. The aura which surrounds and protects the body is forced open and this in turn allows the infiltration of foreign bodies or influences.

So we are beginning to see that this question of the spirit and body being in balance is extremely important to the physical and mental health of each individual. It is this balance which causes you to be well or ill, sane or insane, to live or not to live.

Having established this, what next? You pick up your glass of alcohol and drink it down. Immediately, the physical body begins to quicken but the spirit does not and, consequently, the balance between the two begins to waver. The spirit finds it is no longer able to control its physical counterpart quite as well as before. Remember, your automatic reactions will still function, you will still be able to lift your arm, you will probably be able to walk – maybe in not quite such a straight line but nevertheless your limbs are movable. But that spark, that something within you which dominates your life, is not in such strong control.

The amount of alcohol you consume at any one time obviously affects this control proportionately and, if you went on drinking continuously, your control over your body would soon become negligible. When this happens, alien spirits may try to take over the physical body, and this is why you sometimes encounter abnormal outbursts from a person who has drunk to excess. He has not only lost control of his body but, worse still, it is being temporarily used or influenced by another spirit. Strangely enough, when a spirit loses control of the physical body through inebriation, it is only in extreme cases that an alien spirit can get sufficient control of the physical body to drive away the native spirit. This is indeed very fortunate as you can well visualise what the result would be if it were not so.

In the case of an addiction, a person's physical body can attune itself so that it takes longer for the quickening up process to take effect; but, when it does so, it will be that much quicker and easier for the spirit to lose control. It is detrimental for this to happen too frequently in an incarnation and I would strongly advise anybody against it.

If an individual is actively participating in some form of psychic expression, then I consider it to be potentially dangerous for them to become inebriated to any extent. This particularly applies to anyone engaged in psychic work of a mediumistic nature, but when it comes to those of you who undertake advanced healing work, then my remarks are quadrupled because the dangers there are very great indeed.

If you look back in history, you will see that many famous people have obtained considerable stimulus to their creative powers through an addiction to alcohol. But, unfortunately, as there is no control over what a person picks up in this state, the results may fluctuate between genius and sheer evil, depending upon the prevailing atmosphere at the time.

To sum up, therefore, I would like to say to you that if you want to improve your life, if you want to take the surest step towards improving your creative faculties, do not try to achieve it through alcohol. It is one of those strange things, that alcohol can give you a temporary and quick relief from strain, worry and tension, a quick fillip to your creative faculties; but then it stops you dead and instead of your creations becoming more profound they will become mediocre, in my estimation.

I am not against alcohol, I am not against people enjoying an alcoholic drink, because I can see that used in moderation it can relax you and it can add to the enjoyment of a meal or provide a social meeting point. But if you want to make something worth while out of your life, do NOT drink to excess.

Psychic Pitfalls of Drug-taking

In this lecture I wish to discuss the consequences of drug-taking for so-called uplifting purposes. I intend the word 'uplifting' to include people who take drugs to help them over some difficult situation, as well as those who do so in the hope of gaining some form of psychic or so-called 'spiritual' experience, as the effect is more or less the same.

I view all forms of enforced meditation with suspicion because those who seek this type of short cut to spiritual experience rarely understand what is happening to them; and if they fall into the category of those who think they *do* know the answers, they are even more dangerous.

The 'I', the spirit, ego or psyche, that spark which motivates your body, enters at the moment of conception in order to undergo forms of physical experience. Its controlling mechanism is very sensitive and the liaison or link which connects it with its physical shell is in a delicate balance, to say the least, so that it does not require much to destroy this equilibrium. Most of you have some slight imbalance between the spirit and the body, for as beings incarnate on a physical plane you are not perfect; but it is only when these imbalances become accentuated that serious problems set in. The main factor which affects this delicate balance is modern day living with its noise, tension and false pace of life. Imbalances in the human body bring about some form of illness and this is, in effect, a mutation in itself. A typical example of such an imbalance in mutation form is cancer.

We are moving into the the Aquarian age – the age of the mind – and man is trying to seek into his mind and penetrate the depths of that strange computer-like object he calls the brain. This is not new for he has been engaged in such studies for many years, but he is constantly seeking new techniques to aid him in his quest. Perhaps he is looking for short cuts as well? There are those who suffer under the very false delusion that the taking of drugs is a short cut. On the surface it may appear to be so to some, but a short cut to what? As I see it, it is a short cut to the breakdown of spiritual values and can lead to the complete and wanton destruction of the physical vehicle. So what then is left? To put it in a nutshell, drug-taking is the surest and quickest way of retarding the evolution of the individual.

But am I being too harsh? Am I failing to go with the trend? Any spirit that comes to a planet to throw some form of light into the darkness has to try to keep things moving, for stagnation is retrogression. We cannot therefore condone any form of negative teaching, because negation does not help anybody. If you, individually, are interested in developing yourself spiritually, you must go forward positively with clear-cut thinking.

What happens when you take a drug? The control between the spirit and the physical brain is affected according to the type and potency of the drug and parts of the subconscious are released. Many of you must be familiar with the results of an excessive intake of alcohol when portions of your conscious control are relinquished, with sometimes amusing but more often pathetic results. From a psychic point of view certain drugs induce similar processes, but the difference between drugs and alcohol lies in the speed of the effect on the metabolism of the body. The drug strikes deeper as it were, the lack of control is increased and the spirit immediately leaves the body and enters the astral planes. If a person is trying to achieve a subliminal experience and he takes a drug in anticipation of achieving such an end, his own power of thought will aid the process in the earlier stages.

I cannot emphasise to you sufficiently the effects of the power of thought. When a person dies and the spirit leaves the body, that which is left of the essence of that particular personality lives on in a state of thought, so that the state of mind prevailing at the time of passing is important to further evolution.

When the spirit leaves the body as a result of drug-taking, it is projected onto a thought plane; the connection between the subconscious and the conscious mind is loosened and, consequently, any experiences undergone on the spirit plane are easily relayed upon return to the body. Thus a form of psychic experience is effected. But, unfortunately, the drug is having a deteriorating effect on the body so that the actual mechanism of the brain is becoming slowly enfeebled. Perhaps the first few sessions will prove quite agreeable but, remember, the spirit is being catapulted onto a plane where it has no proper form of control. There is no one there to watch over it and see that it does not come to any harm. By its own actions it has rejected its spirit helpers.

This form of ejection of the spirit from the body is completely unnatural. It causes bewilderment to the spirit because there is still the link to the body while the psychic consciousness is operating on a false freedom. If the person becomes addicted to the drug and then has to increase the dose, the physical body begins to degenerate. Those who have become complete addicts will know within themselves the form of suffering undergone, although to a person who is not a drug-taker this is almost impossible to understand. One of the most destructive aspects of this is the revulsion which addicts feel within themselves for what they have done and are doing.

When the physical body can take no more the spirit finally moves on. It leaves that body knowing, usually, that the drug has prevented it from discharging its karma in that life, for drug-taking does not provide a natural form of experience; it could even be described as a form of anti-experience. You see, that person has systematically destroyed his or her own body by deliberately breaking the elemental patterns of which it was composed.

It seems strange that, although many drug addicts profess love and non-violence, they are unable to extend this philosophy to the preservation and welfare of their own physical vehicle, the elements of which have as much right to consideration as the principles preached!

Let me return for a moment to the question of anti-experience. The spirit experiences physically through a process of reincarnation. It chooses its body for each life and enters it at the moment of conception with the knowledge that that particular life offers a certain type of karma that it needs. This experience begins at the moment the spirit joins the fertilised ovum. The challenge of your life is to carry out your chosen karma within the realm of the cosmic laws which govern physical experience. However, there are certain forms of experience which are entirely alien to the physical body and these include the alienation of the mind from normal physical living; in other words, when the mind does not accept the body but tries to live constantly in the world of the spirit.

I can assure you that no one experiences the higher planes through any artificial or unnatural means such as drug-taking. Contrary to what they may believe, drug-takers do not take a trip to these higher realms; their experiences are usually undergone on the astral planes that offer a spirit a very wide range of experiences, varying from colourful impressions to horrific nightmares of a 'bad trip'. In order to experience on the higher planes it is necessary to ascend through a series of spiritual developments called initiations, which each person meets through their inner crises and challenges. Spirits can only attain such exalted realms when they are ready to go there. It is a process of evolution, of gaining wisdom, for there are no short cuts to spiritual evolution. To unlock the door you must first acquire the wisdom to turn the key and you cannot acquire such wisdom from the effects of a drug. Wisdom is attained over many incarnations through the achievement of karma; and karma is something from which you cannot escape, you cannot avoid it, you cannot cheat it.

From this you can see that a person – let us say, a man – who destroys himself through drug-taking has usually denied himself the karma for which he has entered his body, because he has spent portions of his life going through forms of what are, in effect, anti-experience. To make matters worse, he has abandoned his body for long periods before actual death because the spirit has been forcibly ejected by the action of the drug. Sometimes, while the addict is on a 'trip', the body becomes possessed by another spirit. This is a most unpleasant experience, as the possessor is unable to control the body while it is under the effects of the drug, and it often results in fits of uncontrollable violence for which the person cannot account once the effect of the drug has worn off.

All the time, then, there is this programme of destruction and the spirit is left in a state of complete humiliation, degeneration and bewilderment. Unfortunately, it usually takes a long time before the spirit can work through the karmic barriers it has erected about itself. There is no penitence worse than self-inflicted penitence; there is no torture worse than the torture of a spirit that has completely frustrated itself. Once such a spirit leaves its body there is the additional frustration that it can no longer rely upon the drug to ferry it into a series of astral experiences. Without artificial aids it is reliant upon its own power of thought which it has not been in the habit of using. So the experiences it has enjoyed are denied it for, without a body, they cannot be bought by a 'fix'. Such is the torture of an addict whose supply has been permanently cut off.

Is it possible for a drug addict to benefit from healing? Unfortunately it is much more difficult to help a person who is under the influence of a drug, because the healer needs to connect with the spirit as well as the body and he or she is faced with half a person, in effect. For healing to be effective, it must be absorbed by the spirit which then relays it to the physical body. If the spirit is continually being forced away from the body, it cannot relay the healing power which could bring the body into a state of wholeness.

Before I end this lecture I would like to go beyond the realms of drug-taking and touch on some other psychic pitfalls which are just as dangerous. In the eastern world, forms of meditation have developed over a number of years and many of them have been designed for the uplifting of the soul. Some of these have penetrated westwards but, like most things which come from the East to the West, they have been adapted to meet the way of the westerner. It is important to realise that in the East there is an entirely different approach to spiritual thinking, inherited and developed through the centuries, from that which has evolved in the western civilisation. Certain forms of meditation used in the East can, in my opinion, be extremely dangerous to the westerner, especially if they involve relinquishing mental control. The westerner should always try to think positively but never beyond that of which he or she is capable. Unfortunately, there are types of meditation at the present time which have come from the East and which tempt the westerner to try to step beyond the realms of his or her own capabilities; they encourage meditation of a receptive nature which can ultimately produce a similar effect – from the psychic point of view – to drug-taking.

I shall enlarge upon this a little more because meditation is a subject about which I feel very strongly. I see it as a discipline which should only be carried out in a disciplined way. It is a simple psychological trick to use a form of pseudo-positive meditation and enforce people to over-concentrate on one idea in order to make the mind susceptible. This technique has, in fact, the effect of creating a vacuum in the mind, which in itself can be very dangerous. I do not wish to enter into too much detail on this as I am trying to point a moral rather than give a list of 'do's' and 'don'ts'.

The moral is a simple one. It is that in any form of seeking you must guard himself against your own personal vanity. It is very easy in the beginning to say 'I am going to have a go at this because I can always pull myself out of it at the last moment', or, 'I am going to have that or do this because I know I can always stop'. I am quite sure that most addicts have said this at some time or other.

The same type of vanity unfortunately prevails amongst many spiritual seekers. They see in their astral experiences a form of entertainment or escape which exists purely for their amusement; they convince themselves that it is furthering their spiritual evolution and blindly claim immunity from any evil consequences. Each of you must learn never to push yourselves beyond that which you know in your true self you are capable of achieving. If you follow this principle you cannot go wrong. But at the same time you must think and work positively and progressively within this framework; for this in itself is a step on the ladder of evolution and, as I have always taught, the plan of the universe is evolution, with the Godhead as the Ultimate.

Justice and The Offender

Those of you who are conversant with my philosophy may wonder how my teachings fit in with the present system of social and civil laws and justice throughout your Earth planet. Most certainly there must be social and civil laws, because all the peoples upon Earth are in different stages of evolution and, when living in such a society, a form of common control is essential. But I consider that your present laws need some revision.

First of all, the death penalty, still in existence in many countries of the world, should be abolished immediately for no useful purpose is served by it. As most intelligent and wise people will admit, if a man is in that state of mind whereby he is prepared to kill, he will do so regardless of whether his own life is imperilled or not.

All murderers need psychological help, guidance and healing. No man or woman has the moral right to take the life of another person. And that statement is *not* at variance with my former teaching in which I expressed the view that man is not yet ready for pacifism and, in his present stage of evolution, is entitled to defend his freedom. Although I acknowledge the right for a man to kill to defend that which he believes to be right, it does not make it morally correct that he should do so. On the other hand, if a man commits a murder, it is certainly no answer to take *his* life, for surely that is putting your 'civilised laws' on the same level as that of the murderer.

I would like to go one step further and say that no murderer is beyond psychological assistance and healing. These are but words, you will say, it is easy to theorise, but in practice it is much more difficult. In fact, such assistance will gradually come about and indeed it is most necessary that it should do so. For when a man is killed for committing murder, his spirit is released on to the astral with bitter and resentful thoughts in mind and, in this state, can wield an extremely unfortunate influence upon people still in physical bodies on Earth.

As spiritual healing develops and orthodox psychology advances, you will find that gradually the two will steer towards each other and, eventually, a great deal of help will be available for these people. Believe me, it is in accordance with the evolution of the world as a whole that this should be so.

I am opposed to prison life in general, for it does little to make a man repent, but merely aggravates his bitterness against the world and opens his mind still further to negative and destructive influences. Perhaps you can appreciate from this that, in most cases, imprisonment actually serves to increase the criminal's potential as a menace to the people around him.

This is all very well, you will say, but what is the alternative – how can healing make any impression on a criminal? The people of this planet are slowly awakening to the vast magnitude and importance of the power of thought, the power of healing and the value of psychological assistance; the wonders that *could* be achieved would amaze every man, woman and child.

So, my friends, I say to you: let us not just put a person in prison and conveniently forget about him or her, but let us offer help; for, as most people have begun to appreciate, the urge to commit theft, murder, sadism, or any form of accepted crime, is an illness. It is a mental illness often due to lack of evolution but, in most cases, to the inability of the spirit to control the physical body properly. Most crime has its beginnings in this lack of control alongside certain psychological states which could be classed as mental illness. For instance, I would consider extreme intolerance and greed to be crimes in themselves as, if they are not checked, they can lead to theft, cruelty, physical violence, sadism and murder.

If your neighbour had pneumonia you would not give him six months hard labour, so why give him six months hard labour for being mentally ill? He may need to be contained but such a person needs understanding, psychotherapeutic assistance and healing; and whilst I appreciate that there are few yet equipped to give such healing, I can assure you that, in the not too distant future, there will be many such people. As those who work with me grow, not only in numbers but in healing ability, I intend to see that there are those to whom we shall teach the means whereby, with the will of God, such healing shall be accomplished.

THE WAY AHEAD

‘As Above, So Below’

‘As above, so below’ states the ancient maxim. This reflection between levels applies not only to the state of your planet, but to the state of your mind, your spirit and you as an individual. It is the harmonious blending of your own chakric system. Today’s opportunity for reinstating the ‘light’ means there is a response from the shadow side; and because, over these aeons of time, negative energies have dominated this planet, it has meant that the shadow side of humanity’s personality has been predominant and, through self-indulgence, has not been faced. And when one talks about indulgence, it is amazing how many facets of life that can cover.

So, to welcome God into your hearts you have to face the wrath of those negative influences, reflected within yourselves, that would destroy this world. Many prophecies of catastrophe, doom and destruction have been forecast over the centuries in reference to this day and age. As you approach the turn of the century, it is vitally important that you, individually and collectively, face your own shadow and work to complement each other. The choice is yours. I can give you some cheerful predictions for this period: heightened and irregular weather conditions, economic and political instability, the danger of war, the danger of diseases which mankind will not be able to control. Or I can present you with the flip side of the coin, and say: NEVER HAVE THE OPPORTUNITIES BEEN GREATER TO RISE ABOVE THE NEED FOR DOOM AND DESTRUCTION.

We are moving steadily towards that climax and, dear friends, you have done well; for you are still here, the light is spreading and the shadow is beginning to be acknowledged and faced. Putting it very simply, your shadow side can only triumph while you hate it and suppress it; the more you despise your vulnerabilities, the greater their strength. Accept them. Love yourself as a total being, for you are all light *and* shadow. Be not afraid! Every time you hate, you are feeding the evil of the world. When you find inner balance and can love without denying the negative, then you are strengthening the forces of light and healing the forces of darkness.

You always have to attend to these problems within first, for the more you can cope within, the greater your offering without. So despite the threat of the gathering storm, I still perceive the future with optimism because many like-minded individuals and groups all over the planet are beginning to gain ground. The world is becoming smaller and gentleness is beginning to manifest, despite the destruction.

And let us not forget, during this period ahead, the nourishment of the youth of today. They need an emotional outlet which acknowledges the ego, so that their frustrated energy which often bursts forth into vandalism can be redirected. It requires concerted government action all over the world to try to understand the deeper causes of the situation. I have already expressed my views on crime in which I stated that I consider punishment to be no cure. We need to look deeply into why the violence is taking place and how that shadow energy can be re-channelled into something positive, something good. Such a change can only be a reflection of the combined attitude of all governments, acknowledging that people are not just machines, nor figures on a page of statistics, but individuals. You cannot classify people into numbers or letters and this, of course, is one of the inherent dangers of your computer age and why it is important that those who read these words recognise the unique individuality of each human being. Governments are afraid of thinking that way because they want to maintain power and control. They have yet to see and understand that every person is different and society needs to cater for those differences.

So, dear friends, this is what you have to work on when sending out your positive thoughts over the coming years. Let us show what we can do to help those who would vandalise and destroy in their ignorance and intolerance and, with your help, as you each individually grow in both personal and planetary awareness, we shall reach the year 2,000 and beyond with the symbol of spiritual renaissance standing high over this planet.

Further reading:

WHERE THERE'S LOVE by **Annie Wilson**

The dramatic story of the entrance of H-A into the lives of Tony Neate and his companions, of the growth of The Atlanteans, now called Pegasus Foundation, and of their eventual arrival at Runnings Park on the Malvern Hills, is told by Annie Wilson in this fascinating book. Passages of H-A's teaching, cleverly interwoven into the text, make this a relevant saga of our times.

Published by Gateway Books at £4.95.

THE GUIDE BOOK – A Channelled Teaching of our Time
H-A channelled through **Tony Neate.**
Devised, edited and arranged by **Michael Dean.**

H-A paints an exciting picture of life as it could be on planet Earth and the important role that each of us individually can play at this crucial planetary moment. He speaks directly to us and gives us hope:

> "Planet Earth is going through a deep process of transformation; it is birthing a new energy. Any birth brings pain, trauma and suffering while it transforms the subject from one state of being into another. This process of change is allowing a finer, more compassionate energy to permeate and affect all aspects of society. Everything is being touched by this energy and how you relate to it is vitally important; you have total choice in the way that you integrate it into your life". H-A

This book is ideal for group study and for those who, regardless of background or religion, are interested in exploring spiritual values and their application in daily life.

Published by Pegasus Foundation at £6.50.

If you want to know more about Pegasus Foundation or wish to purchase a copy of *Where There's Love* or *The Guide Book*, please contact:

The Adminstrator
Pegasus Foundation
Runnings Park
Croft Bank
West Malvern
Worcs. WR14 4BP
Telephone: 0684 565253

TONY NEATE is Co-Principal of the School of Channelling and a founder/tutor of the College of Healing. Born in Streatham, South London, he has worked as a sensitive since the 1950's, channelling the wisdom philosophy of H-A upon which Pegasus Foundation (formerly The Atlanteans), was originally founded in 1957. In the late '70's, a deep interest in complementary medicine led Tony into the field of nutrition and he co-founded Nature's Own Ltd., a company that is now in the forefront of nutritional supplements. He has been Chairman of Wrekin Trust, a council member of the College of Psychic Studies, and has led workshops on healing, stress, nutrition and psychic development for many years. He lectures internationally and practises as a counsellor and healer. In 1981, he and his wife co-founded the Runnings Park Conference Centre with three other families. He has a daughter and a son.

DIANE FURLONG trained as a medical secretary and became interested in healing in 1970. She quickly developed a strong intuitive sense which gave her a deep insight into the underlying causes of people's illnesses. In 1975 she started to develop as a channel for a higher level of consciousness, which eventually led to receiving H-A. Recognising the need to expand her therapeutic understanding, she completed the ITEC massage course, then started training in 1985 as a Relate Marriage Guidance Counsellor, subsequently undertaking further training in psychotherapy. She runs a busy practice in counselling, healing and psychotherapy, both at Runnings Park and in London. Diane is a founder/tutor of the College of Healing and has lectured widely on healing, meditation and psychic sensitivity. She is a founder member of the Runnings Park community and has a daughter and a son.

RME

and the SUMMIT COMPLEX

by

Cliff Hayes

Including its connection with

RANDOLPH TURPIN: World champion,

British and British Empire Light Heavyweight Champion

Summit Complex
The Great Orme Country Park
Llandudno Gwynedd LL30 5XF

Published by:

Summit Complex
The Great Orme Country Park
Llandudno
Gwynedd LL30 5XF
Tel: 01492 860963

In association with:

Northern Publishing Services
28 Bedford Road,
Firswood, Manchester
M16 OJA Tel: 0161 862 9399

ISBN 1 899181 61 X

written by:

Cliff Hayes

Acknowledgments

Thanks mostly to the Jones family for commissioning this book, which has brought a lot of pleasure in the research. Thanks to Brian Hurst from 'Collectables,' at Rhos-on-Sea, for his help and pictures. Special thanks to to Tom Leigh my friendly gardening expert and the help given by the staff at the The Great Orme Copper Mines. Thanks to Ron Keeling, hairdresser of Chorlton for lending the photo on page 34.

INTRODUCTION

For many years I have visited Llandudno and have enjoyed the peace and beauty of this seaside resort. I look forward to my visits, two or three each year, and always find something new and interesting in and around the area. I had been visiting Llandudno for quite a few years before I thought of wending my way and finding the little tram that took me on a nostalgic journey, and introduced me to a whole new world - The Great Orme.

If you visit Llandudno and never go up the Great Orme, you cannot imagine just how much you are missing. Apart from the spectacular views, the Orme has a fascinating history. As a merchant seaman I travelled the world, and have enjoyed a quiet drink in the some of the more exotic places the world has to offer, Singapore, Hong Kong, San Francisco, Tonga, I have drank in them all. Sitting outside Randy's bar on a warm summer night is up there with all those places.

Once you get to know the Great Orme you are hooked into finding out more about this enchanting area. It is now designated as a Country Park and area of Outstanding Beauty and this goes a long way to protecting its environment. In telling you about the Orme I feel as if I am betraying a secret. It is like being between the devil and the deep blue sea. Everyone should visit the Great Orme when in the area, but if they did so the tiny road that leads up from behind the Empire Hotel would not cope with the traffic. Taking the tram to the mines and the Summit Complex goes some way to alleviating the traffic problem, but to see the Great Orme in its winter dress or on a bright spring day before the trams start for the season is exhilarating and well worth the effort.

I hope that when you have read this book you feel as I do, that walking on the Orme is walking on thousands of years of history. I feel an excitement when I realise that man was here, working the mines 4,000 years ago. Early man built his crude turf huts here, safe from intruders both from the sea and land.

Walking, climbing, recreation, nature and history, the place that has it all is . . .

THE GREAT ORME at Llandudno.

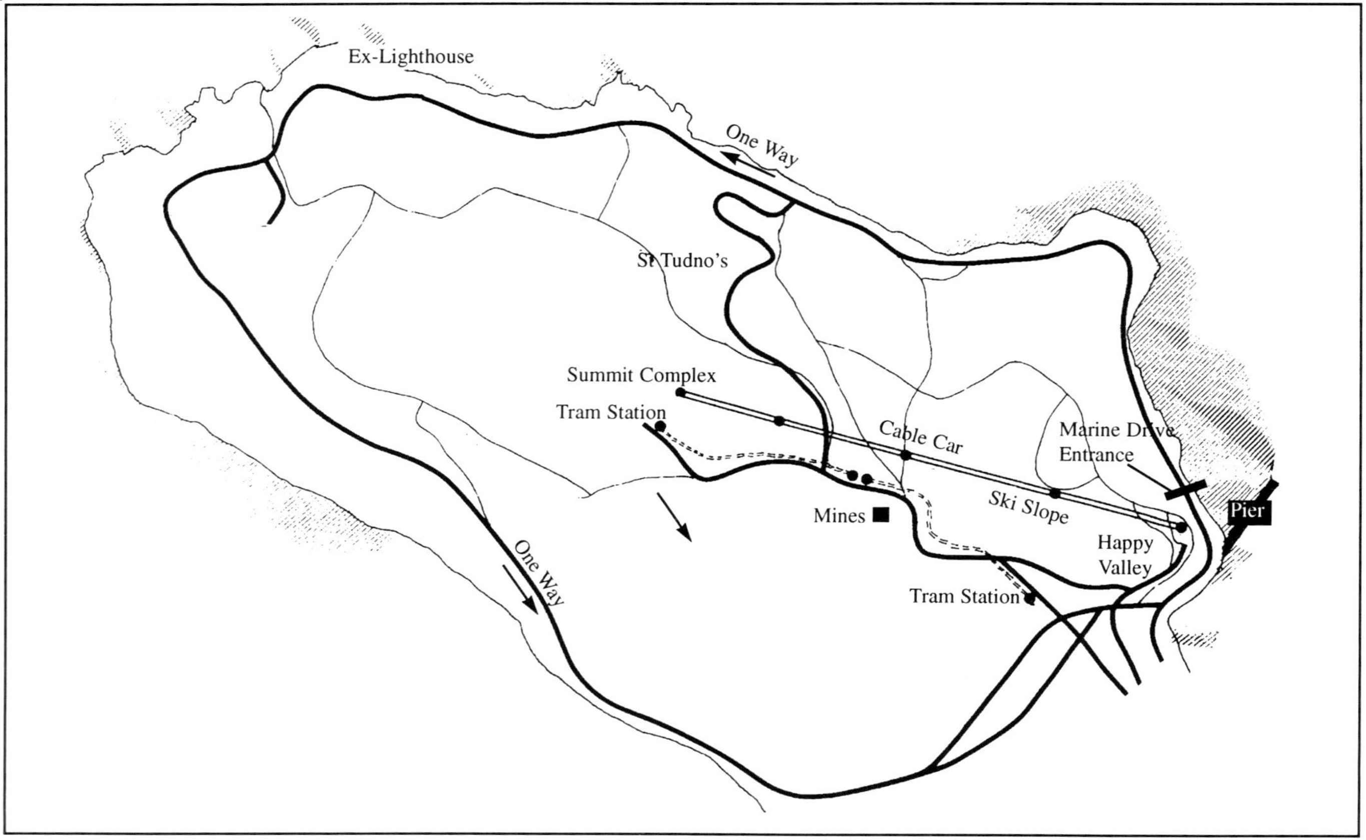

Map of the Great Orme

CONTENTS

LLANDUDNO IN THE 1930's. A tram resting on Mostyn Street after it's journey from Rhos.

LLANDUDNO

THE 'QUEEN OF THE NORTH WALES COAST' is an oft quoted tribute to this elegant and gracious town. A product of the Victorian push for the best of everything and giving the newly emerging 'Middle Class' an affordable version of what the nobility had been enjoying for some time. Llandudno in 1840 was just a collection of workers cottages clinging to the leeward side of the Great Orme. Those who worked on and in the Great Orme, lived in those cottages and a crude inn served their needs. The mines were still bringing out copper ore and at high tides the sea still encroached, trying to make the Great Orme an island once again.

But the winds of change were blowing strongly. People were starting to look on leisure as part of their right. The railway was spreading it's iron rails further and further and travel was undertaking a series of changes from which there was no going back.

The development to a wonderful Victorian town, seemed to have been sparked off by the problems at the Ty Gwyn mine. A meeting of shareholders was called and Liverpool architect and engineer, Owen

Gloddeath Avenue, Llandudno c. 1910 showing a tram negotiating the single track that was there, and can you make out the steamer crossing the bay in the background?

Mostyn Street, Llandudno 1912 again showing two tramcars that provided a service as far out as Colwyn Bay.

Williams, accompanied his friend to the meeting and spent a pleasant few days walking the Great Orme and the shore of what was then called Orme's Bay. At the Company Dinner in the King's Head Inn, he expounded his thoughts of how suitable the area was for development into a specially built 'Bathing and Watering Resort'. Listening to all this was John Williams in his dual role of Secretary of the Ty Gwyn Mining and agent to the local squire and land-owner Lord Mostyn. Another family member the Hon. E. M. Lloyd Mostyn, M.P., pushed an 'Enclosure Bill' through Parliament in 1843, and by 1844 that architect, Owen Williams, was to meet Lord Mostyn and his agent in a hut on the sea shore and put into action the plans to develop the re-claimed land that led to the Llandudno of today.

The Llandudno Junction Branch Railway was started c.1847and by 1849, everything was in place for the land auction. On Aug. 28th, 1849, 176 plots (at 6d a square yard) were offered for sale to business men who wanted to join in this exciting development. Interest was shown, but it was definitely not an overwhelming sell out and only a few plots were actually sold. It may have been a slow start but grow the place did, and the first major hotel to open, the St. George's, opened it's doors in 1854. It was a success, and success breeds success, over the next 30 years the empty spaces filled up.

One interesting "Might Have Been" was the plan in 1853 by the St. George's Harbour and Railway Co. to turn the place into N. Wales' major landing port. The railway would come through the town, and to the area where the Pier starts and the Happy Valley Road is today. Jetties and even docks were to be constructed along this stretch of the Great Orme and the plan started in 1858 with the construction of a 'Working Pier' with berths and cargo sheds.

The great storm of 1859 swept away this pier and some of the jetty work and the plan floundered for lack of money. The need for a modern trading port was still there, but a rival company took over the initiative and transferred the ideas to Holyhead, and developed the Irish link there. The name of the proposed port development in the Great Orme area was Port Wrexham, (Llandudno being the name for just a small area from just above the Empire Hotel to the church of St. Tudno). It really was close, we nearly didn't have a Llandudno as we know it, and it was only a twist of fate and the hand of the sea, in the great storm, which rescued this elegant Victorian town.

An open-topped 'toast rack' tram waits in Gloddaith Street, about 1950.

Looking up Old Road towards the Great Orme tram station, sometime in the 1970's.

THE GREAT ORME

The name Orme comes from an Old Norse Word for sea-serpent, and our name for the common gardeners friend the worm comes from the same base. The 'Wurme' of the Viking era was a large lizard like creature and in Norse Travels off the coast they would liken this head-land and its features as to a Welsh sea dragon watching their movements. The 'W' was lost in time and the name the Orme has evolved over a thousand years.

The Great Orme came about later, when the smaller version of the other end of what was then known as Orme Bay took up the name.

The limestone hill that is the Great Orme consists of a number of carboniferous limestone ridges, sandwich between layers of millstone grit. Boulder clay laid down 300 million years before was rounded off by the effects of the glacial drift of different ice ages and produced what we see today. Faults in these layers have allowed mineralisation and on the Great Orme this is mostly copper with just a little lead.

Happy Valley taken from high on the Great Orme. Early 1950. A sweeping view of the pier, the bay and the Little Orme in the distance.

Dygfylchi and the Great Orme (1950's)

THE GREAT ORME COUNTRY PARK

The Great Orme is a haven for wild life of all kinds. People who have not visited the Great Orme Summit or driven around the Great Orme Drive cannot imagine just how much open space there is. Just how many hidden corners and rugged places the Great Orme has, is a real eye opener, and it is this variation in terrain that enables the Great Orme to support the vast amount of variety in wild life.

On the mammal side, squirrels, weasels, moles, voles, rabbits, mice and foxes can be found, and even badgers have been seen in the past. Pipistrelle Bats are found and Lesser Horseshoe Bats live in the old mine workings. The harmless grass snake is at home on the Orme but is rarely seen due to its shy nature.

The butterflies, moths and insects are of special interest and from late May they can be seen in plenty on the the Great Orme. Some never stray from the area and some winter as far away as North Africa. Among the butterflies the rare Silver Studied Blue and the Grayling are at home on the Great Orme while the Painted Lady and the Red Admiral are among the travellers. Late June will reward the observer with glimpses of some beautiful butterflies including the Peacock, the Holly Blue and many more.

There are moths to be found on the Great Orme including Custus Forester a lovely iridescent green, very rare elsewhere, and the small Silky Wave Moth found only in southern England and on the Great Orme.

Where the bird life is concerned the Great Orme is a microcosm of caves, cliffs, heath and shelter and as such attracts an unbelievable variety of birds. There are specialist booklets on the wild life and birds of the Great Orme and they cater well for the enthusiast. At one time Peregrines and Sparrow Hawks could be seen, and even today the Kestrel can be seen over the Great Orme, and the Fulmar Petrolis a common visitor. Gulls, Turns, Auks, Cormorants and Divers are some of the larger birds seen with many different ducks and waders making up the numbers. Short-eared and Tawny Owls live on the Great Orme and most members of the Crow family are found there. Thrushes, Buntings and Finches are all there along with Warblers, Tits, Pidgeons and Wagtails. The Sky-lark is often heard on the Great Orme and Woodpeckers and Wagtails are seen too. The Swift, the Swallow and the House Martin are yearly visitors.

There are more species of plant life on the Great Orme than can be found in any other area in Great Britain. Again there are specialist booklets available and a visit to the Great Orme Nature Reserve Centre next to the Summit Complex is a must for all those interested in Nature. Exotic trees have 'escaped' from the Haulfre Gardens in Church Walks Llandudno and a large number of medicinal plants from the Herb Gardens of the former Gogarth Abbey. These are now to be found all over the Great Orme, but beware, Hemlock, also grows on the lower levels of the Orme.

Cotoneaster is found, and although some variations are common in Garden Centres the Wild Catonaista is found only on the Great Orme. The tiny Hairy Violet and the rare Nottingham Catch Fly (Silene) can be found. Although the Royal Fern has now apparently vanished it was once one of the Great Orme's plant life that could not be found anywhere else. The rare Hutchinsia with its tiny white flowers is another of the many gems on the crown that the Great Orme wears. Dog Mercury and Cowslips are evidence that there was once an ancient woodland on part of the Great Orme.

The Great Orme Country Park which was formed in 1978 covers over a thousand acres and the whole headland was designated as an area of Heritage Coastline in 1974. This area of outstanding beauty is a nature lovers and walkers paradise, but can be used just as a place to blow away the cobwebs - you will have to go a long way to beat Llandudno's Great Orme.

A close-up of the Queen Victoria Jubilee Memorial, - erected to commemorate her sixty years on the throne.

Looking down on Happy Valley with the Great Orme's Head behind,just over a century ago.

THE KASHMIRE GOATS

When Queen Victoria came to the throne, among the many presents she received was a small herd of Kashmire goats from the Shah of Persia. She had them placed in Windsor Great Park, and she and the children were amused by them for many years. In 1860 she gave away a breeding pair of these goats to Lord Mostyn after he had done something to please her and these he kept at his home at Gloddaeth. The goats bred every year and by 1890 the herd was so considerable that it was decided to release some of them on the Great Orme. Those remaining started to increase their numbers once again so it was decided that they should join the rest and by 1895 there were around 30 goats running wild on the Great Orme.

When Whipsnade Zoo opened, Queen Victoria gave another breeding pair to them and it is from there that most of the mascots for the Welch Fusiliers come from.. On one of the few occasions that they have tried for a kid from the Great Orme, the over zealous soldiers panicked the goats and some were lost in the sea. There have been many problems with the goats, due to the in-breeding of the herd and the headaches they cause gardeners on the edge of the Orme. There was a cull a few years ago which didn't go down very well with some people, but they are at the moment still there, wandering the Great Orme like masters of the mountain ranges these goats originally come from. In the summer they are not that easy to spot, but what a treat if you do see one of the twice-Royal gifts, Lords of Kashmire and The Great Orme.

A picture of the uncovered workings of the Bronze Age Copper Mines on the Great Orme.

THE HAPPY VALLEY.

The area was once a quarry, and part of the working Great Orme. When the 3rd Lord Mostyn assumed the family mantle of duty, he took on his mother's charitable demenour and as well as donating the land for the Llandudno Town Hall he also, to mark the 50th Jubilee of Queen Victoria in 1887, gave the land that was be become 'Happy Valley'. He paid for it to be landscaped etc., which took over a year to complete and the first entertainers appeared in 1890. The place was a natural amphitheatre, and still is today, with Camera Hill on the townside (named after the Camera Obscura that was buit there in 1860 by Lot Williams) with the Unusual title 'Scottish Hill' being given to the other side. I like to think the name was in honour of Alex Munro who was the last of the great summer entertainers and kept the fine tradition going into the 1970's. But the name was in place long before Alex started entertaining. Sadly the theatre in Happy Valley burnt down and there has not been and real efforts to replace it.

A guide from 1920 described the 'Happy Valley' as "A veritable amphitheatre of lovliness, so sheltered the roses bloom until December most years. During the season the ground is appropiated by a first-class troupe of minstrals, and is favoured by ladies who have the care of children." Even in the late 1950's (deck chairs three pence per day, plus a penny deposit) Happy Valley was packed with holiday makers each summer, to watch the entertainers and all the traditional contests (Junior Talent, Glamorous Grandmothers, Knobbly Knees, etc) of the British Sea-side.

The ornate drinking fountain in the middle of the grass area was given by Lord Mostyn's mother, Lady Augusta Mostyn to celebrate the 60th anniversary of the reign of Queen Victoria.The circle of stones which look as if they were placed there centuries ago, by the ancient Druids, were in fact only put there in 1962, in preparation for the Royal National Eisteddford of Wales, which took place there in 1963, the Gorsedd circle being where the 'Welcome, and Opening Ceremony' was held.

Above this area there are enjoyable gardens, with a blaze of colour most of the year and feature some very interesting rock plants and climbers. The area where the Ski slope is today was added to Happy Valley in 1911-2 from the Wyddfyd Estate and was first laid out as a small holiday golf course. Climbing even higher you come to Pen-y-Dinas where there are the remains of an Iron Age hill fort, and low, round stone-built dwellings are to be found, and also the 'Rocking Stone' which rocks no more.

THE SUMMIT COMPLEX

Another sunny day at the Summit Complex.

The highest point on the Great Orme is 679 ft above sea level and is always going to be the focus of attention. The actual highest point of land is roughly one hundred yards away from the Summit Complex and at one time a bronze plaque marked the spot and pointed out the seven counties that you could see in good visibility. Though the plaque has now gone the views have not, and it is said that on a very clear day you can see the Mountains of Mourne. There is of course the old wise crack that no matter how many kingdoms you can see, if you look up you can add one more - the kingdom of heaven. When the trustees of Liverpool Docks decided in 1826 to put in a telegraph system from Holyhead to Liverpool, the Great Orme featured as an important point along that line. News that your ship had come home safely was very important, and news was eagerly awaited, every hour that that news could be delivered earlier was in the owners interest. The telegraph was like two old style (semaphore) railway signals back to back on a mast and two of these masts stood together. Like the hands of a clock one arm at 22 the hour was an 'A', at a quarter-to it signalled a 'B'. These stations were spread along the coast and the Great Orme read the signal from Puffin Island and past it

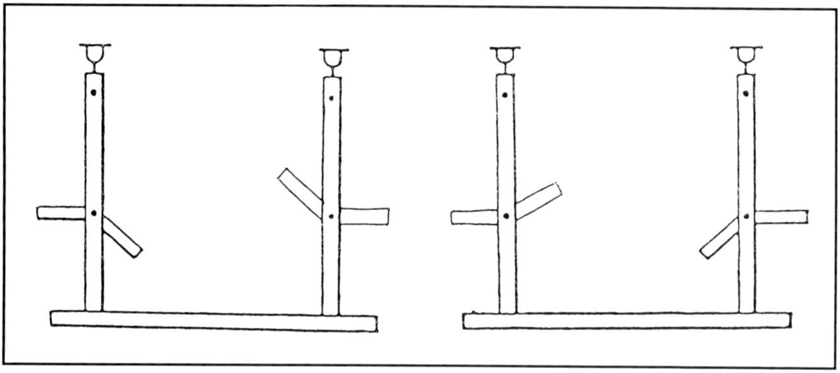

How the telegraph system worked.

on to Llysfan on its way to Bidston Hill and then on to the Tower in Liverpool. Liverpool ship owners could read it for themselves with their spy-glasses or telescopes from their large mansions along the banks of the Mersey. It took on average 4 minutes for a ships name to pass from Holyhead to Liverpool, and the company flag was then run up a large flag pole on Bidston Hill and Liverpool owners, bankers, sweethearts, wives and families all breathed a sigh of relief. The system changed to electric telegraph (morse code) in about 1848, and to a spoken telegraph in around 1900.

A century ago the house where the telegraph keeper, Mr Jones, and his family and workers lived, had a good reputation for hospitality. ''Visitors are accommodated with soda water, lemonade and ginger beer. Afternoon tea is available at short notice." Another advertisement in the local paper advised picnickers to visit the Telegraph House, and went on ''the house is very neat and clean and their garden is in good order and pleasant to sit in." The start of a tradition still kept up today, though on a far larger scale. This old telegraph station building was for a time the Golf Club House and stood until after the Second World War, during which time was used as a radar station. The Summit still plays a part in modern communications with a signal bouncing tower built in as part of the Complex.

At the turn of the century this Telegraph Cafe/ Inn was a very popular place to visit. Mr Thomas McDonald saw the potential and decided to build a new modern Telegraph Hotel near the old building. He incorporated an 18 hole golf course in front of the new hotel and the 'Great Orme Golf Club' was formed, becoming Llandudno's third golf

A rare view of the Telegraph Keepers house

course. Many of the famous golfers of the day played there as well as visiting dignitaries and entertainers who were engaged at the resort. The hotel itself was described as one of the most elegant in North Wales, people who stayed there said that it had a Victorian feel to it, even though it was built after the Victorian era, luxurious, comfy and always smelling of good cigars - a compliment in those days. Ladies and families did stay at the hotel, but it was more of a 'Gentlemans Club', a place where business men would talk of sport, politics, and of course business, over brandy and cigars after a fine dinner.

The hotel carried on - a haven of luxury - despite the beginning of the First World War in 1914. In times of war, places like the Great Orme are natural sites for defence and look-out stations, and during the First World War the Orme was occupied by Army and Naval personnel with visiting top officers, impressed with the relaxation and luxury it offered, staying in the hotel itself. One group of officers who did not 'check in' were German submarine commanders and officers who had escaped from the Dyffryn Aled prison camp in August 1915. They had managed to get a signal back to Germany that they would wait to be picked up on a beach on the Great Orme. August 14th 1915 saw them near Dutchman's Cave waiting to be rescued. They risked a flash-light to send signals out to a waiting submarine, but at dawn they were still there. Sleeping and hiding all day, probably in the cave, they tried again the next night but to no avail, and so they set off over-land for the East Coast. They were not the only ones disappointed and frustrated, the captain of the German submarine who, against all odds, had managed to slip into the Irish Sea and wait off the mouth of the river Conway unnoticed, lay for two nights just off the Orme, waiting for a signal, but the prisoners they were supposed to be picking up were in another bay, only two hundred yards away, and signalling in a different direction. These prisoners were nearly the only Germans to escape from Britain during World War One, but they were soon captured and the event was forgotten.

Between the wars from 1919 to 1939 the hotel and golf course continued to flourish. The golf course opened a special section for the ''working man'' to play on and enjoy this past-time of the 'upper classes'. But the storm clouds of war were once more gathering following the high unemployment of the early thirties, and as 1938 approached, life at the Telegraph Hotel was set to change course for ever.

The army commandeered the Great Orme during the Second World War, and a Coastal Artillery School was started at Llys Helyg September 1940. Later a Wireless Officers Cadet Course was started and by 1942 there were 150 officers, 115 cadets and 445 other ranks all stationed on the Great Orme. The hotel itself was requisitioned by the RAF and used as a radar station. As all of the rooms were taken up by military person-

The Telegraph Hotel viewed from the air when it was a 'Golfing & Sporting Hotel c.1930

A very early postcard of the Summit Hotel c.1908.

nel, the government moved in and ran the hotel. The modern day equivalent of the old telegraph system was still in place, and the Great Orme became a very important link in the communication lines.

After the war, the hotel and complex was slow to be handed back to their owners and even slower to re-open. Billy Butlin and Fred Pontin were showing the way with their new Holiday Camps, and in the end the 'Great Orme International Sporting and Holiday Centre' opened. It seemed to be aimed at married couples who wanted a sporting holiday, with golf and walking as the centre of their annual break, and not for families with young children. It fell between the popular markets and never really reached its full potential. It was put up for sale in 1949 as a 29 bedroom hotel with 163 acres of land, but even at auction it attracted no real bidders. The golf course was soon sold off to Howell Jones from the Pink Farm as grazing land, and returned quickly to the wild pasture it had been, Mr Jones was also a member of the Llandudno Urban District Council.

On July 23rd, 1952, the hotel went up for sale again; shorn of its golf course and with only 15 acres of land with it. The tea rooms were still in use as a summer cafe, but the rest of the package (the public bar, the restaurant, the bedrooms and the old golf club headquarters, were silent and empty). Among the bidders was a Mr Leslie T. Salts and Randolph Turpin who had put úp to £7,500 each into a fund to make a bid for the hotel. In an interview later, Leslie Salts said that amongst his other business interests in North Wales he owned the Great Orme Tramway and this may be one of the reasons why he and the man whose business manager he was - Randolph Turpin, were stood in the dining room that day. The auctioneer Mr N. Adnitt from a company in Chester told the thirty bidders that the place was ready to open tomorrow and it would make somebody a lot of money. He started by asking £15,000 but had to go down to £5,000 to get his first bid. Salts, went in at £7,500 and finally bought the hotel for £10,000. At a press conference the next day Leslie Salts said that he would turn the hotel into a great sporting complex with many amenities and it would be a wonderful benefit to Llandudno. Work began the next day on cleaning up the place and giving it a face-lift.

The hotel had originally been built with castellated walls, but these were removed and its image modernised. The out-door boxing ring and miniature railway at Gwrych Castle also owned by Mr Leslie Salts and which is situated just north of Llandudno, were repeated at the Great Orme, and on Easter Monday, April 1953, the 'Summit Complex' opened. This is the first time the name 'Summit' had been used. It was Randolph Turpin who had thought the name up, and it was Turpin who had put in Randy's Bar where the old public bar had been. The official opening was performed by ex Flyweight World Champion Jimmy Wilde, and telegrams of congratulations came from many well-wishers including boxers, Freddie Mills and Bruce Woodcock, an old sparring partner from Gwrych, cricketer Denise Crompton and MacDonald Bailey the sprinter. Thousands of people turned up to watch the opening and the boxers were mobbed by the crowds for their autographs.

It is difficult for most people today to grasp just how popular Randolph Turpin was at that time. Only twelve months before he had been a world boxing champion, England's hero, the man who had helped lift the gloom of austerity that had hung on after the war. He had knocked out the most famous name in boxing history - 'Sugar' Ray Robinson, and even in defeat at the return match in America he had shown true British bravery and grit. He was even more popular because he was accessible to his public. The man who they were watching fight on the 'Pathe' News' at the cinema had been available to his adoring public as he sparred and boxed at Gwrych Castle and now here he was in Llandudno - what an attraction! In today's terms he was Garry Lineaker, David Beckham and Simply Red all rolled into one. He must have given

Great Orme Holiday Centre, Llandudno.

The Great Orme Holiday Centre in the 1950's with Randolph Turpin's boxing ring.

millions of autographs out at the Summit. Whatever he did, everybody did, if he came out and ordered lemonade the crowd queuede for lemonade, if he asked for a snack, everybody had a snack, things were going well.

Leslie Salts had become Turpin's business manager, and had controlled the purse strings when Randolph had appeared at Gwrych Castle, but at the Summit 'Randy' was left to run things his way. He enlisted the help of willing relatives who enjoyed Randolph's fame and fortune. Unfortunately they had no experience of running such a project, and although everything started off smoothly Randolph's relationship with Salts soon began to sour. Salts pulled out of the deal, leaving Randolph to carry on as the sole owner for a couple of years. Although Randolph was a popular figure in the boxing ring, and with holiday-makers and locals alike, he was no business man, and together with troubles in his personal life, his business dealings began to fail, culminating in him becoming bankrupt in 1961, when the Inland Revenue came down on him for £16,000 in unpaid taxes. Randolph had to sell off all his assets including the Summit Complex. It was the end of his dream! Reluctantly he left Wales and returned, with his wife and children to his home town of Leamington. A few years later in 1966, at the age of 37 he was dead.

It was the Llandudno UDC, led by Councillor Howell Jones, who had earlier bought the golf course, who eventually bought the complex from Randolph Turpin . The council let out the cafe part to a local company, who kept it open for some years before it recently moved to its present holders the Great Orme Summit Limited and although in the 1980's there were complaints that it was looking past its best, it has now undergone a great change, and with a lot of care, attention and renovation, it has become a bright, friendly, welcoming and interesting place to visit to a whole new generation of holiday makers, day trippers and locals. And throughout all the changes, the thing that is still there, and has been since time began is the breathtaking views and exhilarating fresh air.

The beautiful view from outside Randy's Bar complete with a tram that has just arrived

RANDOLPH ADOLPHUS TURPIN

1928-1966

Randolph Adolphus Turpin was born in 1928, in Leamington, the youngest of five children, three boys and two girls. Their father, Lionel Fitzherbert Turpin came to this country from British Guiana, settled in Leamington Spa, and married the daughter of Tommy Whitehouse, a well known bare knuckle fighter. He fought in the First World War, was gassed on the Somme and never fully recovered from this and died prematurely when Randolph was only a few months old. All three boys in the Turpin family were boxers, Jackie Dick and Randolph. Jackie, the eldest was the Midland area Featherweight Champion, Dick was the first black boxer to be allowed to fight for a British title, and became British & Empire Middleweight Champion, and Randolph, the youngest, after winning the British and European Middleweight titles in 1950 and 1951 went on to win the World Middleweight title on that amazing night in July, 1951, when he defeated 'Sugar' Ray Robinson.

The family was destined to be a tough one, but all of them agree, when Randolph was around, he was the boss, and it was always going to be so. Randolphs victories in the A.B.A. championships of 1945 and 1946, showed that he was going to be the best of three very useful fighters, and this proved to be the case. 'Licker' was his early nick-name and he could certainly lick (beat) them all.

Randolph was drawn into the fight game very early, because his brothers were both fighting. He joined his brother Jackie in a 'turn' at a fairground boxing booth when only eight years old, and at the age of 12 was boxing for a local Boy's Club set up to keep these tough youngster off the streets. He served some years in the Royal Navy and as a teenage rating, he was one of the cook's on board ship, he would have seen quite a bit of the world. He married Mary Stack, a local girl and they had a son, but they drifted apart, as Randolph fought his way to success, and they had parted before he fought for the World Championship.

Randolph Turpin turned professional in 1946, aged 18, and five years later he had landed the British Middleweight Championship by beating Albert Finch in five rounds. Sports writers had given him nick-names 'The Dark Destroyer', the 'Black Panther' etc, but Randolph and the Press never got on very well together. 1947 saw him capture the European Middleweight Title in an amazing 48 seconds against Luc Van Dam. Four more victories with-in the distance earned him a fight with the American 'Suger' Ray Robinson, who held the World Middleweight Title and at Earls Court in London, on July 10th, 1951, the two men met.

All the sporting writers gave the fight to Robinson as a walk-over. He had been on a European tour and though the opposition had not been the toughest, he had made light work of these local champions. He was a star with a large entourage (15) and all the trappings of stardom. Randolph and his brother Dick travelled to the fight on the tube. Maybe Robinson didn't take the fight as seriously as he should have, he didn't cope with the unusually long reach of Turpin, and took too many left jabs and left hooks to the head, and when the points were added up at the end of the 15 rounds Randolph Turpin was the clear winner and the new World Middleweight Champion. The crowd went wild: they stood up and sang 'For He's a jolly Good Fellow' and Randolph went home in style.

There was a clause in all title fights that a return match must be fought with-in 90 days, and this re-match was organised for September 12th in New York. Turpin left England by boat and sailed off with the good wishes of everyone behind him. He started well and at one stage, at the 6th round Randolph was well on top and Robinson seemed to heading for a defeat. In the tenth Turpin cut his opponents eye, but rather than stop Robinson it just brought out a killer instinct and he turned on Randolph with what can only be described as a hammering of heavy blows that dazed Turpin enough to make him an easy target for even more punches. The referee stopped the fight in that same round and Turpin's reign as World Champion was over after only 64 days.

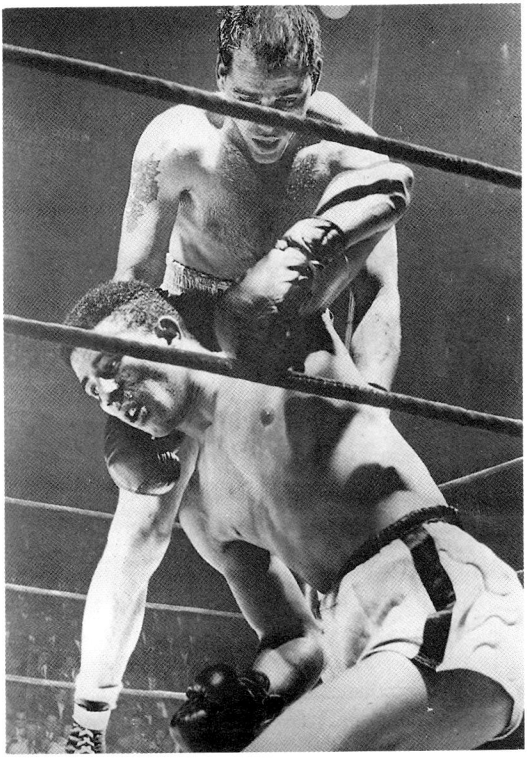

The champ in action.

After a winter of recovery, quite a lot of it spent in North Wales, Turpin was back fighting at the top level and it was on Feb 12th in London that he started a run of eight straight wins, including the British and Empire Light-Heavyweight Titles from Don Cockell in June 1952 and the Britsh and Empire Middleweight Titles in beating George Angelo on Oct. 21 that year. But he was starting to take some punishment and although training at Gwych Castle did revive his inner self, the sports press, always quick to knock, were not giving him the backing he deserved and though he was winning, it was on points etc, rather than on knock-outs.

He could have re-gained the World crown at the end of 1953 in New York, but there was obviously much more to that match than the ordinary man in the street knew about. He got into trouble with the police, he didn't train with his usual verve, and he argued constantly with his brother, and the rest of his party. It was almost as if he was frightened of winning, and when he lost on points to Carl Olson it was as if he was releaved and couldn't wait to get home to Llandudno and Wales. He only had two fights in 1954 and in the second he lost the European Middleweight Title in Rome, stopped in the first round, that had never happened to Randolph before. He successfully defended the British and Empire Light-Heavyweight Titles in April 1955 in London, but later that year he was knocked out for the first time in his professional career and lost for the first time in Britain since April of 1946.

It all started to go wrong for Turpin in 1956, he said after one defeat: "I could see the punches coming, but I just couldn't get out of the way". His last professional fight, the 73rd, was against Yolande Pompey on September 9th, 1958, and he took a battering before being knocked out after only four and a half minutes of the fight. It was all over for him.

Randolph's connection with North Wales started when he decided to move into Gwych Castle, Abergelle, for use as a training camp. This brought him into contact with a Mr Leslie Salts who later became his business manager. In 1952 they heard of the sale of the Golf Links Hotel on the Great Orme, and the two put up the money to buy the place.

The place had been taken over by the forces during the Second World War and not given the care and maintenance that a good hotel requires. The Golf Links themselves had been sold off for farming, but there was still the potential there to make a major attraction for the holiday makers visiting Llandudno. Even with untrained management, Randolph's sister Joan and her husband Johnny Bestin were put in charge, and all the 'friends' that Turpin invited to stay, the place still made money. John admitted later that he went down into Llandudno and bought a book "How to run a Hotel" for 15/-. Everybody wanted to see the world champion, and he would keep them entertained.

He had courted and then married a North Wales girl, Gwyneth

and she brought stability and children, into Turpin's life. They had four daughters, and they seemed very settled in North Wales. After sister Joan and John decided to move out of the Summit, Randolph and Gwyn, more or less ran the place, and lived up there. Gwyn said later that it was there that 'Randy' was happiest and there that they had their best years. Even so when he lost the Summit Complex and the Tax man issued bankruptcy proceedings it was back to Leamington that the Turpins went.

Much against all advice Randolph bought a small cafe, even though it was soon for demolition, and leaving it for his wife to run. He made money when and where-ever he could. Working during the day in a scrap yard, and at night doing the odd exhibition bout, personal appearances and even at one stage, trying the grunt and groan game, wrestling, Randolph tried to make ends meet, but the end that had the tax bill just wouldn't come even close to being solved. His inability to handle money kept coming back to haunt him and the money he had given away and 'lent' just wouldn't be repaid.

On May 17th, 1966, aged 38, Randolph Turpin, former World Middleweight Boxing Champion, was found dead in an upstairs room of his home in Leamington, Warwickshire. In the same room was his youngest daughter, who had been in her cot, she had a bullet in her head but miraculously survived. Randolph had one shot to the head, and one through the heart, either shot would have killed him instantly. The Coroner's Court decided it was suicide, and the verdict has been hotly debated many times since. Whatever happened that day, he didn't deserve to die. Fate had been very cruel to him, and he had some true friends, but not enough. Sometimes he knew, he was his own worst enemy, and was never good at taking advice. Almost everyone who dealt with him said that out of the ring he was a gentleman. He was once quoted as saying: "Back streets, me; and backs streets I want to remain".

He was a man who had given so much pleasure, hope, and entertainment to Britain. A man who had showed all the attributes of a British Bulldog, and whose rare courage in the ring had been an inspiration to thousands of youngsters.

To go up to Randy's Bar at the Summit Complex today and see the pictures of him there is great. But if you know a little more about the man standing there before you, then it makes it all the more interesting. The man who first named the place the Summit, and who first made and named 'Randy's Bar'.

RANDOLPH TURPIN

1946	Sept. 17	Gordon Griffith	London	won	ref.stopped1st
	Nov. 19	Des Jones	London	won	points.
	Dec. 26	Bill Blything	Birmingham	won	ko. in 1st.
1947	Jan. 14	Jimmy Davis	London	won	ko. in 4th
	Jan. 24	Dai James	Birmingham	won	ko. in 3rd
	Feb. 18	Johnny Best	London	won	fight stpd 1st.
	Mar. 18	Bert Hyland	London	won	ko. in 1st.
	April 1	Frank Dolan	London	won	ref. stpd fight, 2nd.
	April 15	Tommy Davies	London	won	ko. in 2nd.
	April 28	Bert Sanders	London	won	points.
	May 12	Ron Cooper	Oxford	won	ref stpd fight.
	May 27	Jury VII	London	won	points.
	June 3	Mark Hart	London	won	points.
	June 23	Leon Fouquet	Coventry	won	ko. in 1st
	Sept. 9	Jimmy Ingle	Coventry	won	fight stpd 3rd.
	Oct. 20	Mark Hart	London	drew	
1948	Jan. 26	Freddie Prie	Coventry	won	ko. in 1st.
	Feb. 17	Gerry McCready	London	won	fight stpd 1st.
	Mar. 16	Vince Hawkins	London	won	points.
	April 26	Albert Finch	London	lost	points.
	June 28	Alby Hollister	Birmingham	won	points.
	Sept. 21	Jean Stock	London	lost	retired
1949	Feb. 7	Jackie Jones	Coventry	won	ret 5th.
	Feb. 21	Doug Miller	London	won	points.
	Mar 25	Mickey Laurent	Manchester	won	ret 3rd.
	May 3	William Poli	London	won	dis.4th
	June 20	Cyrille Delannoit	Birmingham	won	fight stpd 8th.
	Aug. 22	Jean Wanes	Manchester	won	ret 3rd
	Sept. 19	Roy Wouters	Coventry	won	fight stpd 5th.
	Nov. 15	Pete Mea	London	won	ret 4th.
1950	Jan. 31	Gilbert Stock	London	won	points
	Mar. 6	Richard Armah	Croydon	won	ret 6th.
	April 24	Gustave Degouve	Bottingham	won	points.
	Sept. 5	Eli Elandon	Watford	won	ko. 2nd.
	Oct. 17	Albert Finch	London	won	ko. 5th.
		(British middleweight title)			
	Nov. 13	Jose Alamo	Abergavenny	won	ko. 2nd.
	Dec. 12	Tommy Yarosz	London	won	dis.
1951	Jan. 22	Eduardo Lopez	Birmingham	won	ko. 1st.
	Feb. 27	Luc Van Dam	London	won	ko. 1st.
		(European middleweight title)			
	Mar. 19	Jean Stock	Leicester	won	fight stpd 5th.
	April 16	Billy Brown	Birmingham	won	ko. 2nd.

	May 7	Jan de Bruin	Coventry	won	ko. 2nd.
	June 5	Jackie Keough	London	won	fight stpd 7th.
	July 10	Ray Robinson	London	won	points.
		(World's middleweight title)			
	Sept. 12	Ray Robinson	New York	lost	fight stpd 10th
		(World's middleweight title)			
1952	Feb. 12	Alex Buxton	London	won	rtrd 7th.
	April 22	Jacques Harrabedian	London	won	ko.
	June 10	Don Cockell	London	won	fight stpd 11th.
		(British and Empire light-heavyweight titles)			
	Oct. 21	George Angelo	London	won	points.
		(British Empire middleweight title)			
1953	Jan. 19	Victor D'Haes	Birmingham	won	ko. 6th.
	Feb 16	Duggie Miller	Leicester	won	points.
	Mar 17	Walter Cartier	London	won	dis.
	June 9	Charles Humez	London	won	points.
		(World's middleweight title)			
	Oct. 21	Carl Olson	New York	lost	points.
		(World's middleweight title)			
1954	Mar. 30	Olle Bengtsson	London	won	points.
	May 2	Tiberio Mitri	Rome	lost	fight stpd 1st.
		(European middleweight title)			
1955	Feb. 15	Ray Schmit	Birmingham	won	dis.
	Mar. 8	Jose Gonzales	London	won	ko. 7th.
	April 26	Alex Buxton	London	won	ko. 7th.
		(British and Empire light-heavyweight titles)			
	Sept. 19	Polly Smith	Birmingham	won	points.
	Oct. 18	Gordon Wallace	London	lost	k.o. 4th
1956	April 17	Alessandro D'Ollavio	Birmingham	won	ref stpd fight 6th.
	June 18	Jacques Bro	Birmingham	won	k.o.5th
	Sept 21	Hans Stretz	Hamburg	lost	points 10
	Nov 26	Alex Burton	Leicester	won	ref stpd fight 5th
		(British light heavyweight title)			
1957	June 11	Arthur Howard	Leicester	won	points 15
	Sept 17	Ahmed Boulgroune	London	won	ref stpd fight 9th
	Oct 28th	Sergio Barchi	Birmingham	won	ref stpd fight. 2nd
	Nov 25	Owe Janseen	Leicester	won	ref stpd fight 8th
1958	Feb 11	Win Snook	Birmingham	won	points 10
	April 21	Eddie Wright	Leicester	won	ref stpd fight 7th
	July 22	Redvers Sangoe	Oswestry	won	ref stpd fight 4th
	Sept 9	Yolande pompey	Birmingham	lost	k.o.2nd

Randolph Turpin retired from professional boxing

Gwyrch Castle viewed from the east, when it was still a family home

GWRYCH CASTLE

In 1950 as Randolph Turpin was training for the British Middleweight Championship fight he decided to leave the back-street gymnasiums that he had used to train in and find somewhere better, somewhere with fresh air. Randolph had been in the navy and had tasted the salt air and open spaces. This is when he met Mr Leslie T. Salts who had, in 1948 bought the 'mock' castle at Abergele - Gwrych Castle. The castle had been built in the 1790's for a Lloyd Bamforth Hesketh from Merseyside, and the last of family to live there were the Earl and Countess of Dundonald, it was their home until 1928. During the 1939-45 War it was home to hundreds of Jewish refugees.

Leslie Salts had successfully turned Gwrych Castle into a tourist attraction, and it was this success that attracted Randolph Turpin to Gwrych where he joined the other attractions of Pet Zoo, Monkey House, and Aquarium.

Turpin really pulled the crowds in and attendances rocketed. Thousands would come off the train at Pensarn and queue for the buses specially laid on to take them to Gwyrch Castle, there to watch the 'champ' box. World class Heavyweight Bruce Woodcock and Turpin's brother Dick were among his regular sparring partners. The bouts may have been just sparring but Randolph would regularly give out good hidings to his apponents. One day brother Dick decided to play a joke. Keeping his robe firmly tied - right up to the last second, he flung it open as Randolph advanced to reveal he was wearing bra and nickers. Randolph could not hit him hard for laughing; Dick escaped another hiding! The crowd enjoyed this larking about and it became part of their performance - Dick was very grateful for that, and the beatings he did not get.

When ' The Summit' at Llandudno was opened the exhibition boxing by 'Randy' moved there, with just Bank Holidays at Gwrych. When Salts and Turpin split, Leslie replaced his star attraction with visiting T.V. stars, Welsh Choirs, Talent Contests and Baby Shows, and continued to run the castle fairly successfully. In 1968 when local planning officers turned down his plans for a Marina with link roads to the sea, Leslie Salts sold the Castle.

Over the years others have tried to revive this sleeping giant but without success. As we write, yet another plan for the castle is being talked about, this time as an hotel and health farm, perhaps by the new millenium Gwrych Castle will once again be drawing the crowds

Three young visitors, Ron, Jean & Ernie Keeling, proudly holding Randolph Turpin's Lonsdale belt c.1952

MINING ON THE GREAT ORME

THE BRONZE-AGE COPPER MINES.

The Bronze age started roughly 1,900 years B.C. and finished about 500 years B.C. and as it is now nearly 2000 A.D. then we can say it was roughly 4,000 years ago. It wasn't that some ancient man was digging on the Great Orme and found copper ore, meeting someone from Cornwall they mixed the 90% copper with 10% tin and the Bronze age arrived.. The peoples who started the Bronze Age arrived in this land of ours, probably from Southern Spain. They knew about metals and they had been able to smelt metals and mix them for some time. They first settled in Cornwall, and it would not have taken long for them to start bringing out the tin ore, and using the clay for pot making. Moving up the coast, the Orme would have stood out to them, and we surmise that, once they had landed, there would have been places where the copper vein would have been visible on the surface, and they found the place ideal for their needs. Because these new arrivals knew they could mix ores and knew of the tin in Cornwall, that's when North Wales joined in the Bronze Age. There is plenty of evidence for this because Bronze Age Man built low stone-walled circular huts and we have the remains of these on the Great Orme. We also have proof of mining activities we can carbon date to the middle of this age. Firstly open cast and then deep

Visitors waiting to enter the Bronze Age Copper Mines.

The surface excavations above the Bronze Age site.

mining and we can even reconstruct their methods of mining and the fire-setting techniques used on harder rocks sometimes more than 200ft below the surface. It is the advance of technology and our improving knowledge of how our ancestors used to live, and what they did (work) to sustain themselves, which keeps opening up more and more discoveries. The Great Orme is a wonderland of discoveries and I wonder just how much more we are going to learn from this fascinating giant over the next century.

In 1987 the Local Council asked Tony Hammond owner of Ashton Mining to conduct a feasibility study into the stability of the area of the mines. While doing this he discovered a chamber 40' high 70ft' wide and 45' deep. It was thought at first to be part of the workings from the last century. Then experts dated it, and some of the workings round it, to the Roman Period, but further investigation pointed even further back, until finally it was proved to be a cavern that was part of the Bronze Age Mines on the Great Orme. This caused great excitement among historians and academics, and over the last few years the extent of those mines, and the open cast mines that were discovered on the surface above the cavern, has been further clarified and our knowledge of the times and the people has been greatly added to.

The finds were so exciting that a company was set up to excavate the site and to open it up to the public. On April 23rd 1991, The Bronze Age Mines on the Great Orme opened their doors to an eager waiting world. We have there a unique opportunity to see as far back into the past as our imagination will take us. Stonehenge was being constructed at the same time as these mines were being dug, and visitors get a real sense of history and excitement on visiting the mines which are to be found just near the half-way house of the trams. You can visit by car or minibus, and if you dont want to go underground there is a fascinating visitors centre (including the human and animal bones found in the Caverns) as well as pleasant tea room and displays.

OTHER MINING ON THE GREAT ORME

The Bronze Age Mines might have been the earliest attempt at mining and much of the evidence was thought to have disappeared under later workings, but today we find that we can separate the later workings of old galleries, due mainly to the different instruments used in the extraction of the ore. The evidence of bone tools and charcoal embers for the firesetting have remained undisturbed in some of the older workings, though of course others have been re-opened and incorporated into the later mine workings. In 1831, and again in 1849 there were reports of breaking through into ancient cavern workings, and these were soon re-mined and became part of the 'Old' and the 'New' mines from the 19th century.

The Romans were here, we are certain of that, from the coins and artifacts that have been found both in the workings and on the Great Orme. In other sites in North Wales they were mostly concerned with the lead that could be obtained, and maybe it was the same on our headland. There is of course the Roman Well up near the Summit, where, tradition has it the Romans washed their ore before smelting it. At one time the

Bronze Age Mines were thought to be Roman but the advent of carbon dating proved that myth wrong. When you see sketches of the workings inside the Great Orme, it always looks to me like a medical diagram, showing lungs, organs and arteries, and it's romantic to think that the mines have been making the Great Orme into almost a living thing. There is much more to discover about the mine workings under our sleeping giant and we learn more and more as time marches forward. There is a Great Orme Exploration Society and they have done a lot of hard and exciting work, in unravelling these mysteries from the past.

There is evidence of copper mines on the 'Llandudno Mountain' from April 1692, and the formation of the Welsh Copper Company in 1694 was solely to take copper ore from the Great Orme. The two parties who between them owned the Great Orme (the Mostyn family and The Bishop of Bangor) were both giving out leases to mine during the 1700's and it was at the end of that era, roughly 200 years ago that serious attempts were made to take the best out of the mountain. In 1807 we get the first reference to the 'New Mine', near Pyllau and it's existence gave the previous workings the understandable name of the 'Old Mine'. The new mine pushed forward deep into the mountain and also created the Penmorfa level, a drainage tunnel from the New Mine workings over to the West Shore. This was begun in February 1834 but was not completed until the water broke through in October 1842. The mine fizzled out, rather than closed down, in 1863, and when the Mostyn lease ran out in 1864 it seemed to have been abandoned.

There were some very high figures when you look at the amounts of ore taken out of the Great Orme mines. Looking at the books of the 'Old Mine', once the early years had passed, when very large expenditure on cutting shafts and the Penmorfa level and it's pumping equipment had ceased, there were profits of £11,973 in the years 1836-40. Ore sales in 1836 were £4,342 and rose to £22,054 in 1838.

The Ty Gwyn mine was the last to open and yet the first of the three main mines to close. Said to have been started after a cow at Ty Gwyn (The White Farm) dislodged a turf and disclosed gleaming copper ore right on the surface, beneath the grass. The main adit was just west of the Empire Hotel and there was evidence of mine buildings there until very recently. In 1850 the sea broke-in and flooded the whole mine which had for years before been troubled with the sea. In 1836 they installed a Cornish steam engine from the lead mine at Halkyn, and this helped in their constant battle to keep the mine dry. The Ty Gwyn Mine Co. was formed in May 1835, and in the first 12 years they extracted ore worth £93,000. By 1853 the shareholders decided that the mine was not showing enough profit and they called a meeting. It was to this meeting that John Jones the Liverpool woolen draper (who owned 8 shares) brought his friend Owen Williams, who first suggested the building of a resort on the shores of Orme's Bay.

It was decided to close the Ty Gwyn Mine at that meeting and the surface machinery and other assests were sold off at an auction held in 1855. The engine houses were replaced by hotels as Llandudno grew, but one chimney stack managed to out-live all the demolition and stood proudly, behind the Empire Hotel, until 1969. The exact site of the mine entrances and plans of the workings were lost in time and it took a lot of work by the Great Orme Exploration Society and work and research by Mr. Huw Tudno Williams before an entrance was found under a lawn near to the Pier entrance on the Marine Drive.

Even as I write more work is being carried out and there is an attempt to re-open the Ty Gwyn Mine as a tourist attraction. They are finding out much more about . . . .

MINING ON THE GREAT ORME.

A view of St Tudno's Church taken early 1900's.

ST. TUDNO

The Great Orme was the place chosen by the religious man Tudno, a man from a strong and powerful family who could have carried on enjoying the wealth of his father, who, though a good leader had the unfortunate nick-name of 'Seithenyn Feddw' - Seithenyn the Drunken'. Tudno was born c.510 and the religious settlement dates from around the middle of the 6th century. At this time the Head was virtually an island, and only accessible at low tide, so the Orme's inhabitants would have felt safe. The clear views out to sea and over the mouth of the river Conway meant that they knew exactly who was moving up and down the coast or approaching their headland. The word 'Llan' was said, in olden times, to mean "the holy place of". Now-a-days as religion has lost some of its strength it is said to mean "the special place of" so the Great Orme became the ''religious place of Llan Tudno''. Over the years the 't' has changed to 'd' to make a softer easier to say word, and the settlers who came to work the mines adopted the name of the monastic settlement, a tribute to the time when people looked up to their heroes. The small church we see today nestling into the hillside is mainly the rebuilt church from 1859, although there are parts of it dating from 1400. The church lost its roof in a storm in 1835 and lay almost abandoned for twenty years, until the town of Llandudno started to develop. In 1840 a new church, St. George's was started in Church Walks, in the town, and when it was completed attention was again turned back to the old church up the hill. St. Tudno's was restored at the expense of a Mr H. Reece of Birmingham, who was convinced that it was because he had said his prayers at this little church that had returned his young daughter back to health. But the expanding population of the town decided that they did not want the climb the Orme to say their prayers, so in 1862 St. George's was adopted as the parish church and centre for all civic occassions. Strangely enough though, the final journey for many prominent citizens was still up the Orme to St. Tudno's, and when the council decided to open a Municipal Cemetery in 1903, it was up the hill again, and next to the old church of St. Tudno. And the church was was partially restored once again in 1906. Today if you visit St. Tudno's you will see the outside pulpit, built on the lee-ward side of the church, where open air services, were very popular with visitors on fine Summer Sundays, when hundreds of people would sit among the grave stones to listening to the service.

The lighthouse situated half-way round the Marine Drive, a century ago.

THE MARINE DRIVE

AROUND THE GREAT ORME

The Marine Drive at Llandudno stretches for four and a half miles, right round the sea-ward side of the Great Orme. If you arrive in Llandudno in your car you should make a point of heading home via the Marine Drive, or breaking up your stay with a gentle drive right round this sleeping giant taking in some quiet moments on the West Shore. Visitors arriving by coach or train can still enjoy the thrill and beauty of a drive around the Great Orme on one of the vintage buses which leave regularly from Prince Edward Square, during the summer months. It is a great pity that coaches are not allowed to drive round the Great Orme, I know it would mean spending money making the Marine Drive wider etc, but I'm sure, the money would soon be recouped. I think it would bring in more visitors and give these visitors a glimpse of nature in it's wilder and more rugged form. Some years ago the drive was closed to all traffic, and I know it is a costly battle against rocks and the elements to maintain the road to it's present safe standard. We should be very grateful that the Council have not abandoned the Drive and we can still drive around it. There have always been footpaths on the Great Orme, the Monks Path and farm and mining tracks go back many centuries. There would also have been paths to the front of the Great Orme. The collection of sea-bird eggs would have at one time formed a part of the local diet, and the caves of the headland have always drawn people like a magnet. The first real attempt at a track right round the Great Orme was started in 1856 by Reginald Cust, a trustee of the Mostyn Estates. He oversaw the project during it's two years of building and it became known as Cust's Path.

To walk this Path became a must for the more daring of visitors over the twenty years after it was opened in 1858, though it was narrow in places and with some sheer drops down to the sea. Prime Minister William Euart Gladstone was taken round the Cust's Path when he went to visit Dean Liddell at his home on West Shore. He wished he gone down Gloddaeth Avenue and Abbey Road, and admitted that at some parts he was blind-folded and led by the hand. It was because there was a path around the head, that the Liverpool-based Mersey Docks and Harbour Company decided to build a lighthouse on this path in 1862.

The Great Orme's Head Marine Drive Co. Ltd. was formed in

Summer crowds enjoying themselves a hundred years ago. The entrance to Marine Drive can be seen clearly on the right

1872, and in 1875 it obtained Parliamentary permission to construct a drive for carriages and coaches (horse-drawn) around the Great Orme. It was completed in 1878 at a cost of £14,000 and though you must admire the hard work put into the project, they did, in making the roadway destroy some of the iron age sites and one or two other things of antiquity. The company kept contol of the road and it's tolls until 1897 when they sold out to the Llandudno Urban District Council for £10,500 and paid back all their shareholders. In 1910 the Council decided to drop all toll charges for pedestrians. A brave move considering that more than 80,000 people had paid to walk round the Orme the season before. This led to a penny being put on the town's rates, but the Council thought it was worth it as an added attraction to visitors.

There still is a toll house at either end of the 41/2 mile drive, though as all traffic is one way (anti-clockwise) the one at the far end (West Shore) has not been used as such for more than 70 years. It is six miles from Prince Edward Square back to the same spot and this was the scene for an annual footrace which started in Feb 1885, won by E. R.

Daines in 33mins and 46 1/2 seconds, which has been held sporodically ever since. The drive is in some places high on the cliffs with wonderful views and yet dips low in other places, almost a roller coaster of nature, yet always below the traveller is the coastline, the sea, and the caves.

DUTCHMAN'S CAVE, Many books say the source of the name is unknown, but reading about the number of ship wrecks on the Great Orme, it could come from a Dutch East Indies ship wrecked here at the start of the 1800's.

PIGEON'S CAVE Is accessible at low water, but do not get cut off by the tide.

KENDRICK'S CAVE (GULF CAVE) Contained human remains and decorated bones from the Old Stone Age, the Upper Paleolithic Period.

LLECH (or Hiding) CAVE, also called the Monk's Cave it had a stone table with stone seats in it. It was said to have been a meeting place for religious dissenters though how they got there is something of a mystery, and it is now inaccessible.

HORNBY CAVE Jan. 1st 1824, the ship Hornby left Liverpool with 16 crew and two passengers (Mr. Thomas Guest and Mr. Brandreth from Manchester). Capt. Wade was in charge of her and her £50,000 worth of cargo. She was driven towards the rocks and sailors were sent aloft to take in the sails. One young sailor, John Williams was on the jib and suddenly found himself looking down on a ledge in the cliff. He dropped on to it and the ship was swept back into the sea. No one else survived and the local folk soon turned up and helped themselves to all that was washed ashore. The owners were blazing and tried to hire men to guard the beaches, but to no avail, the cargo was never seen again.

Plundering wrecks was a local past-time at one stage and the 'Flora' and the 'Meldrum' were two famous examples. The 'Lady Agnes' went ashore at the Gogarth Abbey ruins on Oct. 8th, 1896 and became a local landmark until broken up by the sea, many years later. The earliest recorded wreck was the 'Phoenix' in January 1642, during the English Civil War. An anchor has been found from a Greek sailing ship of the 1st Century and there are many unrecorded wrecks.

Near to the Pigeon's Cave you will find a flat stone ledge which on an average tide is covered by about two feet of water. This is known as 'The Steward's Bench' and local folk law has it that any steward of the Mostyn Estates accused of wrong-doing a tenant or suspected of embezzlement was bound and placed on this ledge for two tides. If they sur-

vived, they were innocent, if they didn't survive - it didn't matter. Though the story is very positive, I can find no record of this actually happening, and I think it would have been recorded, which-ever way the outcome was. Maybe it was just the threat of it that kept everyone in line.

At the very point of the promontory just above the Hiding Cave you will find the Old Lighthouse. Built in 1862 by the Mersey Docks and Harbour Board it stands like a fortress on the top of a 300ft precipice and was run by Trinity House until it was declared redundant on April 2nd,1973. It used to flash every 12 seconds and it's 18,500 candle-power beam was said to have been visible for 24 miles out to sea. Visitors were proudly told that in the right conditions the light could be seen from Snaefell, in the Isle of Man, 54 miles away. Today it is a guest house, and retains many of the original features. Above it on the main road is the wonderfully-named 'Rest and Be Thankful Cafe' providing somewhere to stop and admire the views.

Bear's Cave, on the lee-ward side of the Great Orme is well known as a home to local eccentrics who have lived there for one reason or another over the centuries.

GOGARTH ABBEY

The Bishop's Palace, which is another, older, name for Gogarth Abbey, which has spent far longer in ruins, than it ever did in it's once former splendour. The Manor of Gogarth takes it's name from Ogof Arth (The Bear's Cave) which is situated near the southern Toll House on the Marine Drive. Land here was, it is said, given to the Bishop of Bangor, Anian, around 1285, by Edward the First, in return for Christening his son, Edward II, who had been born only weeks earlier in Caernarfon. It was this eldest son, whom Edward I used to trick the Welsh princes into a peace treaty only few months later. Edward promised that if they ceased their battles with him he would give them: "A Prince of Wales, through whom they could pass all their grievences etc. This Prince would be born in Wales has never been to England and cannot even speak English." The Princes agreed, and at Rhudlan Castle Edward presented them with his infant son, later Edward II, who fitted the bill perfectly. Still to this day we get our Prince of Wales from the eldest son of the Monarch.

That the Abbey was at one time a large and important religious centre is not in doubt, although most of it's land seems to have been out to sea, and now eaten away by the expanding and changing River Conwy. The Bishops of Bangor continued to use the Abbey as one of their Houses (Palaces) though in the winter the Bishops seemed to prefer the shelter of Bangor to this beautiful but wild spot. No wonder the monks at Gogarth Abbey made a cough and chest remedy using White Horhound as a base. They brought the plant up from Southern England and with it came the Hourhound Plume Moth, another of the Great Orme's rare insects.

The monks would walk from the Abbey to St. Tudno's Church for special services and it is said to be the vast number of 'Holy Feet' that have trodden the path to church which is said to keep 'The Monk's Path' a verdant green, even in the worse drought. A nice story, but the sheep and goats also use the Monk's Path a lot and sheep droppings, washed in by rain is very good for grass. It is from this Palace and the ownership given to Bishop Anian, that we also get the name Bishop's Quarry at the Summit of the Great Orme. Once renound for it's fossils, it seems now just to provide spelling material for groups of younger visitors.

Don't confuse The Abbey's site with the Gogarth Abbey Hotel

A tram with a view

which stands at the very end of the Marine drive. As you travel round the Great Orme from Llandudno, the Bishop's Palace ruins are on the sea-ward side before you pass the old Toll House and the Hotel is on the land-side, a few hundred yards past the Toll House. The Abbey Hotel started life in 1862 as 'Pen Morfa' a private summer residence built for Dean Henry Liddell, of Christ Church, Oxford, who one summer had the Professor of Mathmatics and former theological student, one Rev. Charles Lutwidge Dodgson staying with him. The visitor started to tell stories to amuse the three children of the Dean, and named them after one of the children 'Alice'. 'Alice's Adventures Underground' became 'Alice in Wonderland' and The Rev Dodgson used a pseudonym (Lewis Carroll) so the light nature of the work, wouldn't reflect badly on the serious mathmatical books he had written. I wonder how much the mines and the caves, just behind where he was writing this story, had an influence on the underground part of the stories, or the wide beach of the West Shore had on the poor Walrus and Carpenter, who; "Wept to See such vast quantities of Sand". Lewis Carrol is remembered by an alabaster font inside the Church of Our Saviour on the junction of Great Orme Road and Bryniau Av. over on West Shore and in the 'Alice in Wonderland Memorial Statue', unveiled in the summer of 1933 by David Lloyd George himself.

The Marine Drive c.1960's

One of Llandudno's leading attractions.The vintage trams seen here passing each other.

THE ORME TRAMWAY

The Great Orme Tramway is a great attraction and an integral part of the Great Orme. Fortunately this Edwardian form of transportation has survived the pressures and modernisation of the 1970's and 1980's. When it first opened the trams carried an average of 160,000 persons per year and even between the Wars 80,000 people each summer would ride to the summit. The tramway takes a lot of the pressure off the small steep roads on the Great Orme and visitors can play their part in the conservation of this unique area by using them. Any visitor who wants an enjoyable day can go by tram to the top of the Great Orme and spend a few hours at the Summit, have a drink or snack, and then back down by the chair lift and this would give them a trip with views they will never forget. The tramway which runs on a 3ft 6 ins gauge system consists of two halves, the lower half which is 828 yards opened on the 31st July 1902. The winding machines, which are at the half way house would struggle if the steel ropeway was made into one. The upper half up to the Summit opened on July 8th 1903 and its 850 yard track completed the tramway system from Victoria Station on Church Walks, Llandudno to the top station one and a half miles away.

The tramway is owned by the Conwy County Borough Council who took it over when they absorbed Llanudno UDC. Over the winters of 1996 and 1997 much time was spent restoring the splendid tramway carriages to their original condition. Their efforts were well worth it when you see the hundreds of happy holiday makers heading up the Orme on sunny summer afternoons.

The tramway is open from Easter to Early October, usually from 10. a.m. to 6.p.m. each day.

A ride on the Cable car gives wonderful views.

THE CABLE CAR

The Cable Car on the Orme runs from the end of North Parade, near the entrance to Llandudno Pier. It opened on June 30th 1969 and is the longest cable lift in Great Britain at 1 mile and 40ft long. At a continuous speed of six and a half miles per hour the cars head upwards towards the Summit giving great views on the way. They pass over Happy Valley, the Ski Slopes, the Iron Age Hill Fort and huts at Pen-y-dinas and over the White Farm on its journey. At one point the cars are travelling 160ft above the ground, and on the way back down, views of Llandudno and the surrounding area are breath-taking.

Riding the Cable Car.

THE SKI SLOPE

The Ski Slope which is on the site of the upper part of Happy Valley is a very popular attraction. Opened 10 years ago, it was one of the first dry ski slopes in Great Britain catering for all levels of skiers. For open practice there is no need to book, and any gear you need can be hired on the spot. The Toboggan Run adds an element of excitement and fun to the ski slope and can be used by non skiers. The run only operates during day light hours and during dry weather.

There was at one time, just after the ski slope opened, a plan to build another cable car on the Great Orme, - this time from the bottom of Happy Valley up to the Ski Lodge. When this didn't come to reality, plans were made to make a half way station on the cable car up to the Summit, to service the needs of the Ski Slope. It is a pity this didn't come to pass, as many more people would be able to enjoy the delights of this part of the Great Orme, without subjecting the road up through Happy Valley to more traffic.

Life on the Orme

Riding the Cable car

USEFUL TELEPHONE NUMBERS

The Summit Complex and 'Randy's Bar Opened Daily
Easter - November 1st. Weekends only: November 1st - Easter
Tel: (01492) 860963

Great Orme Tramway & Tours Scenic rides every day.
Easter to October
Tel: (01492) 876749

Great Orme Mines. Open Daily
February to end of October
Tel: (01492) 870447

Llandudno Cable Car. Open Daily
Easter to October
(01492) 877205

Llandudno Museum. Open all year
Tel: (01492) 876517

Llandudno Pier
Tel: (01492) 876258

Ski Llandudno. Open Daily throughout the year
Tel: (01492) 874707

Alice In Wonderland Visitors Centre
(01492) 860082

Great Orme Country Park & Nature Reserve
Guided Walks Sunday and Thursday
May to Mid September
Tel: (01492) 874151

Llandudno Tourist Information Centre
1/2 Chapel Street
Open all year
Tel: (01492) 876413